The Religion Business

Cashing in on God

'Ben' Bennetts

Copyright © 2012 'Ben' Bennetts

All rights reserved. No part of this publication may be reproduced or transmitted in any form or by any means, electronic or mechanical including photocopying, recording or any information storage or retrieval system, without prior permission in writing from the publishers.

The right of 'Ben' Bennetts to be identified as the author of this work has been asserted by him in accordance with the Copyright, Designs and Patents Act 1988

First published in the United Kingdom in 2012 by Atheos Books

ISBN 978-0-9573218-0-9

Dedication

This book is dedicated to my granddaughters who brought me so much pleasure in my later life. Thank you for being you and I forgive you all for not wanting a train set!

Contents

Prologue. A Conversation With A Christian	1
1. Introduction	12
2. The Meaning Of Words Associated With Religion	15
Appendix: The Meaning Of The Word *Religion*	21
3. The Beginnings Of Doubt: A Personal Odyssey	23
4. A Summary Of World Religions: Ancient Religions	38
5. A Summary Of World Religions: Modern Religions	52
6. Evolution Versus Creationism	93
Appendix: A Human Biology Primer	121
7. Christianity: Not What It Seems	141
8. Islam And Armageddon	157
Appendix: Israel And Palestine	195
9. The Need For A God	199
Postscript: The Science Of Faith	237
Epilogue. A Letter From A Granddaughter	245
A Sam Harris/Richard Dawkins Dictionary	247
Acknowledgements And Further Reading	251
Index	254

Prologue
A Conversation With A Christian

What's past is prologue.
William Shakespeare, *The Tempest*

Some time ago, I came across a website[1] that purported to answer questions of a religious nature and, being idle that day, I started an e-mail exchange with one of the advisors. The site advertised itself as 'a safe place to explore questions about who God is and what it might be like to know him'. Here's the transcript of the dialogue that took place over three days. I have changed the name and e-mail address of the advisor to protect his anonymity.

To: <john.smith@domain.com>
Sent: Sat, 2 Jan 2010
Subject: Got a Question? - EveryStudent.com

If God exists, who created him, or her?

Ben

From: john.smith@domain.com
Sent: Saturday, January 02, 2010
Subject: Re: Got a Question? - EveryStudent.com

Ben,

Thanks for visiting everystudent.com
   I don't think there is an answer to your question except to say that God has always existed. If someone were to have created God then that someone, by definition, were to be God! What do you think?
   Hope that helps.

John

To: <john.smith@domain.com>
Sent: Sat, 2 Jan 2010
Subject: Re: Got a Question? - EveryStudent.com

---

[1] http://www.everystudent.com

John:

For me, your answer demonstrates a fundamental weakness for 'proving' the existence of God. You cannot say that he has always existed. That's axiomatic. Where's the proof? My question also becomes recursive. Even if you could, somehow, explain the creation of God, my next question would be 'Who created God's creator?', and so on.

Richard Dawkins hit it on the nose when he asked a similar question recently about unicorns - can you prove the existence of unicorns? The fact that nobody has ever seen a unicorn doesn't prove, or disprove, that unicorns do not exist. It just means exactly what it says - nobody has ever seen a unicorn. So, to base a religious edifice around something whose existence cannot be proved is, to me, a pointless exercise unless there's some other hidden agenda such as power or control over a populace, or greed, or some other human trait.

Here's another question. www.godchecker.com has identified 2,850 different gods, including God/Allah/Yahweh/Jehovah/Jesus and so on. Is 'The God' all 2,850 gods wrapped up into one; or are there really a multitude of gods out there, all different, all teaching/preaching different things; or is The God a sort of Chief God? How does that work?

Just curious,

Ben

From: *john.smith@domain.com*
Sent: *Saturday, January 02, 2010*
Subject: *Re: Got a Question? - EveryStudent.com*

Ben,

To be honest, it sounds like you are trying to pick an intellectual fight with me. I could be wrong (and I hope I am), but if so I don't think anything I say will convince you nor you me. We will just be sending each other links and that won't get us anywhere.

If you are truly interested as you are searching for God I would be happy to answer your question as I do have some extremely rational reasons to your valid questions and objections beginning with the person of Christ and His claim to be God in human flesh.

Let me know how you want this conversation to progress.
God Bless, John

Prologue: A Conversation With A Christian

To: <john.smith@domain.com>
Sent: Saturday, January 02, 2010
Subject: Re: Got a Question? - EveryStudent.com

John:

You said '... it sounds like you are trying to pick an intellectual fight with me.' Well, not really, but I am looking for answers to basic questions and I thought that when I accidentally found your website that I could engage in a fruitful discussion. It sounds, to me, that this is not the intent of your website. Your assumption is that God exists and everything stems from this assumption. I cannot make this assumption because of answerless questions like the ones I've posed. And, I've many more questions which, so far, have never been answered to my satisfaction if the basic axiom of God's existence is not assumed.

I suggest that we stop our discussion and I will look elsewhere for answers. Thanks for taking the time to respond to my e-mails.

Ben

From: john.smith@domain.com
Sent: Sunday, January 03, 2010
Subject: RE: Got a Question? - EveryStudent.com

Ben,

Email is always hard to tell, but it seems that I might have offended you. Please forgive me.

Here is where there is a whole section dedicated to the subject of God's existence. The author of a majority of the articles on this website was Marilyn Adamson who was a former atheist, so hopefully you can appreciate her perspective.

Here is that section in case you are interested:

http://www.everystudent.com/menus/existence.html

John

To: <john.smith@domain.com>
Sent: Monday, January 04, 2010
Subject: Re: Got a Question? - EveryStudent.com

John

You did not offend me. My skin is far too thick for that to occur! I just thought that you did not want to get into a discussion, intellectual or otherwise, about the existence of God. Hence my closure. There's nothing to forgive.

However, since you've re-opened the discussion, I do have some further thoughts.

I had already read Marilyn Adamson's essay before I contacted you. I had some major problems with her position on the existence of God - see later - and I moved from her essay to the Contact page and sent you my opening e-mail.

To illustrate my problems, I have cut and pasted sections of the Adamson essay into the attached document and then inserted my comments, in *italics*, under the sections. Take a look.

I am also quite happy for you to forward my comments to Marilyn Adamson. I don't have her e-mail address. You may have it.

One final question. You say that Marilyn Adamson was a former atheist. Can you tell me her profession and about her background? In particular, has she ever had any scientific or engineering training? I'm just curious, again.

Regards,

Ben

The attachment, containing extracts from Adamson's essay and my interspersed comments in italics.

Is there a God?
By Marilyn Adamson

Does God exist? Here are six straight-forward reasons to believe that God is really there.

Just once wouldn't you love for someone to simply show you the evidence for God's existence? No arm-twisting. No statements of, "You just have to believe." Well, here is an attempt to candidly offer some of the reasons which suggest that God exists.

But first consider this. If a person opposes even the possibility of there being a God, then any evidence can be rationalised or explained away. It's like if someone refuses to believe that people have walked on the moon, then no amount of information is going to change their thinking. Photographs of astronauts walking on the moon, interviews with the astronauts, moon rocks...all the evidence would be worthless, because the person has already concluded that people can't go to the moon.

I don't agree. If the evidence of moon walking is irrefutable, then any sane and intelligent person will change his or her mind. We are built to question but we are built to accept that we might have been wrong.

1. Does God exist? The complexity of our planet points to a deliberate Designer who not only created our universe, but sustains it today.
Many examples showing God's design could be given, possibly with no end. But here are a few:
The Earth...its size is perfect. The Earth's size and corresponding gravity holds a thin layer of mostly nitrogen and oxygen gases, only extending about 50 miles above the Earth's surface. If Earth were smaller, an atmosphere would be impossible, like the planet Mercury. If Earth were larger, its atmosphere would contain free hydrogen, like Jupiter. Earth is the only known planet equipped with an atmosphere of the right mixture of gases to sustain plant, animal and human life ...

... as we know it. This is post rationalisation. This is like saying that the human hand is exactly right to grasp an orange therefore the hand has been designed correctly. If the orange turns out to be a pocket of air or a large bubble of water, then the hand has been designed incorrectly.

The Earth is located the right distance from the sun. Consider the temperature swings we encounter, roughly -30 degrees to +120 degrees. If the Earth were any further away from the sun, we would all freeze.

Not if we had all developed in such a way so as not to freeze. Human beings cannot live at the extremes of our planet, such as the Arctic and Antarctic – well, not without considerable help from artificial aids such as clothing, generated warmth, brought-in food and drink and so on. Darwin claimed that our development was based on natural selection. If it's very hot, we adapt, or die. If it's very cold, we adapt, or die. If there's very little oxygen, we adapt, or die. I'm convinced that evolution is a natural thing, not something controlled by a master designer. But, it's not sufficient just to say this because you could say the exact opposite and neither of us would know who was correct. However, there's a wealth of scientific provable evidence to support my statement. The idea of a master designer is not yet proven.

The human brain...simultaneously processes an amazing amount of information. Your brain takes in all the colors and objects you see, the temperature around you, the pressure of your feet against the floor, the sounds around you, the dryness of your mouth, even the texture of your keyboard. Your brain holds and processes all your emotions, thoughts and memories. At the same time your brain keeps track of the ongoing functions of your body like your breathing pattern, eyelid movement, hunger and movement of the muscles in your hands.
...
The eye...can distinguish among seven million colors. It has automatic focusing and handles an astounding 1.5 million messages -- simultaneously. Evolution focuses on mutations and changes from and within existing organisms. Yet evolution alone does not fully explain the initial source of the eye or the brain -- the start of living organisms from nonliving matter.

Standard biology and becoming more understandable every day as science progresses. Our understanding of how the brain and the eye work is always increasing. We know more now than we knew, say, 100 years ago or 200 years ago, and there's no evidence to suggest that we have hit a barrier in our understanding. Every now and again, we pass a milestone. I would suggest that the development of the modern solid-state computer – a science that is only 60 years old – has given us tremendous insight into how the brain processes the electrical signals it receives from our receptors – ears, nose, eyes, mouth, hands, feet, and so on. The organisation of hierarchical memory; the storage of data; the retrieval and use of this data in a computer have all led to a better understanding of how the brain might do the same things. This, in turn, has led to insight into many other branches of science that affects our life – linguistics for example.

Our appreciation of how languages evolve has increased enormously as our understanding of cognition improves. And our understanding of cognition is, in turn, linked to our comprehension of why it is difficult to program judgmental resolution into a computer. My point is that science is progressing at an unprecedented rate and, so far, has not come up with the idea of a master designer. The need for such a figurehead is not there yet. It may become a requirement at some future date but, so far, I've not seen it.

2. Does God exist? The universe had a start - what caused it?

Scientists are convinced that our universe began with one enormous explosion of energy and light, which we now call the Big Bang. This was the singular start to everything that exists: the beginning of the universe, the start of space, and even the initial start of time itself.

...

The universe has not always existed. It had a start...what caused that? Scientists have no explanation for the sudden explosion of light and matter.

I agree, but this doesn't prove the existence of some mythical supernatural force as the creator of the universe. It simply says that the scientific community has so far failed to explain how it all began. But that is not to say that it will continue to fail in the future.

As a simpler analogy, consider the force of gravity. A few centuries ago, gravity was something that happened but which was not explainable. If you dropped something, it just fell to the floor. That's the way it was – a natural phenomena. Why didn't the object rise? Why didn't it just stay where it was, in a state of suspension? Why didn't it disintegrate? And another million 'Why didn't it ...' questions. We did not know the answers to any of these questions until Isaac Newton, and others, figured out the forces associated with spinning objects and mathematics gave us the framework for expressing these forces and hence, finally, understanding gravity. But our lack of understanding did not cause us to create a Gravity God, not as far as I know (although the Egyptian deity Shu *comes close) so why is there the need to create a master creator simply because, so far, we don't understand the root causes of the creation of the universe?*

3. Does God exist? The universe operates by uniform laws of nature. Why does it?

Much of life may seem uncertain, but look at what we can count on day after day: gravity remains consistent, a hot cup of coffee left on a counter will get cold, the earth rotates in the same 24 hours, and the speed of light doesn't change -- on earth or in galaxies far from us.

How is it that we can identify laws of nature that ***never*** change? Why is the universe so orderly, so reliable?

Why indeed, but why not? And is it true to say 'that never change'? Einstein rocked our boat with his insights into the relationship between time and space and what were considered to be fundamental laws certainly changed as a result of his work. Darwinian evolution is another example of laws that are constantly changing. The universe is not so orderly, not so reliable. *The Hadron Collider is on track to discover some very fundamental changes to our understanding of atomic physics. Black holes were postulated as far back as 1783 but not shown to exist until the twentieth century. We now believe that there are at least fourteen black holes in the universe and there's speculation that white holes may also exist. Both black holes and white holes were first proposed by mathematical models that were later tempered by changing laws. I have yet to see a mathematical model, even a very coarse one, which proves the existence of God.*

4. Does God exist? The DNA code informs, programs a cell's behavior.

All instruction, all teaching, all training comes with intent. Someone who writes an instruction manual does so with purpose. Did you know that in every cell of our bodies there exists a very detailed instruction code, much like a miniature computer program? As you may know, a computer program is made up of ones and zeros, like this: 110010101011000. The way they are arranged tells the computer program what to do. The DNA code in each of our cells is very similar. It's made up of four chemicals that scientists abbreviate as A, T, G, and C. These are arranged in the human cell like this: CGTGTGACTCGCTCCTGAT and so on. There are three billion of these letters in every human cell!!

A similar argument prevails. Our understanding of genetic coding is increasing every day, some say at a frightening rate and others say in a way that emulates a creator. DNA engineering, coupled with stem cell research, puts bespoke human creation into the realms of possibility. We can eliminate disease. We can create super athletes. We can enlarge the computing capacity of the brain and, with it, intelligence. Whether we agree with these possibilities and even want to do these things becomes irrelevant. Very soon, we will be able to do these things – in fact, some may have already happened unbeknown to most of us – and, if we do, it puts us on a par with a master creator, doesn't it? What role then for God? And was he (I will assume male for convenience) ever needed anyway? Research projects such as the Hadron Collider, genetic engineering through manipulation of DNA, and many other scientific activities are stripping away the mystery of creation at a very fast rate. Once stripped, once understood, do you really think that a master creator will be revealed? I will keep an open mind but all the evidence so far says 'No'. Look what happened to Shu once the true laws of gravity were understood. He was no longer necessary.

Prologue: A Conversation With A Christian

5. Does God exist? We know God exists because he pursues us. He is constantly initiating and seeking for us to come to him.
I was an atheist at one time. And like many atheists, the issue of people believing in God bothered me greatly. What is it about atheists that we would spend so much time, attention, and energy refuting something that we don't believe even exists?! What causes us to do that? When I was an atheist, I attributed my intentions as caring for those poor, delusional people...to help them realize their hope was completely ill-founded. To be honest, I also had another motive. As I challenged those who believed in God, I was deeply curious to see if they could convince me otherwise. Part of my quest was to become free from the question of God. If I could conclusively prove to believers that they were wrong, then the issue is off the table, and I would be free to go about my life.

Okay. I admit it. I'm an atheist. I also have a scientific background plus I'm an engineer and a researcher. But, the issue of people believing in God did not bother me as much as intrigued me, just like 'Why does a cup of coffee cool down if left alone?' intrigued me in my student days. Why do people believe in God? Why are there so many gods (2,850 according to www.godchecker.com).[2] Why did different cultures develop their own god system – the Greeks, the Egyptians, the Incas, the Aztecs, and so on? What does a god provide that is not provided elsewhere? And, most importantly, is there any proof that any of these gods really exist and, if so, where's the proof?

6. Does God exist? Unlike any other revelation of God, Jesus Christ is the clearest, most specific picture of God revealing himself to us.
Why Jesus? Look throughout the major world religions and you'll find that Buddha, Muhammad, Confucius and Moses all identified themselves as teachers or prophets. None of them ever claimed to be equal to God. Surprisingly, Jesus did. That is what sets Jesus apart from all the others.
...
   What proof did Jesus give for claiming to be divine? He did what people can't do. Jesus performed miracles. He healed people...blind, crippled, deaf, even raised a couple of people from the dead. He had power over objects...created food out of thin air, enough to feed crowds of several thousand people. He performed miracles over nature...walked on top of a lake, commanding a raging storm to stop for some friends. People everywhere followed Jesus, because he

---
[2] Now up to 3,700 one year later.

constantly met their needs, doing the miraculous. He said if you do not want to believe what I'm telling you, you should at least believe in me based on the miracles you're seeing.

Hearsay, mythology and the stuff of entertaining but fallacious stories. I can say to you that, three weeks ago, I turned a red snapper fish into a beef steak but that I then went on and ate the steak so there's no evidence of my miracle. But, I'm prepared to swear before the highest court in the land that what I did was the truth. I'm also prepared to state, under oath, that I'm related to God and that he gave me this power. Thus starts a belief that I enacted a miracle and I am in some way divine. Two hundred years later, this belief becomes a 'fact' that can never be proved, or disproved, unless scientific evidence shows irrefutably that the DNA structure of a red snapper fish can never be morphed into that of a beef steak. It just ain't possible. The morphing will go through an intermediate stage where all cells become water and the ex-snapper will dissolve into a puddle on the floor before it can assume the shape and texture of a T-bone.

There are many stories from the past that were passed down word-of-mouth and then eventually recorded for posterity but which were so warped that any residual truth had become embellished and distorted beyond all recognition of what really took place. The Bible is such a collection. Events were not recorded as they happened. Errors crept in at every re-telling. More errors crept in as major translations occurred. And, in the end, we cannot look to the Bible as a factual account of events that occurred thousands of years ago. The Bible is just a collection of well-worn stories. You cannot claim that they are factual. They are just stories; some entertaining, some horrific, some conjecture, some of historical interest, but in the end just stories.

To conclude my comments on Marilyn Adamson's essay ...

As I said earlier, statements about the existence of God always turn out to be axiomatic: first, let me assume that God exists and now I will prove to you that God exists. This cuts no ice with me but if you show me a piece of moon rock that hasn't travelled here by way of a meteorite, then I will believe, after further probing, it was brought back by an Apollo astronaut.

I have come up with my own ideas as to why religions develop, either centred around one god such as Christianity and Islam, or centred around a collection of gods such as many of the ancient religions or a modern religion such as Hinduism, but that's another essay. I am not against God. I just don't believe that he exists in any traditional sense and I see no evidence that he exists in any other sense even though we cannot formulate the other sense. Scientific progress keeps explaining things in rational terms that we thought were inexplicable and if I have any faith at all, it is that science will continue

Prologue: A Conversation With A Christian

to peel away the mysteries of life and that there'll not be a master creator at the end of the road.

I could be convinced otherwise but I need a lot more than the arguments put forward by Marilyn Adamson.

Ben

The dialogue stopped at this stage. 'John Smith' never responded to my last e-mail and its attachment.

This dialogue lay dormant in the recesses of my computer's hard drive for a year until I read, and re-read, two books written by prominent atheists Richard Dawkins and Sam Harris– *The God Delusion* and *The End of Faith* respectively.

The book by Dawkins impressed me with its calm and precise scientific analysis of the evidence for and against the existence of God whereas the Harris book frightened the living daylights out of me with its thesis that we're fast heading towards Armageddon because of what Muslims believe, truly inherently unquestionably believe about what happens when they die and what they should do to those who do not follow their religion.

As a result, I feared for the future of my granddaughters and was motivated to write my own book. It is dedicated to them and I hope that they all live to a ripe old age rather than be blown up or in some other way destroyed by the blind and unassailable beliefs of people who believe in a Supreme Creator called God and a hedonistic afterlife throbbing with sexually-available virgins and unlimited food and wine.

Now read on …

(^_^)

Chapter 1
Introduction

> **Faith Warning!**
> Do not read this book if you have a blind faith in the existence of God, or any other god(s), and you don't want your faith shaken, stirred or otherwise disturbed.

Why write this book?

This book started out as an essay to my four granddaughters who, I hope, will survive me by many years and, consequently, will inherit the effects of the religious intolerance that now affects the world in which we live.

Religion is a hot topic, especially among mostly-secular Western Europeans, many of whom fear the ever-increasing encroachment of Islam into their traditional cultures, and among Americans concerned about the sometimes secretive influence of Christianity on both the education of their children (the teaching of Creationism rather than Darwinism, for example) and the formulation of dogmatic State and Federal laws based on religious beliefs. (Up to 2003, sodomy was classed as illegal in at least fourteen States in the USA thereby forcing homosexuality to be illegal.[3])

Over the last ten years, we have seen the publication of some extremely interesting and provocative analyses of modern-day religion written by authors such as the evolutionary biologist Richard Dawkins and the neuroscientist and philosopher Sam Harris. Their best-selling books, *The God Delusion* and *The End of Faith* respectively, although erudite, thought-provoking and profound in their content, are, in parts, difficult to read if you are not an evolutionary biologist or neuroscientific philosopher, or do not have a lexiconic vocabulary[4] equal to theirs. Nonetheless, their analyses and conclusions deserve to be heard by, let us say, the common man.

---

[3] http://en.wikipedia.org/wiki/Sodomy_laws_in_the_United_States
[4] By which I mean a very wide vocabulary of both ordinary and scientific words. In the case of the Harris/Dawkins books, I had to look up the meaning of almost 100 words in order to make sense of their prose! I've listed these words, and their meanings, in a Harris/Dawkins dictionary at the end of the book.

Other books have achieved similar prominence – *God is not Great* by Christopher Hitchens and *In God we Doubt* by John Humphreys, for example. Although more approachable than the Dawkins and Harris books, they lack the scientific rigour of *The God Delusion* and philosophical structure of *The End of Faith*. But, taken as a set of books, they all raise fundamental questions about the very existence of God, the influence of modern religious faiths and tenets on our societies, and the future of a world in which certain dominant and aggressive religions that are tightly coupled to the state, especially Islam and especially Iran, now have access to weapons of mass destruction, including the nuclear bomb or the wherewithal to make a nuclear bomb. Indeed, according to Harris, the future is bleak. I will have more to say on this aspect of modern religions later in the book.

My personal journey from being a relatively devout Christian in my youth to a devout atheist in my more senior years was based on my education as an electronics engineer and the background in analytical analysis intrinsic in such training.

Before I retired, and thus had time to read books by Dawkins and others, I had already spent many hours cocooned in aircraft and in hotel rooms thinking about the nature of religion and subjecting its beliefs to my analytical thinking. My conclusions were that, in the end, there was no evidence to support the belief that God has ever existed and that religion, stripped of this belief, was merely another money-making business similar in to any business that manufactures, distributes and sells a commodity product.

Consider this.

There is a product. In fact, there are several products, very similar in nature but coming from an organisation whose history includes violence and life-threatening addictions. There are also several myths perpetuated about the product, including its origin, its make-up, holders of secret knowledge, and what it can do for you. In fact, there is considerable mystery as to the exact nature of the product but there is a very capable, some might say ruthless, marketing team coupled with an efficient distribution channel such that the product is readily recognisable and available in every corner of the world. But despite this, people consume this product with an implicit belief that it solves an immediate problem and does so in a way that does not harm the consumer. There are also competitive products, including abstinence from any of the products, and sometimes the market chooses to adopt one of the competitive products in preference to the real thing but, in most cases, the differences between the various products are slight or even indiscernible. But, despite which product you consume, the variety of products is ubiquitous, always available, comforting and very lucrative for the merchants and peddlers involved.

Did I just describe the creation, manufacture, marketing, distribution and consumption of a mass-produced commodity product, such as Coca-Cola; or of God?[5]

My purpose in writing this book is to introduce you to my thinking and conclusions. In so doing, I will rely on the findings of authors like Richard Dawkins and Sam Harris when I need scientific authority to justify my own, sometimes subjective, conclusions. My intention is to present the main conclusions of Dawkins and Harris embedded in my own thoughts on the multi-faceted topic of religion. If I succeed, then it will be due, in part, to my reliance on their scholarly research and treatises. If I fail, then it will be due to my own inadequacies as a researcher or author.

One last thing before we start – a note about the references included in this book. Websites are like quicksand – forever changing.[6] For this reason, I have not listed all the websites I visited while researching the contents of this book. Instead, I will assume that you are skilled in the use of search engines and can dig around, much as I did. I have included references to a few major websites however, usually as footnotes, plus a list of books recommended for further reading. These recommendations can be found at the end of the book.

(^_^)

---

[5] The original working title for this book was 'God and Coca-Cola: what's the difference?' Unfortunately, Coca-Cola lawyers objected to the use of their trademarked name in the title on the grounds that it suggested that the Coca-Cola Company was setting itself up as a religion. Perish the thought!
[6] All websites listed were visited sometime between February and July, 2011.

Chapter 2
The Meaning Of Words Associated With Religion

'When I use a word' Humpty Dumpty said in rather a scornful tone, 'it means just what I choose it to mean - neither more nor less.'
Lewis Carroll, *Alice in Wonderland*

'If I asked for a cup of coffee, someone would search for a double meaning.'
Mae West, American Actress

'We can define a word how we like for our own purposes, provided we do so clearly and unambiguously.'
Richard Dawkins, *The Selfish Gene*, p. 28

In my former career as a teacher to people in the electronics industry all over the world, I learnt one basic fact of life very quickly: always predefine what you mean by the technical words that you'll be using. I have had several discussions with groups of electronic designers, and more so, managers, in which it turned out that our basic definitions of a word were fundamentally different. One example is the word *system*. To a designer of microprocessors, a *system* is the final device or, nowadays, collection of devices, that become the microprocessor. To a designer of an internet backbone router, the system is a huge assembly of component-loaded printed-circuit boards sitting in metal racks and connected by vast collections of cables, with the whole construction occupying a room big enough to house an elephant, or two! How would a group of microprocessor designers converse intelligently with a group of router designers if they both use the same word but, unknown to either group, assign different meanings to it? The answer is either not to use the word *system*, or to agree up front what the word means in the context of the discussion.

Taking this lesson to heart, here are my meanings of common words associated with religion that I have used in the book. The definitions are mostly based on Merriam-Webster's dictionary but sometimes coloured by my own intentions, as per Humpty Dumpty.

Agnostic: Someone who admits neither to the existence of a god, nor the nonexistence of a god. Basically, someone who says 'I don't know if a god exists, or not.'
Allah: See **God**.
Animism: A belief that all objects, animate and inanimate, possess a spirit or soul and that they are at least worthy of respect and, in some cases, worship.
Apostate: One who renounces or abandons a religious faith.
Armageddon: Variously known as the *Day of Judgment*, the *End of Time*, the *Second Coming of Christ*, the *Day of the Lord*, and *World War Three*. Basically, it's used as a generic term for any end-of-the-world scenario.
Ascetic: One who practices strict self-denial as a measure of personal and especially religious (spiritual) discipline.
Atheist: One who denies the existence of God or any other god, and who therefore has no religious beliefs.[7] People can be atheists by default - that is, because they have never been introduced to such beliefs – or by reasoning - for example, because they have decided the existence of God cannot be proved and therefore that such a belief would be false.
Avatar: Originating from Hinduism, an *avatara* (Sanskrit) describes an intermediary form between man and God: a divine manifestation altershape. *Vishnu*, the preserver, has visited earth nine times in the form of an avatar. The eighth avatar was *Krishna*.
Belief: An absolute conviction of the truth of some statement irrespective of whether any evidence exists to substantiate it. Harris states that a set of beliefs underlies everything we do, how we react to certain situations, how we think about anything and how we position our thoughts in our view of the world. In other words, our beliefs become the very core of our interaction with anything and everything in the world. An unquestionable belief in God therefore becomes central to our behaviour.[8]
Blasphemy: The act of insulting or otherwise showing contempt or lack of reverence for God
Cosmology: A study of the nature of the universe and its contents.

---

[7] This assumes that the word religion automatically infers a belief in a mythical being called God, or a set of gods, and is the sense in which I generally use the word. But, religion is a hard word to define. See the **Religion** entry in this chapter for more discussion on the possible alternative meanings of the word.

[8] An interesting philosophical question arises from this statement. Is it also true that an unquestionable falsehood (disbelief) can also be central to our behaviour? I'll let the philosophers answer this question.

The Meaning Of Words Associated With Religion

Creed: A set of fundamental (religious) beliefs.

Darwinism: Ascribing to the theories of Charles Darwin, and others, relating to the evolution and survival of a species by a process of transmutation and natural selection with no divine intervention.

Deism: A natural form of religion that argues that reason and observation are sufficient to explain the existence of God and the creation of the universe. A deist's God is a one-time creator. Subsequently, he, she or it is passive. God's work has been done. **Deity**: The property of being either a god or a goddess. A deity is also called a Divinity.

Diaspora: A scattering and resettlement of a nation or race or religious group into different parts of the world.

Divine: Possessing the attributes of a deity.

Dogma: A doctrine, or body of doctrines, concerning faith and morals formally stated and authoritatively proclaimed by a church. Dogmas are statements that, usually, cannot be proven: 'Jesus is the Son of God sent to die for the sins of the world'.

Epistemology: A study or theory of the nature and evidence of knowledge, usually with reference to its limits and validity. Epistemology answers questions such as 'What is meant by knowledge? How is it acquired? How is it validated?'

Eschatology: A system of beliefs about what happens when you die – an afterlife belief. Eschatology also implies a belief concerning the end of the world and the ultimate destiny of mankind.

Fact: Something that can be proved to be true by experimentation, evidence and existence.

Faith: A state of mind that leads people to believe something – it doesn't matter what – in the total absence of any supporting evidence (Dawkins, *The Selfish Gene*, p. 330). Faith is often used as a synonym for belief and is usually related to a religious order, for example a faith in the beliefs associated with Christianity.

fatwa : An authoritative Islamic opinion on some question of religious interpretation.

god (lower case g): A being, object or entity believed to have more than natural attributes and powers and usually the object of some form of adoration, adulation or worship, examples being Zeus or the Blarney Stone.

God (upper case G): A supernatural being perfect in power (omnipotence), wisdom (omniscience) and always present

(omnipresence) who is worshipped as the creator, ruler and maintenance superintendant of the universe and all its contents.[9]
Hadith (report): A narrative set of the sayings and customs of Muhammad the Prophet, largely used to interpret the statements in the Qur'an. The Hadith is described by Harris (*The End of Faith*, p. 116) as 'the lens through which to interpret the Qur'an'.
Heaven: In the Christian faith, the dwelling place of God and one of the final resting places for human souls when they depart from their bodily trappings. A similar place, called Paradise, exists in the Islamic faith. In both cases, the place is characterized as a good place for your soul to spend the rest of its afterlife existence, being 'a place of happiness'. The alternative to Heaven is **Hell**: a 'place of purgatory, suffering and misery' and in the Christian and Judaism faiths, presided over by the fallen angel Satan, also known as the Devil.
Heresy: An opinion or doctrine contrary to a specific church's dogma.
Hell: See **Heaven**.
Incarnation: The conception and birth of a sentient being, human or animal, as the material manifestation of a mythical being such as a god. Jesus Christ was said to be the incarnation of God.
Infidel: One who is an unbeliever with respect to a particular religion or who admits to no religious beliefs.
Innate:
1 : Existing in, belonging to, or determined by factors present in an individual from birth : NATIVE, INBORN
2 : Belonging to the essential nature of something: INHERENT
3 : Originating in or derived from the mind or the constitution of the intellect rather than from experience

Innate applies to qualities or characteristics that are part of one's inner essential nature and not acquired after birth.
Instinct: An inherent inclination of a living organism towards a particular behaviour: something that is performed without prior experience.

(Chapter 9 adds a second part to this definition: An instinct is a subconscious process involving the cerebral cortex in the brain, and based on a primitive reaction that we may or may not be able to control.)
Jihad: A call to war. A holy war waged on behalf of Islam as a religious duty. A crusade for a principle or belief

---

[9] In this book, if I've need for a pronoun to identify God, I'll use the pronoun he or him. Since we don't know the sex of God, or even if he has any sexual characteristics, he/him, she/her or it would all be appropriate pronouns but the usual convention is to assign God to be a male but note that this does not confer maleness on God.

Koran: See **Qur'an**.
Laity: The followers of a religious faith as distinguished from its clergy.
Martyr: Someone who voluntarily or otherwise suffers death as a penalty for refusing to renounce or confess to a religious belief.
Meditation: An altered state of consciousness which is induced in a controlled manner.
Mendicant: A member of a religious order owning neither personal nor communal property.
Miracle: An extraordinary event manifesting divine intervention in human affairs.
Monotheism: A religious doctrine or belief that supposes that there is only one God, not many gods. For example: Judaism, Christianity, and Islam.
Muslim: A follower of Islam.
Pantheon: A set of gods and goddesses officially recognised by a social group. For example, the Greek gods, the Roman gods, and many similar groups of deities.
Paradise: See **Heaven**.
Polytheism: Religious doctrine or belief that supposes that there is more than one God. For example: Hinduism, some branches of Buddhism, all the ancient religions (Greek, Roman, Celt, and so on).
Qur'an: A book recording the word of God allegedly handed down by the angel Gabriel to Muhammad the Prophet. Qur'an is often spelt Koran.
Radicalise: Advocating extreme measures to achieve or restore a political or religious ideal. A radical is one who has extreme views.
Religion: A notoriously difficult word to define.[10] I use the following general definition.

An institutionalised system of attitudes, beliefs and practices based on the belief of a God or set of gods – Christianity, Islam, Judaism or Hinduism, for example – practiced either by an individual or by a community of people who might gather in special buildings or places for worship and meditation.

See the Appendix to this chapter for further elaboration of the word.
Schism: Formal division in or separation from a church or a religious body.
Secularism: Relating to worldly non-religious sentiments. A secularist is someone who believes that a government/society/organisation

---

[10] Pornography is similarly a difficult word to define. The only definition I know that works is: 'Pornography? You'll recognise it when you see it!'

should be free of any religious influences – separation of church and state, civil laws not religious laws, no discrimination based on religious beliefs. Secularism is the opposite of a **theocracy**. The original Constitution of the United States was a secular constitution.

Soul: Another difficult word to define. A simple definition is 'an immaterial essence, animating principle, or actuating cause of an individual life' (Merriam-Webster). Or a person's inner self awareness that, possibly, survives death. All religions include the concept of a soul but give it different names and meanings: soul (Judaism, Christianity, and Islam), *atman* (Hinduism), *karma* (Buddhism), *jiva* (Jainism), *chi* (Taoism), *kami* (Shintoism), and so on. See Chapter 9 for more discussion.

Superhuman: Possessing human properties exceeding normal human power, size or skills.

Supernatural: Possessing properties beyond those of the laws of nature and attributed to possession of divinity.

Supreme Creator: Often used by non-Abrahamic religions to denote the creator of the universe and all its contents. Supreme Creator avoids using the name God, which is seen to relate to Judaism, Christianity and Islam.

Syncretism: The combination of beliefs, doctrines and rituals originating from two or more different religions.

Theism: A belief in the existence of one or many supernatural beings called gods who have the power to intervene directly in worldly affairs.

Theocracy: A government of a state that is guided and directed by the doctrines of a religion and by those considered to be either divine or divinely guided. The Islamic Republic of Iran is an example of a theocracy.

Theology: The study of a God or set of gods and the associated nature of their godness (divinity).

Totemism: Similar to **animism** (see above), but a belief that there's a single primary source of life, typically the land itself, rather than multiple sources.

Transubstantiation : A Roman Catholic belief that the wafer and wine partaken at Communion really is converted into the flesh and blood of Jesus Christ although they retain the appearance and taste of bread and wine.

Transtheism: Applied to religions that have no deities and yet claim to be a religion, examples being Theravada Buddhism and Jainism. The word bridges the gap between theism and atheism.

Appendix: The meaning of the word *Religion*

As already noted, the word *religion* is notoriously difficult to define. In this book, I've used the word in its most simple form: an institutionalised system of attitudes, beliefs and practices based on the belief of a God or set of gods. But when you get to the section on Buddhism (Chapter 5), you will note that I ask the question 'Is Buddhism a religion?' The original version of Buddhism, now called Theravada Buddhism, did not assume nor need a mythical Supreme Creator. So, is Buddhism a religion? We can decide 'yes' or 'no' depending on how we want to think about religion in all its aspects rather than just conveying a belief in God.

While I was researching the meaning of the word *religion*, I frequently came across references to the *Seven Dimensions of Religion* as expounded by Ninian Smart (1927 – 2001). Smart identified what he called *para-historical* and *historical* aspects of religion. Para-historical means attributes that are based on something that cannot be proved whereas historical means attributes that can be substantiated. Here is a summary Smart's seven dimensions.

Para-Historical Dimensions

1. Doctrinal. The system of doctrines (principles, beliefs) concerning the nature of a Divinity (such as God) and the relationships that exist between the Divinity and humans.
2. Mythological. Sacred stories passed down from generation to generation that tell stories about the Divinity, reveal the nature of the Divinity, or reveal the underlying reasons for certain traditions.
3. Ethics. The set of rules and guidelines for behaviour within a community and the basis for judging good or bad, innocent or guilty.

Historical Dimensions

4. Rituals. The way in which the community institutionalises its beliefs in the Divinity, expressing their beliefs through actions such as group prayer, festivals, fasting, abstinence from sex, and so on.
5. Experiential (based on experience). The capacity of religious actions such as prayer and other forms of worship to induce feelings of security, comfort, awe, inexplicable presence, mystery or ecstasy.
6. Social. The impact of the religious traditions on social organisation – for example, the organisation of religious orders and those who

exemplify the religious traditions - monks, nuns, priests, and so on. The interactions between church and state.

7. Material. The material manifestations of the religion – sacred buildings, sacred places, sacred objects, paintings, statues, books, music, clothing, and so on.

If we accept that these seven dimensions pretty much define the attributes of any religion, then the next question is 'How many boxes should we tick to define some organisation to be a religion?' I'll leave this question unanswered but in the case of Theravadic Buddhism, we can tick all but the first box. So, does that make it a religion?

(^_^)

Chapter 3
The Beginnings Of Doubt: A Personal Odyssey

'I used to believe in God, until I reached the age of reason.'
George Carlin, American comedian, author, social commentator

'Have you noticed that no matter how sick the Pope gets, they never consider taking him to Lourdes?'
Tom Dunker, American author

'My best advice to anyone who wants to raise a happy, mentally healthy child is: keep him or her as far away from a church as you can.'
Frank Zappa, American composer, musician, film director

I used to be a Church-of-England (C-of-E) Christian. That is, I went to Sunday school when I was a young lad still in short trousers growing up in post Second World War England and, for a time, in Ceylon (now called Sri Lanka). I believed in the existence of God as a friendly benevolent and bearded father figure who lived somewhere up in the sky in a place called Heaven. I occasionally prayed to this benevolent figure, either when I wanted something (a train set, a smile from the girl next door) or when I was told to do so (at church – 'let us now pray'). I believed that Jesus Christ was the son of God, just as I was a son to my own father, and that after Jesus was crucified, he rose again and went up to his father's place. And I believed that God could see everything I did, hear everything I said, monitor everything I thought, and was basically in total control of my life and my actions.

Why did I believe all this? Because I was told that it was true by people I knew and respected: my parents, some of my teachers at primary school, but mostly by the people I met in church and who conducted the various church services – the priests, the curates, the lay preachers. And, I have to admit, the thought of an all-seeing all-hearing and always-present 'super being' called God was comforting as I developed my own awareness of the world around me.

When I entered puberty and my early teenage years, I began to allow other activities to take priority over my religious sentiments: sport, academic studies, a growing interest in girls, reading exciting books, seeing exciting films. In short, I began to enter the adult world. My faith didn't leave me: it just shrank into the background, but I still went to church and, until my voice broke, I was a member of the local church choir. I even performed a couple of treble solos. 'Oh love that wilt not let me go' (Hymn 359 in Hymns Ancient and Modern, Revised) was my speciality. I was incredibly nervous when I sang these solos at Evensong, but proud of the fact that I had been selected to sing the praises of God in public and in front of an audience.

At age fifteen, I entered the boarding school section of my grammar school (*The King's School, Grantham*; a school founded by Bishop Richard Foxe in the sixteenth century and formerly attended by a young Isaac Newton back in the 1650s[11]) and for the next four years, until I left school, I was obliged to attend Sunday's Morning Service in St. Wulfram's Church just behind the school.

By now, I was entering the rebellious stage of my teenage years, questioning everything that I was doing or being told to do. I was also starting to specialise in scientific and mathematical subjects in my academic studies, learning how to acquire a critical and analytical approach to just about everything that was coming my way. (This included the opposite sex which, I must confess, absolutely refused to succumb to any form of critical or logical appraisal and has so remained all my life! But, I digress.)

One of the pupils in my class was not a C-of-E Christian. He was a member of another religious group – I forget which one but it was monotheistic (one that admits to only one god)[12]– and because he was not C-of-E, he was excused the need to attend compulsory school services in St. Wulfram's church. This set me thinking. First, why was he not Church of England? Second, why was he excused attendance even though his God was the same as my God? Third, if he was unable to attend my church, where did he go to offer up his prayers and subservience to God? Fourth, was his religion better than mine? Fifth ... The questions came in thick and fast with no easy answers. In retrospect, this small incident in my religious life was to become a major turning point in my personal understanding of God and religion, and all its ramifications. But, it didn't happen overnight.

---

[11] Isaac Newton's statue stands in the centre of Grantham. I was once severely admonished by the Head Master of my school for walking past the statue wearing my full school uniform, including my cap, and holding hands with a girlfriend. Such disrespect! I was probably sixteen or seventeen years old at the time. Isaac Newton is said to have scratched his name in the window of what was the old school hall. I've seen the scratching but I doubt if it really was the work of Newton. More likely a prank by some mischievous scholar well before my time!

[12] He was Hungarian, arriving at the school in 1956, the year of the Hungarian Revolution – the attempt by Hungary to break free from the USSR. Thus he was probably a Roman Catholic rather than a C-of-E Protestant.

The Beginnings Of Doubt: A Personal Odyssey

At age eighteen, I left school with higher-level qualifications in mathematics and physics – the classical subjects to support a scientific or engineering career – and I started a process of higher education at university level. First, I qualified as an aeronautical engineer, then I converted to electronics engineering and, ultimately obtained a doctorate in what was blandly and incorrectly called 'computer science' but in reality was a specialist topic in electronics.[13] By the time I finished my university education, I was well skilled in the application of the *scientific method* to technical problem statement and solution and religion was about to remove itself from my view of the world simply because it was consistently failing to stand up to rigorous scrutiny.

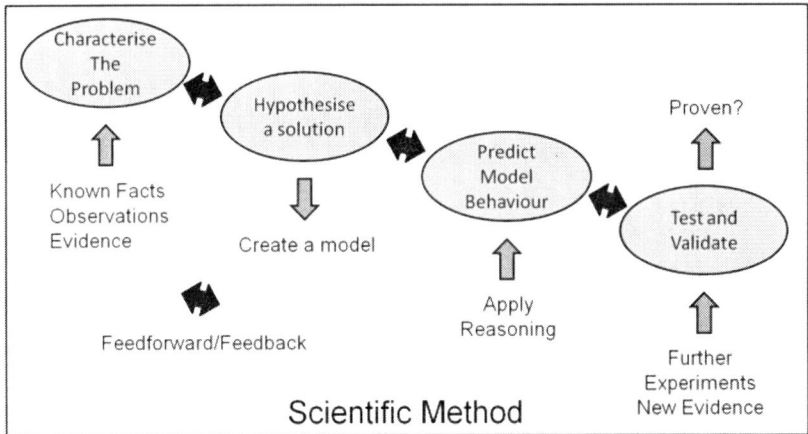

The scientific method, also known as the *scientific approach*, for proving or disproving a hypothesis to explain a phenomenon can be summarised in the following way:

Step 1. Characterize the phenomenon by means of evidence: known facts, observations, definitions and repeatable measurements. That is, define the problem.

---

[13] The topic was to become known as Design-For-Test; the ability to design very complex electronic devices and component-loaded boards in such a way that they could be tested after manufacture in a short and economical amount of time but with enough confidence to predict that the unit was without any manufacturing defects and would function as intended. The topic was in its infancy when I started my doctorate in the late 1960s. It's now a huge topic throughout the whole electronics industry and has been the subject of my entire post-doctoral professional career.

Step 2. Put forward a hypothesis (an explanation or a model) to explain the phenomenon characterized in Step 1. Ensure that the hypothesis fits all the evidence so far known. The hypothesis can be mathematical, physical or simply a statement.

Step 3. Use the hypothesis to predict further behaviour by deductive, inductive or abductive (guessing) reasoning.

Step 4. Conduct tests (experiments producing yet more evidence) that confirm, or otherwise, the predictions in Step 3. If the tests confirm the hypothesis, publish the results and all accumulated experimental data and experimental procedures (called a full disclosure) so that others can conduct independent experiments to confirm the results. If the tests do not confirm the hypothesis, return to Step 2, modify the hypothesis and repeat Step 3 (different or additional predictions) and Step 4 (different or additional experiments) until either a satisfactory result is obtained or you've succeeded in disproving the hypothesis.

A key point about the scientific method is the need for evidence – something that furnishes an undeniable and unquestionable proof of an existing fact or a new fact. If evidential proof is not forthcoming, we have two mutually-exclusive courses of action: either declare that the original hypothesis cannot be proven and thus remains false, or accept the hypothesis without proof, in which case it becomes a belief. Of course, this pre-supposes that we live in a Boolean world – one in which something, such as a hypothesis, can only be either TRUE or FALSE. In the real world, this is not true. There are many shades of result between the Boolean end-stops of TRUE and FALSE and greater minds than mine have pondered upon the philosophical nature of all the in-between results. I will say more about this conflict of evidence with result in a later chapter when I discuss cause-effect analysis but, for now, let us accept that the scientific method gives us an analytical, albeit maybe recursive and never-ending way of getting to the validity of a statement, especially an unsubstantiated belief.

Questions, questions, questions

In my own development, my education in the scientific method had begun to raise very serious questions in my mind about my religious beliefs. In retrospect, and with some embellishments, here are some of the questions.

- Where was the proof that God exists or existed in the past? And, who created God? Another even-more superior God, or did God just happen? If so, how can this be? We are close to validating the hypothesis that *home sapiens* evolved from self-created minute organisms that burst into existence in a primeval pond somewhere. Is there a similar evolutionary process for God? If so, where is God now? We can identify ourselves as the product of an evolutionary process but we cannot do the same for God. Does he (I'll use the male pronoun for convenience) have other attributes that we, as yet, don't know about? Or are we chasing a will-o'-the-wisp?
- Why is it that my prayers never worked? Did God not hear me? If he did hear me, did he think that my requests were not important enough in the greater scheme of things? (I could live with that if it were true!)
- Can the evidence for God's existence be found in the so-called holy books: the Hebrew Tanakh, the Christian Bible or the Islamic Qur'an? If the Qur'an is considered to be the true word of God as told to Muhammad by the angel Gabriel, how should one interpret the Bible? Can the Bible be taken literally? There's much contradiction and, in the Old Testament, descriptions of violence, revenge and retribution, and multiple incitements to violence against those who do not adhere to the Christian faith. The Qur'an is even more forceful on 'killing all unbelievers'. Does this mean that the God of Islam, also known as *Allah*, requires that all Christians, also believers in the same God, should be killed for not living according to the tenets of Islam? Where's the sense in that?
- Was Mary a virgin when she became pregnant with Jesus and did she remain so up until the birth? Is such an occurrence possible? No sexual intercourse? No artificial insemination? No fertilization of a female egg by a male sperm? (My emerging sexuality had taught me that it takes two to tango!)
- Did Jesus truly arise from the dead three days after he died on the cross?
- Did Jesus really turn two fishes and five loaves into a feast for 5,000 people?
- Did Jesus really walk on water without any flotation aids?
- Is there really a good place called Heaven with a corresponding bad place called Hell and would my soul, if it truly exists, end up

in one of these two places when I die? How can I prove the existence of my soul anyway? Does it have any tangible form?
- Why were there different forms of religion all worshipping the same God? Even though Islam accepts that Jesus Christ was a prophet, Muslims do not afford him the special status of Messiah nor Son of God, whereas Christians do. Why?
- Why did the Roman Catholic Church ban contraception whereas the Church of England (my faith at the time) allow it? Contraception reduces disease, reduces unwanted pregnancies, and allows sex for pleasure as well as for procreation. Why did the Catholic Church force many women all over the world to bear large families and thus live in poverty all their lives and at the same time contribute to the explosion of the world's population?
- At Communion, was the wafer and wine really converted into the flesh and blood of Jesus Christ? It didn't taste so to me! (This belief, known as *transubstantiation*, is particularly strong in the Roman Catholic Church and, in the past, has caused the death of those who denied it.[14])
- What about other gods, present and past?[15] Were they replaced by the present God? Was *Brahma*, the Hindu creator god, really the Christian and Islamic God in disguise? Or was he a different creator god to God? How can there be multiple creator gods anyway?
- If the present God has replaced earlier gods, is it possible that he too, in due course, will be replaced? If so, when and by whom or what, and why?
- Why does God who, we are told, loves us all allow savage acts such as war, rape, genocide, pestilence, natural life-destroying disasters (tsunamis, earthquakes, volcanic eruptions, hurricanes, floods), child abuse, genital mutilation, man-made fatal accidents (car accidents, aircraft crashes, ship sinkings), deadly cancers, concentration camps, and so on ...?[16]

---

[14] The belief was established by the Roman Catholic Church in 1215. If wafer and wine are truly converted into flesh and blood that makes all partakers cannibals!
[15] The Godchecker website www.godchecker.com currently lists 3,700 different gods, goddesses, spirits, demons and saints known to human civilizations, past and present. Where did they all come from? Where have they all gone? Are they all manifestations of the one true God?
[16] After I wrote this list of questions, I revisited John Humphreys' book *In God We Doubt*. On page 210, Humphreys presents a short list from one of his correspondents. The list contains questions similar to mine but does contain one further interesting question – what is the fate of all those who lead exemplary lives and yet do not believe in God, the existence of a soul and life after death?

There are no easy and immediate answers to these questions and there's a huge body of literature, mostly written by philosophers, theologians and advocates of a particular religion that attempts either to provide answers or demonstrate the symbolic aspect of the belief or refute the claims. But, for me, these types of questions began to raise doubts – serious doubts – about my religious beliefs and, quite frankly, I gave up worrying about them. Other events had overtaken my life: my marriage (in a church, by the way, probably more out of convention and to please my existing and new families), my three children (all baptised in a church, probably for the same reasons) and my professional career. I punted theological questions into the sidelines but I had already taken major steps towards atheism – a disbelief in the existence of any and all deities, including the Christian God. I was also developing a personal understanding that, ultimately, religion was all about money-making and control: the governance of a large group of people by a small group of people based on a set of unfounded beliefs that could be used to restrain and regulate by means of irrational dogmas and fear of the unknown.

That all happened in the 1960s -1970s and my conversion to atheism remained fairly static but resolute for 30 years while I got on with my life. My fundamental view of religion, any religion, was that it was a business like any other business. I stopped going to church. I stopped all private worship (prayer). I did not instil religious beliefs into my children. Basically, I gave up on God and assumed that he was merely a figment of someone's lively mind on a par with Father Christmas, the Tooth Fairy, the Seven Dwarfs, and trolls, leprechauns and goblins. And then something interesting occurred.

In 2001, my wife and I went to Sri Lanka on holiday – the country I had lived in as a young boy, when it was called Ceylon. One morning I woke up early in my hotel room and decided to go outside and sit on the beach so as not to disturb my still-sleeping wife. Before venturing outside, I opened the drawer in the cabinet by the side of my bed looking for some reading material and expecting to find a Gideon Bible, which I would have ignored. But, there was no Gideon Bible. Instead, I found a small book called *Buddhism in a Nutshell* written in 1933 by Narada Maha Thera. Being curious, I took the book and read it cover-to-cover on the beach. I was entranced by its contents and when my wife finally woke up, I informed her that I was a Buddhist, albeit a meat-eating one![17] That book mirrored everything I believed in for comporting myself with others – don't steal, don't kill, don't covet, be nice, don't harm animals, and so on – and with the exception of the philosophical discussion on the *karma*,[18] made perfect sense to me. But, the bit that really hit home about Buddhism was that it was created by a man, a Nepalese or possibly Indian prince, without the assistance of a mythical being. Buddhism in its truest original form is a religion without a God if that is not an oxymoron (depends on your definition of the word 'religion' – see Chapter 2).

When I returned from the holiday, I bought the book determined to revisit its contents when I had more time but this did not happen for a few more years – that is, until after I had retired on the last day of 2007.

In the meantime, certain events had caused me to consider the nature of religion and its influence on the behaviour of my fellow humans. These left a deep impression on me.

Events that influenced me
1939 – 45 Second World War

I was born during the Second World War and, although I've no recollection of the war itself, my father was a member of the Royal Air Force and one of my uncles, my father's brother, had served in the British Army and been captured by the Japanese army when Singapore fell in 1942. He spent, and survived, more than three years in various Japanese prisoner-of-war camps.

Both my father and my uncle told me stories about the war and so it was very real to me.

The Second World War is not considered to be a war fought on religious principles – was Hitler a Christian?[19] – but the persecution

---

[17] At the time, this was my first introduction to Buddhism and the *Buddhism in a Nutshell* book, although written in 1933, does not elaborate on the many developments and alternative forms of Buddhism that will be described later in Chapter 5. Knowing what I now know about Buddhism, my 2001 pronouncement would have to be slightly modified to say that I was a Theravada Buddhist. More on this when we reach Chapter 5.

[18] John Bowker, in his book *World Religions*, defines karma to be the moral law of cause and effect. Narada Maha Thera, the author of *Buddhism in a Nutshell*, defines karma to be something that survives our death and which is an amalgamation of our inherited past actions and our present deeds. I'll elaborate in Chapter 5.

[19] Hitler is purported to have said 'National Socialism and religion cannot exist together.... The heaviest blow that ever struck humanity was the coming of Christianity. Bolshevism is Christianity's illegitimate child. Both are inventions of the Jew. The

and elimination of the Jews, and other so-called undesirable social groups such as gypsies and homosexuals, was based on Hitler's desire to rid the world of what he considered to be inferior social and ethnic groups in order to allow the pure Aryan race to flourish.

In this sense, the Jews were seen to be of an inferior group simply because that's the way they had always been regarded since the death of Jesus Christ. In other words, the original religious stigmas associated with Jewry had morphed into a general hatred of all Jews, now considered to be a race of people rather than just a religious order, for a multitude of reasons – perceived religious and social arrogance, ruthless merchants, intolerance to other religions (an accusation that can be levelled at other religions, by the way), and land-grabbers.

My thought at the time was how could God, this benevolent father figure in the sky, allow the death of six million of his *Chosen People* in such a horrible and inhumane way?

1978 Jim Jones and mass suicide in Jonestown, Guyana

Jim Jones, a citizen of the United States, was an ardent communist, atheist and hater of all religions. He was the leader of a cult called the Peoples' Temple who practiced *apostolic socialism* – a belief that the only way to combat religion was to lead religious people down the path to enlightenment called socialism. To do this, he set himself up as a reincarnation of many religious leaders – Jesus Christ, Mahatma Gandhi, Siddhartha Gautama (Buddha), Father Divine (1876 – 1965, an Afro-American spiritual leader who claimed to be God), and even Vladimir Lenin (not a religious leader unless you believe that communism could be defined as a religion without a god). Basically, Jones adopted the *persona* of God to combat God.

Jones's increasingly militant stance began to upset many influential people in the USA and to escape his persecutors he fled to the South American country of Guyana in 1974 and started to build a sanctuary – Jonestown. In 1978, a US Congressman, Leo Ryan, arrived with a small party to conduct an investigation into stories of human rights abuse. Ryan was physically attacked by a member of the Temple and withdrew to the airfield, taking fifteen other members of the Temple who had said that they wanted to return to the USA. Jones made no

---

deliberate lie in the matter of religion was introduced into the world by Christianity.... Let it not be said that Christianity brought man the life of the soul, for that evolution was in the natural order of things.' *Hitler's Secret Conversations 1941-1944* published by Farrar, Straus and Young, Inc., 1953 pp. 6-7

attempt to stop the deserters as they left the encampment but, subsequently, Jones's Red Brigade armed guards fired on the group at the airfield, killing the Congressman and four others including an NBC reporter and NBC cameraman.

Later that day, 909 members of the Temple, including 303 children, committed mass suicide by taking a cyanide-laced drink. In recordings of the death scene, Jones is heard telling his followers that, in effect, they were not dying – they were 'just stepping over into another plane'.

It turned out that Jones had practiced dummy runs of mass suicide in training events he called White Nights. The children died first, probably by being encouraged to drink the poisoned grape-flavoured concoction by their parents, and then the adults committed suicide. It was all very orderly with families lying down in their own groups. Jones himself was found dead with a gunshot wound in the head that could either have been self-inflicted or administered by another member of the Temple.

What's grimly fascinating about the story of Jonestown is how Jones was simultaneously both a Marxist and a religious zealot and how he was able to convince nearly a thousand people to commit suicide voluntarily. What power did he have over them and what need did he fulfil for them? We will ask the same questions of Muslim extremists who commit suicide in the name of their faith.

1993 David Koresh and the siege at Waco, Texas

David Koresh, born Vernon Wayne Howell in 1959, became the leader of a religious sect called the Branch Davidians, a breakaway group of the Protestant Seventh Day Adventist Church. The Davidian group, originally led by a self-proclaimed prophetess Lois Roden and her son George Roden, had their headquarters at a ranch just outside Waco in Texas. Koresh joined the sect in 1981 and by 1983 had started claiming that he had the gift of prophecy.

Following the death of Lois Roden in 1986, Koresh entered into an intense power struggle with George Roden and eventually became the leader of the group in 1989. Seventh Day Adventists, and Branch Davidians, believe in the imminent second coming of Jesus Christ coupled with the infallibility and literal truth of the Scriptures. Koresh had declared himself first to be the final prophet and eventually to be the 'Son of God, the Lamb who could open the Seven Seals',[20] aligning himself with Islam's Prophet Muhammad by virtue of his family name, Koresh, a westernised version of Muhammad's family name, Quryash. There are many stories of complete subservience and polygamous sexual relationships with many underage girls, some as young as twelve years old, and yet Koresh somehow managed to attract the unquestionable support of many followers.

In February 1993, the US Bureau of Alcohol, Tobacco and Firearms (BATF) raided Koresh's compound at Mount Carmel following allegations of possession of illegal firearms and explosives. In the ensuing fire fight, four BATF agents and six Davidians died. As a result, the FBI took over and set up a siege lasting 51 days, claiming that those inside the compound were hostages rather than willing followers of Koresh. Eventually, the US Attorney General, Janet Reno, approved an all-out assault on the Davidian's building and 76 Davidians, including 17 children under the age of seventeen,[21] and Koresh himself, died in the fire that was said to have been deliberately started by the Davidians. The true story of what went on during the siege and the final storming of the ranch may never emerge but it does seem true that some of the dead Branch Davidians had either committed suicide or been killed by other Davidians inside the building.

Subsequently, in video tapes sent out by the Davidians during the siege and revealed in the later enquiry, adult and child Davidians explained in lucid terms that they were not hostages and that they stayed with Koresh of their own free will. The question here is how did Koresh convince himself that he was the Son of God, and then convince others that this was true to the point where they willingly accepted death rather than rescue?

2001 New York 9/11

On September 11th, 2001, the now notorious suicide attack on the Pentagon in Arlington and the Twin Towers of the World Trade Centre in New York by al-Qaeda terrorists took place. The day is now

---

[20] The Seven Seals are described in the Book of Revelation, the last book in the Christian New Testament. Each opening of a Seal is accompanied by a significant event. The first four Seals produce the Four Horsemen of the Apocalypse; the fifth Seal produces a vision of martyrs; the sixth Seal produces various cosmic disturbances of mammoth and catastrophic proportions; and the final seventh Seal produces seven angels with trumpets sounding the beginning of Armageddon and the Last Judgment.
[21] Some say 76/17; others say 80/22.

universally known as 9/11. On the day that it happened I was at home and my daughter-in-law called me and instructed me to turn on the TV. I was appalled at what I was witnessing. At the time it was not known who the perpetrators were, but I have to confess that the thought flashed through my mind that only a Muslim suicide group could plan and commit such a deed. It was a seminal moment in time; our lives have not been the same since. Three thousand people lost their lives. Islamophobia was fuelled,[22] Afghanistan was invaded in the name of the 'war on terror', and air travel, once a great pleasure, was blighted as all sorts of airport security measures and carry-on restrictions were introduced. Political correctness overtook commonsense where multiculturalism was concerned and the non-Muslim world, in general, began to fear for its future as Muslims encroached into their territories and their consciousness.

2004 The death of many children in Beslan

In 2004, Muslim extremists, male and female, from Ingushetia and Chechnya, entered a kindergarten and primary school in Beslan, North Ossetia in Russia and took some 1,100 hostages, 777 of whom were children attending the school. Russian security forces stormed the building on the third day of the siege with heavy artillery, tanks and incendiary devices and in the ensuing fire fight, 334 hostages were killed, including 186 children. Why?

The Ingush and Chechen hostage-takers were members of an Islamic group and were sent by a Chechen war lord in an attempt to influence the outcome of the second Chechen war that had been raging in Chechnya since 1999 following Chechnya's attempt to establish itself as an independent republic, unfastened from Russia's control. The world, of course, was outraged by the death of so many children and although blame was laid at the door of the Muslim extremists for creating the situation in the first place, it was also apportioned to the Russian security forces for the heavy-handed way in which they attacked the school building.

The question here however is why the extremists did not allow the 777 children to go free?[23] Over the three days incarceration, the children were forced to witness executions, deprived of food and drink (some drank their own urine), refused medicines, forced to

---

[22] Sam Harris states that he started writing his book, *The End of Faith*, the day after 9/11. It was an automatic reaction to the event and originally intended to be a letter to a friend. Subsequently, the letter grew into the book.

[23] Eleven nursing mothers and fifteen babies were released on the second day.

stand for long periods, deprived of sleep and human contact (all mobile telephones were confiscated), told they would be shot if they cried, and used as human shields in the final shoot out. The militants must have known that there would be casualties in the event of a fire fight and that although the loss of any lives would be regrettable, the loss of children's lives particularly would not do anything to support their cause – quite the opposite, in fact. But something in their mentality denied the children even this consideration. I did not understand how any religion would allow such treatment of children in order to further a political agenda.

2005 London 7/7

On July 7th, 2005, four radicalised Islamic extremists exploded their bombs in underground trains and a surface bus in London, killing 56 people, including themselves. Three of the bombers were of Pakistani origin but were born and raised in the UK. The fourth bomber was Jamaican born but had lived in the UK for most of his life. One bomber was married and had a young child: another similarly so, with a second child on the away. Clearly, the attack was motivated by political requirements – 'Pull your forces out of Afghanistan and Iraq' '... stop your financial and military support to America and Israel' – but, ultimately, the ability to blow themselves up, and others close by, was based on a blind faith in their religion – 'Our religion is Islam, obedience to the one true God and following the footsteps of the final prophet messenger.'[24]

2008 LRA massacre in Faradje, DRC

In December 2008, the Ugandan Lord's Resistance Army (LRA) massacred 189 people and abducted 120 children attending a concert organised by the Roman Catholic Church in Faradje in the Democratic Republic of Congo. The LRA has been in existence since 1978 and, at the time, was led by Joseph Kony. The LRA's purpose in life was to usurp the Ugandan Government and Kony considered himself to be a spokesperson of God and a medium for the Holy Spirit. The LRA itself is founded on apocalyptic Christianity with a dash of mysticism and traditional African black magic. Kony taught his troops that

---

[24] These statements are extracts from video recordings made by two of the bombers, Mohammad Sidique Khan, and Shehzad Tanweer.

drawing a cross of shea nut oil on their chests would protect them from bullets.

What struck me about the massacre by the LRA (which wasn't their first by the way) was the brutality of the deaths and the abduction of the children. Machetes and other long knives, plus clubs, were used to batter and hack the victims to death and the boys and girls were taken away to become soldiers and sex slaves respectively.[25] Once again, I saw religious ideals and beliefs used to justify atrocious barbaric behaviours, especially towards children.

Recent wars, such as the Bosnia-Serbia conflict in Kosovo, including the appalling 1995 slaughter of 7,500 Muslim Bosnian men and boys by mostly-Christian Bosnian-Serbian militia;[26] the non-religious but ethnically-motivated genocide of the Tutsis by the Hutus in Rwanda and neighbouring Burundi; the civil war between Arab and non-Arab Muslim groups in the Darfur region of Sudan; and so on has inured us to the fact that lots of people die on a regular basis to support some political aim justified by a religious belief.

The role of religion

Together with other events, these acts of barbarity caused me to consider the role religion plays in the actions perpetrated by those who murder others. Religion and barbarity seem to go hand in hand, and there appears to be no respite. As Richard Dawkins puts it (*The God Delusion*, p. 316), 'I cannot think of any war *or similar act of barbarity (my addition)* that has been fought in the name of atheism.' This is an interesting statement warranting a deeper inspection.

We can argue that not all wars are caused by religious beliefs – First World War, Second World War, the Korean War, the war in Vietnam and the war in Cambodia, for example – but, often, religious beliefs are used to characterize or in some other way justify the aggression.

The conflict in Northern Ireland, *The Troubles* as they are often euphemistically called, may have been portrayed as a political war

---

[25] In 2005, the International Criminal Court issued an arrest warrant for Kony, citing 33 charges against him - 12 crimes against humanity and 21 war crimes, including murder, sexual enslavement, rape, cruelty, pillaging, and the forced enlistment of children into his army. At the time of writing, Kony has not been arrested and his whereabouts is unknown.

[26] The massacre was carried out by troops commanded by the Bosnian-Serb General Ratko Mladic. He was found and arrested in May 2011, while I was writing this book. He is now in detention in The Hague awaiting trial by the International War Crimes Tribunal.

couched in religiosity – Catholics versus Protestants – but it was really a war about land acquisition masquerading as unification.

So, are all wars caused either by political ideologies, including land-grabbing and enslavement, with religion used as a justification, or vice versa? Is there in fact, a single conflict that led to the death of many humans that was caused solely for atheistic beliefs - that is, a belief that there is no God or gods?

To answer these questions, we first have to find the atheists who perpetrated the conflicts and then examine their motivation.

I have searched the Web and, like Dawkins, I can find no such occurrence. But I did find a lot of discussion along the following lines: Stalin was an atheist, Hitler was an atheist, Mao Tse-tung was an atheist, Pol Pot was an atheist, Kim il-Sung was an atheist – need I go on? – therefore atheism has been the cause of millions of deaths in the twentieth century alone.

What nonsense! If Stalin, Hitler ... Kim il-Sung had all been vegetarians with one leg and raging syphilis, would this prove that all monopedic syphilitic herbivores are *ipso facto* evil by default? Of course not. It would be very difficult to point to any of these characteristics as being the root cause of their behaviour. Similarly, it would be difficult to identify a disbelief in God, or any gods come to that, as the root cause of the behaviours of all these despots. Their behaviours are far more likely to have been caused by a mix of greed, racialism, political ambition, ethnic hatred, revenge, misplaced patriotism and psychosis, none of which can be traced back to atheism if you believe that we're born with an innate sense of what's right and what's wrong rather than that we need religious instruction before we appreciate morality.

These, and many other thoughts and observations were what prompted my personal odyssey from being a Christian to what I am now, an atheist. I don't recall going through an agnostic stage. (Later on, I will claim that it's impossible to be an agnostic. You either believe, or you don't – there's no half-way house.) My changeover wasn't instant, however. It was a gradual sense of awareness based on the accumulating evidence for not believing, or better put, based on the accumulating lack of evidence for believing.

In the next two chapters, I will survey the world's religions, ancient and modern, as objectively and dispassionately as I can. Judgment of some of the religions will then follow.

(^_^)

Chapter 4
A Summary Of World Religions: Ancient Religions

'Religion is an insult to human dignity. With or without it, you'd have good people doing good things and evil people doing bad things, but for good people to do bad things, it takes religion.'
                    Steven Weinberg, Nobel Prize-winning physicist

'All religions are founded on the fear of the many and the cleverness of the few.'
            Marie-Henri Beyle, French author, also known as Stendhal

Foreword

While writing this book, I had to both refresh and top-up my knowledge of the world's religions, past and present.

This chapter and the next summarise what I learnt. Each summary abridges the religion's historical development and main events, lists the names and functions of its principal gods and prophets, outlines the main beliefs, and includes any other intriguing information that caught my eye.

As you'll see, I have expressed dates as either BCE (Before Common Era) or CE (Common Era) instead of BC (Before Christ) or AD (Anno Domini – the year of the Lord). BCE/CE dates are identical to BC/AD ones but are not specific to Christianity. The reason I have presented them this way is to achieve the religious equivalent of political correctness.

Origins of religion

We can trace religious concepts back as far as when records of civilization started – to cave drawings made up to 35,000 years ago that depict people worshiping the sun, the hunting of animals, the use of animals, especially birds, as guides to a better place, half-animal half-human depictions, and a general belief in an Underworld, one half of a Heaven and Hell duo.

Also thousands of years old, the ritualistic burial of the dead can be viewed as an indication of some form of religious belief – an eschatology based on the existence of a soul (something that survives death) and an afterlife.

It is not difficult to imagine such beliefs blossoming into full-blown religions complete with gods and goddesses, a concept of heaven and hell, symbolic artefacts, communal worship and ceremonies including both animal and human sacrifices.

Neanderthals (who lived 600,000 to 30,000 years ago) are considered to be the earliest species of man that buried its dead. Often, they did this in shallow graves in which they also placed *grave goods* such as stone tools and the bones of animals. We can but speculate as to why such items were placed in graves but a belief in an afterlife in another world is as plausible as any other explanation. Coupled with cave drawings, it suggests that religion was alive and well and flourishing in Western Europe, in the Middle East, in China and even in Australia many thousands of years ago.

The development of language[27] followed by writing[28] gave a major boost to the development of religions, among other things. With language, a set of rules, attitudes and beliefs could be constructed and passed down through the generations with the risk of all sorts of distortions and embellishments: a Chinese Whisper[29] development of religion. With writing, texts could be created that would serve to stabilize the various belief systems. Once these recording systems were in place, religions flourished and, in many cases, have inspired great works of art.[30]

In the summaries that follow, I have illustrated the ancient polytheistic (multiple gods) religions with some of their more-popular or outrageous deities. In making the selection, I've been influenced by the truly amazing website www.godchecker.com. Among other things, the site is compiling a list of all known deities. At the time of writing, some 3,700 – three thousand seven hundred! – gods and goddesses have been identified. That's a lot of deities!

Some have many different names or subtle variations on the spelling of their names or even names that cannot be pronounced (see the Aztec deities, for example). Earlier deities have, in some cases, been

---

[27] Arguably, language development can be traced back as far as 200,000 BCE when *homo sapiens* evolved in Africa but such a language would be classed as a proto-language, a pre-cursor to language as we know it today.
[28] Picture writing has been traced back to around 6,000 BCE whereas phonetic writing, based on some form of an alphabet, can be traced back to a system invented by the Canaanites around 1,700 BCE (Steven Pinker, *The Language Instinct*, p.189)
[29] A children's pass-the-story game, also known as Telephone and Pass The Message.
[30] Possibly because that's where the money was rather than some deep-felt spiritualism?

inherited or absorbed by later mythologies and so keep re-appearing through a process of deity mutation, replication and regeneration. Many have conflicting stories and even more conflicting genealogy – was the Egyptian goddess *Nut* a sister-wife to her twin brother *Geb*; was the Celtic god *Dagda* both the husband and son of *Danu*? But, one thing's for sure – there were many gods and goddesses and they certainly had many stories to tell.

Ancient religions

I'll start with what are now called ancient religions, mostly outdated or long gone, and then move on to the major current religions in the next chapter.

Egyptian religion

The Egyptians started their religion about 2,000 BCE with a pantheon based on dynasties of gods, some male, some female with offspring, some part human part animal, each dedicated to some religious function and each with a story to tell. Examples are:

- *Ra*, the Sun God, a major self-creating deity who morphed into various new forms and assumed new responsibilities via mergers with other gods such as *Atum*, *Horus* and *Amun*.
- *Geb*, the Earth god and both twin brother and husband of *Nut*, and able to create good impressions of farmyard animals!
- *Nut*, the Sky goddess and in an incestuous sister-wife relationship with her twin brother *Geb*.
- *Isis*, the goddess of Motherhood, Magic and Fertility, and daughter of *Geb* and *Nut*. *Isis* was a popular goddess who was adopted by both the Greeks and the Romans and even said by early Christians to be the *Virgin Mary*.
- *Osiris*, the god of the Afterlife, the Underworld and the Dead and the son of *Geb* and *Nut*. Also the possessor of a golden phallus thanks to the ingenuity of *Isis*.
- *Bast*, the goddess of Protection, Fertility and Sensuality and daughter of *Ra*.
- *Anubis*, the god of Mummification and Afterlife.
- *Morpheus*, the god of Dreams from which comes the name *morphine* for the narcotic derived from opium poppies.
- *Hathor*, goddess of Love, Beauty, Motherhood, Music and Joy.

- *Thoth*, the arbiter of godly disagreements, the god of Arts of Magic, the development of Science and Writing, and Judgment of the Dead. He was also considered to be at the heart and tongue of *Ra*, the Sun God.
- *Set*, the god of Deserts, Storms, Foreigners, Darkness and Chaos – an eclectic mix!
- *Min*, the god of Fertility and Lettuce. The Egyptians thought that wild lettuce, *Lactuca Serriola*, was an aphrodisiac. This has now been disproven by a lot of very slim people!

And so the list continues. At the time of writing, the Godchecker website listed 173 Egyptian deities.

The worship of the Egyptian gods and goddesses was accomplished by festivals, offerings (ranging from mediocre offerings such as fruit or animals up to human sacrifices), sacred buildings and monuments, lavish tombs (witness the Pyramids and Catacombs), a hierarchy of priests, the acceptance of evil spirits and a belief in some form of afterlife. Many of the Pharaohs considered themselves to be reincarnations of gods and were treated as such in their lifetime.

Zoroastrianism

Next up is the monotheistic religion of Zoroastrianism, based on the teaching of the prophet Zoroaster (Greek), also known as Zarathustra (Persian). The religion was created circa 1,200 BCE.

Zoroaster lived in the northern part of what is now called Iran (formerly Persia). Having experienced a vision at age 30, he changed his beliefs from the earlier polytheistic gods of ancient Persia to the monotheistic belief in God, known then as *Ahura Mazda*, and his evil counterpart *Ahriman*.

Zoroaster considered God to know everything, be everywhere, be all powerful (once he had defeated *Ahriman*), and be the source of all goodness and happiness, unchanging and impossible for humans to imagine. His teachings subsequently influenced the beginnings of Judaism leading to both Christianity and Islam, and Zoroastrianism is considered to be the root of the Abrahamic religions.

The religion lives on even today, mostly in India where it is now known as Parsis from the name of the people who fled Persia following the invasion of the Muslims in the eighth century CE.

Greek religion

Circa 1,300 BCE, the Greeks developed a polytheistic religion based on a pantheon not dissimilar to the Egyptian deities. These Olympian deities lived on Mount Olympus and were ruled by *Zeus*, the king of all gods and well-known philanderer. He is reputed to have fathered close on 100 children, some by divine mothers and some by nymphs and earthly mothers.

Other Greek deities included:

- *Apollo*, the god of Light, Sun, Archery, Poetry, Plagues, Music and much more.
- *Athena*, the goddess of Wisdom and War (an interesting mix!) and a famed do-it-yourself practitioner.
- *Hades*, also known as *Pluto*, the god of the Underworld.
- *Aphrodite*, the goddess of Love, Beauty and Sexuality, born as an adult, nubile and infinitely desirable!
- *Pan*, the god of the Countryside and of Fornication with a liking for orgies with nymphs. His image, a male goat with horns, may have inspired the popular image of the Judaic/Christian/Islamic *Satan*.
- *The Fates*, a trio of white-robed goddesses symbolising Destiny.
- *Atlas*, a Titan[31] deity who had great strength and supported the Earth on his shoulders.
- *Ares*, god of War, later adopted by the Romans and renamed *Mars*.
- *Nike*, the goddess of Victory and possibly a fast runner!
- *Heracles*, later to become *Hercules*, the personification of masculinity with extraordinary strength, courage, ingenuity and most of all, sexual prowess with both male and female partners!
- *Dionysus*, the playful god of Wine, Intoxication and Fornication and later adopted by the Romans and renamed *Bacchus*.
- *Eros*, god of Love, Desire and Fertility, carrier of a lethal bow and arrow, and not depicted by the statue in Piccadilly Circus in London. (The statue is of *Eros's* twin brother, *Anteros*.)

According to Godchecker, there are many more Greek deities – a total of 370, double that of the Egyptian religion.

---

[31] The Titans occupied Mount Olympus before being overthrown by *Zeus* and the Olympian gods.

Roman religion

Not to be outdone, the Romans entered the fray around 900 BCE with a pantheon to rival and parallel the Greek deities, but that was more closely aligned to the politics of Rome. It was what we would nowadays call a theocracy.[32]

Chief among the Roman gods were:

- *Jupiter*, the Roman equivalent of *Zeus*.
- *Venus*, the Roman equivalent of *Aphrodite* and only female planet in Earth's solar system.
- *Faunus*, the Roman equivalent of *Pan*.
- *Apollo*, a shared god with the Greeks.
- *Bacchus*, the Roman equivalent of *Dionysus*.
- *Diana*, goddess of the Hunt, the Moon and, eventually, Childbirth, Feminism and Women's Liberation; a local goddess absorbed into the pantheon when the Romans occupied the Aricia area of Italy.
- *Pluto*, a shared god with the Greeks.
- *Mars*, the god of War nowadays immortalised in the relentless pulsating rhythm of the first movement of Gustav Holst's orchestral suite *The Planets*.
- *Cupid*, the god of Desire, Affection and Erotic Love and based on the earlier Greek god *Eros*.
- *Saturn*, the god of Justice, Strength, Agriculture and Dance and based on an earlier Greek god called *Cronus* renowned for eating his own children.
- *Neptune*, the god of Water and Sea, seen on his back in a remarkable photograph entitled *Neptuno na Horta* taken in the Azores by José-Henrique Azevedo on the 15th of February 1986 during a storm.

Like Greek deities, Roman ones were symbolic of the daily needs of the Romans: warmth, rain, shelter, food, wine, love, sex. The

---

[32] Modern day Iran, more correctly named The Islamic Republic of Iran, is a theocracy. The various governing political bodies all report to the Supreme Leader who, as the name suggests, controls the armed forces and security operations, appoints the heads of all TV and radio stations, has the sole power to declare war or not and has the final say in anything to do with governing the country. The country's legal system is based on the Islamic Sharia law and the present Supreme Leader, Ali Khamenei has the religious rank of Ayatollah, (literally 'Signs of God') one of the highest ranks for Islamic clerics, although some dispute whether he is entitled to claim this rank.

mythology that accompanies them is distinguished by the many complex and intertwined stories about their various doings, but there was no holy book, or set of books, that defined the attitudes, beliefs and practices imposed by either gods or goddesses. Indeed, the actions and reactions attributed to them were subject to the whims of the priests and, eventually, of the Roman Emperors. Gaius Julius Caesar claimed he was descended from the gods on his father's side, for example.[33] He was declared a god, *Divus Iulius* (Divine Julius), by the Senate after his assassination in 44 BCE.

Caligula (died 41 CE) also claimed various divine forms, often dressing up as one of the gods *Hercules, Mercury, Venus* or *Apollo* to reinforce the image of divinity and even claiming that his horse *Incitatus* had become a priest![34]

Eventually, the polytheistic beliefs of the Roman Empire gave way to the monotheistic belief of the Roman Catholic Church, and one of the major modern religions began its expansion into the many splinter sects that exist today. But, we should not neglect the polytheisms of Northern Europe and, especially, the Norse and Celtic religions.

Norse religion

Norse mythology owes a lot to earlier Germanic deities and is more a series of long science-fantasy stories than the more-classical Egyptian, Greek and Roman religions. The stories were handed down word of mouth before finally being captured in two classic Nordic documents, the *Poetic Edda* and the *Prose Edda*, circa 1,200 CE.

Although by this time Christianity was flourishing in Western and Northern Europe, the Norse deities, called the *Æsir*, were said to have pre-dated the Christian God. The mythology tells of nine different worlds, each inhabited by their own denizens:

- *Asgard*, world of the *Æsir* and 'top' world inhabited by the one-eyed chief god, *Odin* and his wife *Frigg*. Also living in Asgard were:
    - *Tyr*, the god of Victory, Heroic Glory and Single-Handed Combat (he had one hand bitten off by *Fenrir*, a monstrous wolf).

---

[33] According to the scriptwriters and researchers of the 2005 joint BBC/HBO 12-part series, *Rome*, Caesar claimed to be a descendant of the goddess *Venus*.

[34] There's some doubt about the veracity of this claim but the joint US/Italian producers loved it in the controversial 1979 film *Caligula*, directed by Tinto Brass and, in parts, by Bob Guccione.

- *Thor*, the hammer-wielding god of many things associated with great strength.
- *Loki*, a shape-shifter, mischief-maker and sometimes do-gooder; also a male reproducer (he gave birth to an eight-legged stallion called *Sleipnir*).
- *Baldr*, chiefly known for the manner of his death. He was killed by a mistletoe dart hurled by a blind god called *Hod* under the guidance of *Loki*.

and many other gods all cohabiting and procreating in a hall called *Valhalla*. *Valhalla* was also the home of the dreaded *Valkyries*, the female figures who chose the ones to die in battle in order to become defenders of the gods.

Odin was the grandson of the very first god, *Buri*, created on *Asgard* by the action of a cow licking a rock to get at the embedded salt. And so the stuff of legends is born!

- *Niflheim*, world of those who died from age or sickness. *Niflheim* was created out of ice, frost and fog and the first of two worlds to exist before world-creation really took off.
- *Muspellheim*, world of fire, and the second of two worlds to exist before world-creation got started.
- *Midgard* (Middle World), world of humans.
- *Álfheimr*, world of the *Álfar* (elves).
- *Svartálfaheim*, world of the *Svartálfar* (black elves)
- *Vanaheimr*, world of the *Vanir*, the gods of Wisdom, Fertility and Divination.
- *Jötunheimr*, world of the *jötnar*, a species of hideous nature spirits with superhuman strength, now more commonly called trolls.
- *Helheim*, the netherworld, populated by dwarfs and presided over by the goddess *Hel*, the daughter of *Loki*.

These nine worlds are connected by the world tree *Yggdrasil* - a giant tree with *Asgard* at its top. *Asgard* can also be reached by *Bifrost*, a rainbow bridge guarded by *Heimdall*, a god who can see and hear for a thousand miles.

Norse legend also foretells the end of the world, *Ragnorak* (the Twilight/Doom of the Gods, known as *Götterdämmerung*[35] in the German language), in which all the major gods will die in a great battle after which the world will become totally submerged in water (presumably to wash away all the sins) and then be reborn with just two inhabitants, *Lif* (male) and *Lifthrasar* (female) who will repopulate

---

[35] The inspiration for Richard Wagner's opera of the same name.

the new world. If you detect echoes of the Christian belief in the Final Judgment, the floods that set Noah off on his journey, and Adam and Eve you are right, but the jury is still out as to whether these Christian beliefs and stories influenced the development of the *Ragnorak* concept in Norse religion. It could have been the other way round!

The North European Norse religion was gradually replaced by Christianity. There was no strong culture of temples, priests and formal methods of worship but some of the history lives on today, notably in the naming of the seven days of a week:

Old Norse name	Meaning	Modern Name
Mánadagr	Moon's day	Monday
Týsdagr	Tyr's day	Tuesday
Óðinsdagr	Odin's day	Wednesday
Þórsdagr	Thor's day	Thursday
Frjádagr	Freyja's day	Friday
Laugardagr	Washing day	Saturday
Sunnudagr/Dróttinsdagr	Sun's day/The Lord's day	Sunday

And, as we know, composers such as Richard Wagner and authors such as J R R Tolkien have immortalised the Norse mythology in their seminal works *Der Ring des Nibelung*, including the ever-popular *Ride of the Valkyries* (Wagner), and *The Silmarillion* and *Lord of the Rings* (Tolkien).

Celtic religion

At about the same time as the Norse religion flourished, the Celtic religions were also developing in the British Isles and parts of Gaul,[36] with variants of Druidism, Celtic Christianity and, more recently, Celtic Neopaganism (literally, 'a revival of old paganism' and nowadays known as *Wicca*).

Very little is known of the ancient Druid religion but it is thought that Druids practiced human sacrifice,[37] believed in an afterlife and a form of reincarnation, and held high office in Gaulish society.

---

[36] An ancient region including modern-day France, Belgium and the Po Valley of Italy.
[37] The 1973 so-called horror movie, *The Wicker Man*, is based on a druid sect practicing their arts on a remote Scottish Island. The hero, a policeman from the mainland, played by Edward Woodward, is finally sacrificed (burnt alive) inside a large wooden effigy

Celtic religions are awash with gods and goddesses however, some of the better known or more interesting being:

- *Morrigan*, the shape-shifting goddess of Fate, War and Death and one of the founders of the Irish Celtic movement called *Tuatha-Dé-Danann*.
- *Aonghus*, an Irish god of Love, Youth and Poetic Inspiration – a Celtic Cupid (a nice alliteration).
- *Danu*, the fairy mother of the Irish Celtic deities and goddess of Fertility and Plenty and founder and high priestess of *Tuatha-Dé-Danann*.
- *Dagda*, the fairy father of the gods and god of Time, Magic and Protector of Crops; also both the husband and son of *Danu*. (The Egyptians weren't the only deities to indulge in sister-wife brother-husband relationships!)
- *Cuchulainn*, a great warrior, the Superman of the Celtic gods and on a par with the Greek god *Hercules* (although one suspects that *Cuchulainn* was strictly heterosexual).
- *Brigit*, the goddess of Fire, Heating, Fertility and the patron of blacksmiths. She was adopted by the Christians and became *St. Bridget*.
- *Cernunnos*, possibly the god of Nature or Fertility.
- *Accasbel*, most likely was an early God of Wine or Mead.
- *Achtland*, a goddess queen who no mortal man could sexually satisfy, so she took a giant from the fairy realm as her mate.
- *Aeval*, the goddess of Sexuality who in popular legend is a fairy who held a midnight court to hear the debate on whether the men of her province were keeping their women sexually satisfied or not. She commanded that the men bow to the women's sexual wishes. I believe the men acquiesced!
- *Albion*, a god who was once said to rule the Celtic world. His name became the poetic name for Britain.
- *Breasal*, high king of the entire planet who made his home in the Otherworld. It is said that when Portuguese explorers reached South America they mistakenly thought they had landed on Breasal's world and named the land they discovered 'Brazil' in his honour.
- *Scathach*, a goddess of the Underworld. A warrior woman and prophetess who taught the martial arts although it is not known if

---

known as a Wicker Man while the villagers sing *Sumer is icumen in*, a song considered to be rooted in paganism.

Bruce Lee, Jet Li, Jackie Chan or Tony Jaa were influenced by her skills.

Inca religion

Finally, I'll summarise a couple of religions that emerged in the central and southern parts of the American continent: the Inca religion of Peru and Colombia in the thirteenth century CE and destroyed by the Spanish in the sixteenth century, and the Aztec religion of the Mayans living in central Mexico in the fourteenth - sixteenth centuries.

The Inca religion was centered in the Cuzco area of Peru. As legend tells it, the founder of the Inca tribe, *Manco Capac*, wandered the earth and underworld and eventually settled in Cuzco. First he built a temple to honour the sun and then he conquered or otherwise persuaded all the local tribes to join his tribe, expanding out to Lake Titicaca and, at some point, building the famed hilltop dwelling of Machu Picchu. The Incas were finally defeated by the Spanish Conquistadores in the sixteenth century. At its peak, the Incan empire embraced Peru, Bolivia, and parts of Ecuador, Chile, Argentina and Colombia.

Inca deities lived in one of two worlds. The inner earth, *Uku Pacha*, was the home of *Pachamama*, the Earth Mother. The celestial realm, *Hanan Pacha*, was the home of *Inti*, the Sun God. It was also the residence of *Mama Quilla*, the Moon Goddess and *Inti's* wife, and of many other deities related to natural events or the need for food, warmth and rain. Humans were relegated to the outer earth, *Kay Pacha*.

The Inca religion was dominated by a belief that the king was divine; sacrifices (with animal or human sacrifices reserved for special occasions), festivals (at least one a month);[38] god acquisition from those defeated in battles; sacred objects or places called *huacas*; and divination based on the occurrence of natural events such as an eclipse or the coming of the rains.

Incas also believed that the human body contained two souls: one that would return to its place of origin depending on what sort of life

---

[38] One of the festivals was a nine-day Festival of the Sun, called *Inti Raymi*. This festival is still celebrated as a one-day event on June 24th at a place called Sacsayhuamán (pronounced Sexy Woman!), just outside Cuzco. Having witnessed the event, I can attest to its majesty and cast of thousands. Fortunately, the sacrifice of live humans or animals is no longer included.

the person had led and on the nature of his or her death, and one that would remain with the dead mummified body.

The king's divine wisdom was derived from his priests who, along with the priestesses (virgins destined to become either wives or concubines to the king), lived in temples. One of the principle responsibilities of priestesses was the making of *chicha*, the name given to a wide variety of fermented drinks usually, but not always, made from maize. Virgins were kept busy while awaiting their fate!

Aztec religion

The Aztec people, speakers of the Mexican *Nahuatl* language, occupied the lands we now associate with Central America: Central Mexico to Belize, Guatemala, El Salvador, Honduras, Nicaragua, and Costa Rica. The Aztecs were at their height between the fourteenth and sixteenth centuries before succumbing to the Spanish Conquistadores, led by Hernán Cortés, in the sixteenth century. The Aztec religion was polytheistic with a pantheon of at least 99 deities associated with seven major categories. Here are some examples:

- Culture
    - *Quetzalcoatl*, god of Priests, Rulers, Wind, Life, Death and Resurrection.
    - *Tlaloc*, the god of Fertility, Water, Rain, Storm and Thunder.
    - *Tezcatlipoca*, a rival to *Quetzalcoatl* and probably one of the most versatile gods being responsible for Night Sky, the Night Winds, Hurricanes, the North, the Earth, Obsidian[39], Enmity, Discord, Rulership, Divination, Temptation, Jaguars, Sorcery, Beauty, War and Strife. It's not known whether he was responsible for all these things at the same time, or whether he cycled from one to the next.
- Forces of Nature
    - *Tonatiuh*, the Sun god.
    - *Metztli*, the Moon god.
    - *Tlaltecuhtli*, the Earth goddess.
    - *Chantico*, goddess of Precious Things, Fires in the Hearth and Volcanoes.
    - *Tecuciztecatl*, originally the god of Worms but later elevated to become another Moon god. Good promotion!

---

[39] A very hard volcanic glass used to make sacrificial daggers.

- Creation
    - *Coatlicue*, earth goddess of Life and Death.
    - *Huitzilopochtli*, god of War, Sun god, son of *Coatlicue*.
    - *Ometecuhtli*, the male half of the original creator god and *Omecihuatl*, the female half.
- Excess and pulque[40]
    - *Tepoztecatl*, god of Fertility and Drunkenness.
    - *Mayahuel*, goddess of Alcohol (dispensed through any one of 400 breasts!).
    - *Xochipilli*, god of Gambling, Dancing, Music and, apparently, Haemorrhoids!
- Fertility and maize
    - *Xipe Totec*, god of Spring and Agriculture.
    - *Cinteotl* and *Xilonen*, god and goddess of Maize.
- Underworld and death gods
    - *Mictlantecutli* and *Mictlancihuatl*, god and goddess of Death.
    - *Acolmiztli*, god of the Underworld.
- Trade
    - *Yacatecuhtli*, god of Commerce and Travellers.
    - *Patecatl*, god of Healing and Fertility.

Many of the Aztec deities demanded human sacrifices in order to fulfil their godly obligations. Some deities just asked for death whereas others were more specific such as *Tlaloc* who had a penchant for new-born babies and *Tonatiuh* who quite liked fresh beating hearts. As a result, there are many accounts of human sacrifices. One suggested that the 1487 reconsecration of the Great Pyramid of Tenochtitlan, located in what is now Mexico City, included 84,400 human sacrifices over four days.[41] Even though the temple was used to worship both *Huitzilopochtli* and *Tlaloc*, both of whom revelled in human sacrifice, the figure of 84,400 sacrifices has been discounted on the grounds that the sheer logistics of sacrificing this number of people in just four days is impossible. I did some calculations. Assuming the killings were non-stop, fifteen people would have been killed every minute! As a result, the consensus among historians is that the total number of sacrifices was around 2,000 – 'just' one sacrifice every three minutes.

---

[40] Pulque is an alcoholic drink made from the fermented sap of the maguey (agave) plant.
[41] http://en.wikipedia.org/wiki/Aztec

Regardless of the quantities involved, warriors, babies, and young girls assumed to be virgins,[42] were the most favoured for sacrifice. The usual method was to stretch the victim across an altar while he or she was still alive, open the chest with an obsidian knife, rip the beating heart from its moorings and hold it aloft for all to witness.[43] The skin of the corpse was then offered to a nearby priest or dignitary to wear as a symbol of the power of the sacrifice. Sometimes, the victim was drugged and roasted alive before the heart-ripping stage. Auto sacrifice (self harm) and cannibalism were also part of the sacrifice rituals in the temples dedicated to the more blood-thirsty deities of the Aztec religion.

The Aztec priests were clearly an unlovely bunch but no worse than the persecutors and torturers of the Holy Inquisition of the Roman Catholic Church in the Middle Ages. We will come to them in Chapter 6.

(^_^)

---

[42] An Aztec father could sell his daughter for sexual slavery or as a candidate for sacrifice for between 500 to 700 cacao beans, the beans used today to make cocoa, chocolate and cocoa butter. To put this in perspective, 300 to 600 cacao beans will make around 1 kg (2.2 lb) of chocolate. So the life of a young girl was worth between one and two large bars of chocolate at today's prices. Aztecs made and enjoyed cocoa drinks and even had a goddess called *Xochiquetzal* associated with the chocolate drink.

[43] Mel Gibson's 2006 film *Apocalypto* about the Mayans, the predecessors of the Aztecs, depicts such sacrifices. Even though we know it not to be real, the imagery in the film makes uncomfortable viewing.

Chapter 5
A Summary Of World Religions: Modern Religions

'The concessions we have made to religious faith – to the idea that belief can be sanctified by something other than evidence – have rendered us unable to name, much less address, one of the most pervasive causes of conflict in our world'
Sam Harris, The End of Faith, p. 29

'Believers, make war on the infidels who dwell around you. Deal firmly with them. Know that God is with the righteous.'
Qur'an 9:123

'The day will come when the mystical generation of Jesus by the Supreme Being as his father, in the womb of a virgin, will be classed with the fable of the generation of Minerva in the brain of Jupiter.'
Thomas Jefferson, 3rd President USA, author of the Declaration of Independence.

In this chapter, I'll take a look at modern religions. There are plenty, so I will restrict attention to the dominant Western, Middle East, Indian and Asian denominations. I will also comment briefly on what are loosely termed Native Religions and finish with New Religious Movements.

First, though, a disclaimer. Religions start small but many grow, split, diversify and become huge organisations with many branches and offshoots. This makes it dangerous to make sweeping generalisations about the generic characteristics of a particular religion. If I speak of Buddhism in general terms, am I referring to Theravada or Mahayana forms? Similarly Islam – Sunni or Shi'a? Or Christianity: Catholic or Protestant? In this chapter, I will associate particular characteristics with particular branches of religions where that's appropriate. Otherwise, it is safe to assume that all branches embrace the same characteristic.

Indian sub-continent religions
Hinduism

Hinduism, a polytheistic religion with a rich pantheon, is the name given to a major coalition of Indian religions formed in the nineteenth century. As such, it incorporates elements of many earlier Indian religions and has absorbed many gods. The word *hindu* is a Persian word meaning river and it used to refer to the people living in the Indus valley in India. Nowadays, some 80% of people living in India consider themselves Hindus.

Because of the multi-religion origins of Hinduism, there's no single founder (unlike, say, Jesus Christ for Christianity or Muhammad for Islam) and there are many sacred texts. For example, the very ancient *Vedas*, considered to be the primary texts of Hinduism; the *Shruti* containing the central doctrines of Hinduism, coming from the gods; and the *Smriti*, similar but not of divine origin. These texts contain epics, poems, hymns, prayers and guidance on how to conduct oneself in this life, and the next.

Hindus believe in a soul, called *atman*, that lives in one human carrier and is rehoused in another after death – a process called rebirth. They search for good ways to behave, called *dharma*, in the present life. Merriam-Webster defines *dharma* to be 'an individual's duty fulfilled by observance of custom or law'. We can think of it as leading a good life according to the rules and regulations of both our earthly and spiritual existences. Achieving good *dharma* means that either the soul has a good rebirth following death or a final release from rebirth, called *moksha*.

Hindus have four goals in life:

- *Dharma*, as above. Basically, to lead a good life.
- *Artha*: the pursuit of legitimate worldly success, the work ethic and associated morality.
- *Kama*: the pursuit of sensual, sexual and aesthetic pleasures; hence the *Kama Sutra*, literally 'a concise statement of the principles of love making'.
- *Moksha*: a final release of the soul from the endless cycle of birth-life-death-rebirth. This cycle, called *samsara*,[44] is present in just about all religions that have originated from the Indian sub-continent, as is the concept of a final release. *Moksha* is achieved in

---

[44] *Samsara*: a Sanskrit word meaning continuous flow or endless wandering.

one of four ways using various yoga techniques: *Bhakti*, the way of devotion, similar to the Muslim Sufis (see later); *Karma*, the way of action; *Jnana*, the way of knowledge and insight; and *Raja*, the way of meditation. Wandering holy men called *sadhus*, dedicate their lives to achieving *moksha* by living on the edge of society, shunning all worldly possessions except a begging bowl (for food or money), and undergoing all sorts of ritual penances such as fasting, yogic exercises and solitude. In addition, there are many other gurus, sects and guides who'll help you achieve *moksha* and, in some cases, relieve you of most, if not all, your worldly goods!

These four goals are heavily influenced by the teachings and examples of the various deities and the Hindu religion is very intertwined with the more secular day-to-day behaviours.

At the top of the Hindu pantheon sit three gods known collectively as the *Trimurti*, the Hindu Triad or Great Trinity:

Brahma: the creator of the universe and its contents;
Vishnu: the preserver of the universe and its contents;
Shiva: the destroyer of the universe and its contents.

A powerful triumvirate by anybody's reckoning!

Brahma, the creator, even created himself, thereby explaining one of the great paradoxes of theistic religions – who created the creator? *Brahma* is not worshipped as much as the other members of the *Trimurti*, possibly because his job is done or, as legend has it, because he was cursed for not attending to a request from one of the great wise men of the *Vedas* texts.

Vishnu, the preserver, has visited earth nine times in the form of divine manifestation alter-shapes called avatars. *Avatara* in Sanskrit means *descent* and the word is used to describe an intermediary form between man and God. The purpose of the avatars was to restore law and order or in some other way save the world from destruction. *Vishnu* has one final *avatara* visit left, in the form of *Kalki*, the destroyer of foulness, ignorance, confusion and darkness. There's some controversy about earlier avatars of *Vishnu*. *Krishna* is listed as the eighth avatar but some regard *Krishna* as superior to *Vishnu*.[45] Gautama Buddha, the original Buddha, is listed as the ninth avatar.

---

[45] The *Hare Krishna* movement, renowned for their Maha mantra, is a monotheistic development of polytheistic Hinduism with Krishna elevated to the status of the one

Shiva, the destroyer, probably the most feared of the *Trimurti*, lives on top of Mount Kailash in Tibet with his wife *Parvati*, two sons *Ganesha* and *Karthikeya*, and two daughters *Saraswati* and *Lakshmi*, all deities in their own right. *Ganesha* is the familiar elephant god, worshipped as the 'Remover of Obstacles' and 'Lord of Beginnings'. *Lakshmi* is the goddess of wealth, prosperity (spiritual as well as material), light, wisdom, fortune, fertility, generosity and courage. She is the embodiment of beauty, grace and charm – clearly a goddess to be worshipped on a regular basis! *Shiva* is often depicted deep in meditation, an ascetic yogin (one who practices yoga), and with a third eye in the centre of his forehead – the eye of enlightenment and a symbol of a higher consciousness.

In his 1961 book *Hinduism*, K M Sen argues that Hinduism could be regarded as a monotheistic religion: each of the many deities is but a divine reincarnation, an avatar, of the Supreme Creator. In this sense, even the members of the *Trimurti* are avatars. I would imagine that most modern practicing Hindus would not agree with this exegesis.

As with other religions, Hinduism has many sacred places and pilgrimage is an important part of achieving *dharma* – the pursuit of the good life. The principle places of pilgrimage are:

- Varanasi, on the bank of the river Ganges, and formerly known as Benares when India was under British rule. Varanasi is another home of *Shiva* and probably the holiest of Hindu pilgrim sites. Hindus believe that if you die in Varanasi, you will be released from the *samsara* cycle of death followed by rebirth. You will achieve *moksha*. Consequently, Varanasi is full of old folk waiting to die – a bit like Bournemouth in England!
- Kurukshetra, the site of a great tribal battle in ancient times and origin of the *Bhagvad Gita*, another sacred Hindu scripture.
- Ayodhya, the capital of an ancient Indian region and the birthplace of *Rama*, the seventh avatar of *Vishnu*.
- Mathura, the birthplace of *Krishna*.

Finally, there's a multitude of festivals to cheer people up by mixing worship with pleasure, notably:

---

true God, 'the Supreme Personality of Godhead', and source of all avatars including, possibly, Jesus Christ.

- *Holi*, usually in March and originally a fertility festival. *Holi* is now a Hindu New Year festival lasting up to sixteen days and designed to welcome Spring, the symbol of new birth.
- *Diwali*, the 'festival of lights' is a five-day festival held between mid-October and mid-November to celebrate the return from exile of *Rama*, *Vishnu's* seventh avatar. Nowadays, Diwali is used to celebrate the start of the financial year.
- *Dussehra*, an autumn festival designed to celebrate the harvest and reinvigorate the earth with vigour and fertility for the next year. The festival is based on *Rama's* ancient victory over *Ravana*, the devil king, and so also symbolises the victory of good over evil.

Overall, Hinduism is a very complex and diverse religion with many sacred texts from different proto-religious sources; many subdivisions into sects; and many gods with confusing ancestry, coverage and importance. Worship is largely individual, either at home or in the multitude of temples that exist throughout the Indian subcontinent and other parts of southern Asia. To be a Hindu is to profess a belief in an afterlife through rebirth and so we would imagine that the sanctity of an existing life would be paramount to the religion. And yet the 1947 division of northern India into the Islamic Republic of Pakistan, a Muslim country, and the Republic of India, a largely Hindu country, saw religious tolerance rapidly give way to religious intolerance with massacres and wholesale slaughter causing the deaths of somewhere between several hundred thousand to more than a million lives.[46]

Jainism

Jainism is an Indian religion founded just before Buddhism. Its main tenet is non-violence to all living things, even the tiny ant under your foot or the fly that settles persistently on your nose. Jains claim that their religion has always existed and will always exist but historians put a start date of between 900 BCE and 600 BCE. The religion currently attracts over four million adherents, most of whom live in India.

Jains believe every living creature, and plant, has a soul, called a *jiva*, that's a conscious living entity that possesses infinite wisdom and

---

[46] Estimates vary in the literature that documents the bloody partition. For an excellent, albeit fictional, account of the effects of the 1947 Muslim versus Hindu conflict, I recommend you read Khushwant Singh's acclaimed book *Train to Pakistan*, first published in 1956. It makes for very sober reading.

knowledge and never dies. When the current bodily carrier dies, the *jiva* and its *karma* (see next point) migrate to another bodily carrier. This is rebirth.

Souls attract both good and bad *karma*. Essentially, the Jain *karma* is considered to be a physical substance that attracts *karma* particles, good or bad, based on the actions, words and thoughts of the human possessor of the soul. Build up of *karma* can be avoided by purifying everything we do or think. *Karma* can be reduced by behaving well and by maintaining the right state of mind.

A soul can only reach liberation (*moksha*) from the endless *samsara* cycle of birth-life-death-rebirth by divesting itself of all *karma*, good and bad. A liberated soul, called a *siddha*, possesses infinite knowledge, infinite vision, infinite power, and infinite bliss - in effect becoming a perfect being.

Karma is not controlled by any god. In fact, there are no gods in Jainism. There are no creators. The universe has no beginning and no end. There's no good *karma*/bad *karma* reward/punishment system. In Jainism, a liberated soul (*siddha*) is the closest thing to a god but unlike, say, the God of Judaism/Christianity/Islam, a liberated soul cannot create or destroy, reward or punish. It cannot be contacted, nor will it contact you. It won't intervene with events on earth or in other ways cause things to happen, and it doesn't make demands on living things. It doesn't impart words of wisdom. It isn't a ruler and it doesn't demand worship. All a liberated soul can do is inspire!

This last point raises the question – if there are no gods in Jainism, is it really a religion in the traditional sense of the word (see the definition and discussion in Chapter 2), or is it atheism? Jainism and Buddhism in its purest Theravada form subscribe to spiritual entities, *jivas* (souls) in Jainism and *karma* in Buddhism, but do not assume, need or allow the existence of any higher-level authority called God, Supreme Being, *Allah*, Yahweh or similar. Thus, the 'religions' bridge the gap between theism and atheism and have been labelled transtheisms.[47]

The path to liberation is based on the Triple Gems of Jainism: Right Vision, Right Knowledge and Right Conduct. The Triple Gems are prescribed in the teachings of enlightened leaders called *jinas* (literally, a 'victor') whose sayings have been revived by the

---

[47] Transtheism: something between a pure theism and a pure atheism, first coined by the Indologist Heinrich Zimmer following his early 1900s in-depth study of Jainism.

Tirthankars,[48] 24 special *jinas* who have reached liberation but who chose to stay and teach others.

The five-way path to liberation, called the Five Vows requires:

- Non-violence, not only to fellow humans but to every living thing. (Remember, Jains believe that every living thing has a soul, *jiva*, and souls, especially liberated souls, *siddha*, are venerated.) Non-violence goes beyond physical forms. It includes mental forms as well; emotions such as anger, lust, pride, deceit, and greed. Even thinking about causing harm (anger), including intolerance to the beliefs and opinions of others, will attract bad *karma* and decrease the ability to achieve liberation of the soul.
- Truthfulness. Always be truthful unless to do so will cause violence. In which case, remain silent.
- Non-stealing, including things that you have found or things that are improperly priced such as stolen goods.
- Celibacy/chasteness. For monks and nuns, absolute celibacy is required. For the laity, a sexual relationship with his or her spouse is permitted but not with anybody else.
- Non-possession, or more correctly, non-materialism. Ownership of an object is allowed but attachment to the object is not. Monks and nuns have no possessions, similar to the Hindu *sadhus*.

Non-violence is the highest of the Five Vows and, in the case of conflict, all other vows are subservient to it.

Because of the Five Vows, all Jains are vegetarian and Jain monks and nuns walk barefoot and sweep the ground in front of them to avoid killing small creatures. There are no priests in Jainism; just ascetics (monks and nuns) who achieve liberation of the soul through self-help only.

Mahatma Gandhi, the leader of the Indian move to independence that resulted in the creation of the Republic of India and the separate Islamic country Pakistan in 1947, was heavily influenced by the non-violence aspect of Jainism. Although he was a Hindu, he studied Jainism and followed many of its tenets: non-violence, vegetarian, an adherence to truthfulness, celibacy (even though he was married[49]) and simplicity of dress.

---

[48] Literally, 'those who have shown the way to salvation from the river of births and deaths' or, more usually 'ford builders'.

[49] At age 36, Gandhi decided to become celibate and, so the story goes, constantly tested his will power by going to bed naked with nubile young girls, also naked (as you do!).

Jains have no temples, icons or ritual worship routines. Their symbols are very simple: an up-stretched open hand symbolising non-violence and incorporating a wheel symbol representing the desire to end the cycle of reincarnation; and a right-facing (clockwise) swastika, literally 'good well-being', specifically a symbol representing the seventh *Tirthankar Suparsva* but more generally symbolising the quest for liberation of the soul.

One last point... Because of the central tenet of non-violence, there are no known instances of a war created by the Jains. There is no other religion, other than Buddhism which is conceptually very similar to Jainism, for which this statement is true as far as I know.

Buddhism

> *'(Buddhism) is neither a religion in the sense in which that word is commonly understood, for it is not "a system of faith and worship owing any allegiance to a supernatural being".'*
> Narada Maha Thera, *Buddhism in a Nutshell*, 1933, p.21

Buddhism is based on the life and teachings of *Siddhartha Gautama*, a prince born 623 BCE, or possibly 566 BCE depending on who you believe, in the Nepalese town of Lumbini. He was the son of a Nepalese King and Queen. He married a cousin when both were age sixteen and they had a son named *Rahula*. Gautama and his family continued to live in the palace until he reached the age of 29. As legend has it, during his twenty-ninth year, he rode out and saw, for the first time, the poor, the sick, the dead and the devoted (ascetics). He was overwhelmed by these scenes and decided to leave the luxury and comfort of the palace and devote his life to improving first himself and subsequently the spiritual lives of others. Thus, he wandered around for six years, living as a mendicant,[50] and achieved enlightenment at the age of 35. He then spent the rest of his very long life (he died at age 80 in Kushinagar in India) assembling his philosophy and passing it on to a group of disciples called *Bhikkhus*, male Buddhist monks, and *Bhikkhunis*, female Buddhist monks.[51]

He claimed that he did this 'for bodily warmth' or 'to correct her sleeping posture'. Whether he succumbed to the temptation of the flesh, or not, will probably never be known. He claimed 'Not'. If he was true to the truthfulness vow, then we can but believe him. His wife's comments are not recorded!

[50] Literally, a beggar, comparable to modern-day *sadhus* in India.
[51] Gautama created *bhikkhunis* at the request of his foster mother, Mahapajapati Gotami, who then went on to become the first ordained *bhikkhuni*. Mahapajapati Gotami was

So much for the man and his life: but what did he teach? He taught that there were two extremes in life - self indulgence and self mortification - and that the way to enlightenment was by a Middle Path based on self dependence. Enlightenment (*bodhi* in Sanskrit) is defined to be 'awakened, aware, and knowledgeable'. The title *Buddha* means the Enlightened One. Gautama became Buddha after he'd achieved *nirvana*, the ultimate state of enlightenment. But, Gautama never claimed divinity nor did he claim to be a reincarnation, an avatar, of *Vishnu*. He said that any images of him or other symbols of faith should be seen to be external objects of reference to concentrate the mind. They were not to be worshipped in their own right.

Buddha left no written record of his teachings but just after he died, his disciples, a group called the *Sangha* (Buddhist Council), began a process of preserving his legacy by learning standard chants and other ways of committing the words to memory. Some 500 years later, the Fourth Buddhist Council meeting in Sri Lanka created the first written records of his teachings, on palm leaves. The records, called the *Pali Canon* or *Tripitaka*,[52] literally 'three baskets', were in three parts: the basket of disciplines (rules and regulations for the monks and nuns[53]), the basket of discourse (the sermons and teachings of Buddha and of some of his disciples), and the basket of ultimate doctrine (philosophy and foundation for achieving enlightenment).

The foundation of Buddha's teaching was the Four Noble Truths, obtained by Buddha while meditating under a Bodhi tree (a species of the fig tree considered to be sacred by Buddhists) in Bodh Gaya, India. Bodh Gaya is a major place of pilgrimage for Buddhists.

The Four Noble Truths are:

- Suffering. To live is to suffer, physically and mentally, and there is no way to avoid the pain.
- Craving. A desire to own material things and to want abstract entities such as inventions and ideas. But ownership of physical and intangible items is always transient and thus their eventual departure will contribute to suffering.
- *Nirvana*, the cessation of suffering: the ultimate goal of a Buddhist. *Nirvana* is a state of mind where nothing matters anymore. All

---

Gautama's maternal aunt and she raised Gautama when his mother, her sister, died seven days after giving birth to him.

[52] It's said that the word count of the *Tripitaka* is eleven times that of the Bible.

[53] These rules and regulations are often called the Buddhist *dharma* – the teachings of Buddha.

suffering is banished. There is freedom from all worldly desires, worries, complexes and ideas. Achieving *nirvana* through enlightenment releases the soul from the endless *samsara* cycle of birth-life-death-rebirth, and signals the end of suffering. Thus an Enlightened One achieves what the Hindu religion calls *moksha*.
- The Middle Way. A process of gradual self-improvement defined by the Noble Eight-Fold Path and leading to *nirvana*.

The Noble Eight-Fold Path is based on:

- Having the Right Understanding: to understand things as they really are and not as they appear to be. Basically, to accept the teachings of Buddha.
- Having the Right Thoughts: the elimination of evil thoughts and the cultivation of good thoughts.
- Making the Right Speech: abstinence from falsehoods, slander, anger and insults. Always tell the truth and stay calm.
- Making the Right Actions: abstinence from any action that could harm either another human or any animal.
- Living with a Right Livelihood: abstinence from any trade that violates the Right Actions path. This includes abstinence from trading in arms, trading in humans, slaughtering animals, consuming intoxicating drink and drugs.
- Making the Right Efforts: basically, discarding evil, preventing evil, promoting good and creating new good actions.
- Having the Right Mindfulness: being constantly aware of all bodily and mental functions.
- Achieving right efforts and right mindfulness by Right Concentration: usually by some form of yogic meditation.

Basically, lead a good life by the use of wisdom (paths 1 and 2), morality (paths 3, 4 and 5) and concentration (paths 6, 7 and 8). This eight-point *dharma* is often portrayed by an eight-spoke wheel symbol called the *dharmachakra*.

Buddhism employs the concept of *karma*, inherited from earlier Indian religions, notable Jainism, but slightly different in meaning. Buddhists define *karma* to be the moral and natural law of cause and effect: something that survives our death and passes to another life form, human or animal, and which is an amalgamation of the qualities of our inherited past actions and our present deeds. Buddha taught that cause and effect are cyclical: a cause creates an effect and the effect in turn becomes a new cause thereby creating a new effect which could turn out to be the original cause! Confusing? Yes, but the concept appears in many other religions originating in India – Hinduism, Jainism and Sikhism, for example. The Buddhist notion of *karma* is in opposition to the belief of a higher-level creator. *Karma* is a natural and universal law that steers one's destiny and requires no higher-level intervention. Cyclical never-ending cause-effect explains it all! Some branches of Hinduism believe that gods like the *Trimurti* (*Brahma*, *Vishnu* and *Shiva*) are simply dispensers of good *karma* rather than the originators of all that exists. Other Hindus believe that *Brahma* was truly the creator and that *karma* relates more to who you are and what you do.

Whatever the philosophical truth of the never-ending cyclical cause-effect law, the *karma* concept offers an interesting explanation of such phenomena as:

- Child prodigies. The new-born child inherits the *karma* of someone who was already highly skilled in some activity before he or she died: for example, music, mathematics or art.
- Memories of a past existence, often vivid and very accurate.
- Geniuses, similar to child prodigies.
- Split personality. Two *karma* battling it out inside one human body.
- The often very-strong sense of *déjà vu*. You haven't been there but one of your inherited *karmas* has.
- And even the accuracy of clairvoyants, astrologers and fortune tellers, assuming that their pronouncements come true!

From these simple beginnings, Buddhism spread far and wide around the Indian and Asian countries with many variations developing. For example:

- Theravada ('Original Teaching') Buddhism: probably the closest to the original form and still to be found in Sri Lanka, India, Thailand, Myanmar (formerly Burma).
- Mahayana ('Great Vehicle') Buddhism: to be found in China, Korea, Tibet, Mongolia and Japan.

Mahayana Buddhism has renamed the original Buddha as *Shakyamuni* and emphasises his teachings through the use of *sutras*,[54] revealing

---

[54] Sutras are short pithy statements (aphorisms) summarising a truism or principle and designed to be memorised: 'If it ain't broke, don't fix it' (attributed to American businessman Bert Lance writing in Nation's Business, 1977).

new sutras on an as-needed basis. Mahayana also creates and uses *bodhisattvas* - monks and nuns who are on the brink of *nirvana* but who remain active by teaching others how to become enlightened. *Bodhisattvas* are similar to Jainist *tirthankars*. A *bodhisattva* is a Buddha-in-waiting and, on death, becomes yet another Buddha. And so are created legions of Buddhas all with their own teachings and resulting in many sub-branches of Buddhism:

- In China: Pure Land, Ch'an, T'ien-t'ai, Hua-yen;
- In Japan: Soto, Rinzai, Jodo, Zen, Nichiren;
- In Tibet: Bon, Nyingmapa, Sarmapa;[55]
- In Korea: Popsong (really!), Son.
- Tantra Buddhism: found in Tibet and India and based on meditation, ritual, symbolism and magic. Tantra techniques are found in several other religions including Hinduism, Bon, Jainism, and Sikhism. Tantric techniques are considered to offer an alternative and faster way to achieve *nirvana*.[56] Tantra Buddhism contains many deities and uses divine power to achieve personal material or spiritual goals.

Mahayana Buddhism builds on the ideas that other deities exist, such as *Mother Earth* and *Mara* (the evil one) who, allegedly, tried to prevent the original Buddha from achieving *nirvana*. Some Mahayana Buddhist sects talk of Buddha's existence in the *Tushita Heaven*,[57] prior to his birth on earth. Thus Buddha himself now becomes a god probably much to the chagrin of the original Buddha, Siddhartha Gautama if he still exists in some shape or form somewhere. With these developments, the Mahayana version of Buddhism can no longer be regarded as a religion without a god.

If we take the Theravada form of Buddhism to be mostly a way of conducting your life for the good of everyone, including yourself, and reduce the importance of the more mystical aspects of *karma* and the need to achieve *nirvana*, then Buddhism has a lot of appeal. In particular, Theravada Buddhism has not resulted in warfare for

---

[55] The exiled fourteenth Dalai Lama, Tenzin Gyatso, belongs to a subset of Sarmapa called Gelugpa and some say that he is the reincarnation of a highly revered *bodhisattva* called Avalokiteshvara, the embodiment of compassion.
[56] The techniques are also said to heighten the pleasures of sexual intercourse as attributed to a certain well known performer of popular music. Tantra Buddhism has been described as the cult of ecstasy, neo-tantra and even pop tantra!
[57] In Mahayana Buddhism, a temporary heaven where *bodhisattvas* go before reaching final enlightenment.

territorial gain, wholesale slaughter of followers of other religions, terrorism, or any other acts of aggression as described in Chapter 3. It was this aspect of Buddhism that attracted me ten years ago on a beach at Bentota in Sri Lanka.

Sikhism

First, some facts. Sikhism was founded by Guru[58] Nanak Dev (1469 – 1539 CE). In the original Sanskrit, the word *Sikh* meant a disciple or student but in Sikhism, it refers to 'One who believes in God'. Guru Nanak Dev was followed by nine other human gurus, the last being Guru Gobind Singh (1666 – 1708 CE), and then by the creation of a virtual guru in 1708, a book called Guru Granth Sahib. This voluminous text was initially compiled by Guru Arjan Dev, the fifth guru, and contains many hymns and poetry attributed to the first four gurus. The book was elevated to guru status by Guru Gobind Singh. He also founded the *Khalsa*, the name of the community of dedicated Sikhs. A member of the *Khalsa* is committed to five outward symbols of faith, known as the five *Kakars* (the five Ks):

- *Kesh*: uncut hair to show acceptance of God's will and the perfection of God's creation.
- *Kangha*: a comb to show controlled spirituality and used twice a day to comb the uncut hair.
- *Kirpan*: a steel dagger to show determination to defend the faith and to cut through untruths.
- *Kara*: a steel wrist bangle to show binding with the Gurus and a reminder to carry out righteous deeds.
- *Kaccha*: a boxer-like undergarment to show moral strength and control sexual desire.

Guru Nanak Dev founded Sikhism during the Hindu–Muslim conflict that arose at the beginning of the Mughal Empire. He based his teachings on a desire to create a religion that transcended the conflict - one true path to God. He believed that there was only one God and that he did not manifest himself on earth, unlike the avatars of *Vishnu*. As in Hinduism and Buddhism, the concept of *karma* and rebirth exists in Sikhism and, similarly, there are stages of purity

---

[58] One who has great knowledge, wisdom and authority and who guides and teaches others.

A Summary Of World Religions: Modern Religions 65

starting with wrong-doer, *manmukh*, and finishing with devotion to and absorption in God and release from rebirth, *moksha*.

Sikhism places a strong emphasis on family life and regular attendance at the *gurdwara* (temple) in which resides a copy of the Guru Granth Sahib. Similar to the holy water used by Christians as a baptismal initiation symbol, Sikhs have a holy water called *amrit* – the nectar of immortality – used to initiate a person into the *Khalsa* (Sikh community). The Indian city of Amritsar, literally the 'pool of nectar', in the Indian region of Punjab was founded by Guru Ram Das, the fourth guru, and contains the gurdwara *Harmandir Sahib, the* famed Golden Temple, completed in 1601 CE and a major place of Sikh pilgrimage. The *Harmandir Sahib* contains the original version of the Guru Granth Sahib book.

Sikhs have long campaigned for their own kingdom, which they refer to as Khalistan, but at the time of writing, Punjab is still a part of India. Amritsar is occasionally the scene of conflict between Sikhs and the Indian government. The last time was in 1984 when India's then Prime Minister, Indira Gandhi, ordered the Indian Army to attack the *Harmandir Sahib* to arrest a Sikh militant accused of complicity in murder and other anti-social acts. The temple was damaged and the event shook the world of Sikhs. In 1998, Sonia Gandhi, the daughter-in-law of Indira Gandhi and wife of Prime Minister Rajiv Gandhi, officially apologised on behalf of the Indian Government.

Far East religions

Before moving on to the major religions of Christianity and Islam, I'll say a brief word about some of the religions that developed in the Far East, starting with China.

In China, most religions are more like philosophies and ways to live a good life than traditional deity-based religions. The most popular philosophies are Confucianism, Taoism and the Chinese version of Buddhism.

Confucianism

Confucius, 551 BCE – 479 BCE, real name *K'ung Fu-tzu*, was a philosopher and sage who emphasised loyalty to the family, respect of the elders (specifically children to parents but also young to old), ancestor homage and good governance based on the principles of family loyalty. He is reputed to be responsible for many wise sayings[59] including what I would call the principle of reciprocal altruistic behaviour – do to others as you would want others to do to you – but more commonly called the Golden Rule. The Confucian way is characterized by creating and practicing order and harmony out of disorder and chaos; balancing the opposing forces of *yin* and *yang*: light with dark, male with female, hot with cold.[60] There are elements of mysticism in the teachings of Confucianism, for example the concept of a Heaven and the acceptance of a god or set of gods, but Confucius taught that these were very personal beliefs and created in accordance with whatever you needed to achieve the right *yin yang* balance in your life. Accordingly, Confucian temples were created to assist personal meditation and remembrance of ancestors rather than to support mass ceremonies of devotion.

Chinese Confucians, and many non-Confucians, believe that Emperors who die go to Heaven and from then on control the destinies of those still on earth. Thus, they must be worshipped as royal ancestors in order to secure good harvests, a good balance of *yin* and *yang* in the community, the regularity of the four seasons, and a continuation of the royal dynasty. These four items are called the Heavenly Mandate. A ruler who pleased the ancestral gods by due piety, worship and sacrifice would obtain the power to exercise the Heavenly Mandate and so become the manifestation of the gods on earth. Consequently, Chinese Emperors were revered as living gods in addition to their more earthly responsibilities and resided in vast Imperial Courts, attended by a cast of thousands.

Taoism

The second great Chinese philosophy is Taoism, known also as Daoism. Tao means 'the way' and emphasises compassion, moderation and humility as exemplary ways of conducting one's

---

[59] Although he left no written records, there's an abundance of 'Confucius, he say ...' expressions in existence. Many may not have originated from him, including such aphorisms as 'Man who drive like hell will surely get there' and 'Man with one chopstick go hungry'!

[60] *Feng Shui*, 'wind and water', is the Chinese practice of balancing *yin* and *yang*. It was originally developed for the positioning of houses and graves (housing ancestors) in a way that maximised the accordance with divine and natural forces called *chi*. The term is now more loosely used to mean any form of harmonious arrangement that pleases the eye and has been applied as New Age ways for arranging furniture and fittings inside a room, or plants and ornaments in a garden: interior and exterior decorating in disguise. This interpretation of *feng shui* is frowned upon by true practitioners of the art.

moral and physical life. Taoism goes deeper into the forces and acceptance of nature and how such forces interact with the natural life forces within the body, called *chi* (also spelt *ch'i*). This latter point has given rise to Taoism being associated with traditional medicines, healing processes, acupuncture, alchemy, rituals, exercises (such as the martial art form called *t'ai chi ch'uan*[61]) and other practices designed to improve one's *chi*.

Taoism admits to a pantheon with various factions defining the deities in different ways. For example, popular Taoism considers the *Jade Emperor* to be the Ruler of Heaven and all realms below including that of Man and Hell whereas the Celestial Masters version of Taoism considers *Lord Lao* to be the head of the pantheon. It seems as if Taoist pantheons are always in a state of flux with constant recruitments, promotions, demotions and even assassinations!

Chinese Buddhism

Buddhism made its way to China sometime in the first few hundred years after the birth of Christ and the rise of Christianity. The Chinese were particularly attracted to the concept of *karma* and linked it with their homage of ancestors. The attainment of *nirvana* and, with it, the eventual release from torment, was attractive to the Chinese Buddhists and was used to obtain the final settlement of ghosts, that is those who had not been properly cared for as ancestors and who were still wandering looking for peace. Various schools of Buddhism developed, such as Pure Land and Ch'an, each with their own new set of deities and teachings. Pure Land Buddhism derived from Indian Mahayana Buddhism, focuses on the teachings of a Buddha called *Amitabha*, 'infinite light'. Amitabha Buddha postulated that there was a pure land of bliss, called *Sukhāvatī*, which, once reached, ensured enlightenment and a final resting place from the world of birth, death and rebirth. But, an entrant into *Sukhāvatī* always had the option of returning as a *bodhisattva* (a Buddha-in-waiting) to assist others achieve *nirvana*.

There are many Pure Land forms of Buddhism, all stemming from the basic Mahayana root. Each form has its own chief Buddha, its own 'pure land' and its own special way of achieving *nirvana*. The various forms may be found in China, Japan, Korea, Tibet, Taiwan and Vietnam at least.

---

[61] *T'ai chi ch'uan* was used with great effect in director Ang Lee's highly-acclaimed 2000 martial art film *Crouching Tiger, Hidden Dragon*.

Japanese Shintoism

Religions in Japan are not really religions in the sense that I have defined the word in Chapter 2: an institutionalised system of attitudes, beliefs and practices based on the belief of a God or set of gods. Similar to Chinese religions, they are more a philosophy for a way of life, based on good ideas drawn from other religions such as Taoism, Confucianism, Buddhism and, more recently, Christianity, but flavoured by their own indigenous folk views of the sacredness of nature, respect for ancestors and strong family loyalties. There are elements of mysticism and a belief in deities but these aspects are subservient to the familial and ancestral loyalties. The original indigenous folk traditions, called Shinto, a word meaning 'way of the gods', have come from folklore associated with ancient Japan. Central to Shinto is the concept of a *kami*. The concept is difficult to define in English and sometimes the word is simply translated as 'soul', 'spirit', 'life force' or 'spirits of nature'.[62] Motoori Norinaga, a nineteenth century Japanese scholar and Shinto revivalist, offered the following definition: 'any thing or phenomenon that produces the emotions of fear and awe, with no distinction between good and evil.'[63]

Shintoism stems from animism; the belief that all objects, animate and inanimate, possess a spirit or soul and that they are at least worthy of respect and, in some cases, worship.[64] Animate objects embrace not only humans but also all members of the animal and plant kingdom. Inanimate objects include:

- permanent natural objects such as rocks, rivers, mountains and oceans;

---

[62] The notorious Second World War *kamikaze* suicide pilots were so named from the words *kami*, here meaning spirits and *kaze*, meaning wind – 'spirits on the wind' or 'divine wind' – and stemmed from the traditions of the samurai warrior and associated bushido code of conduct; death before dishonour, including capture.

[63] http://en.wikipedia.org/wiki/Kami

[64] Animism and totemism are similar in their world views. An animist believes that all life is fostered by the individual spirits that reside within all objects whereas a totemist believes that there's a single primary source of life, typically the land itself. The Inuit beliefs are typical of animism whereas the Australian Aborigine beliefs are typical of totemism. The way that a small child will assign human characteristics and even life to a favoured doll or an imaginary friend is animistic in origin, and probably innate. In fact, animism is considered by some to be one of the fundamental roots of all religions. See Chapter 9, especially the postscript, for more discussion of the possible innateness of religion.

- transient natural objects such as thunderstorms, rain and wind; and
- abstract objects such as names, fertility, occupations, skills and even other gods and Buddhas.

Shintoism has its own pantheon including *Izanagi-no-Mikoto* and *Izanam-no-Mikoto*, the male and female Creators of Japan, and *Amaterasu Omikami*, the Sun Goddess, but Shintoism is not necessarily separate to philosophies based on the religious teachings of, say, Buddhism or Confucianism. Shintoism influences the interpretation and associated practices of these religions. In many cases, life events are handled by Shinto beliefs whereas death events are handled by Buddhist beliefs – a process of belief combination called syncretism.

There are many forms of Shintoism, depending on focus:

- Shrine Shinto: focused on shrines and associated paraphernalia such as festivals, amulets, making wishes, and ceremonies in praise of Japan as a nation.
- Imperial Household Shinto: rituals performed exclusively by the members of the Imperial Household.
- Folk Shinto: based on the folklore of deities and performed by *shamans* - priests and priestesses who use magic to divine the hidden, cast out evil spirits, and accomplish other religious tasks.
- Sect Shinto: based on a particular object of worship such as Mount Fuji whereon lives the goddess *Sengen-Sama*, or a particular activity such as healing and purification, or a particular fusion of Shintoism with another religion such as Confucianism.
- Old Shinto (Koshinto): a reconstruction of Shintoism before the influence of Buddhism.

In 1868, the Japanese government attempted to formalise Shintoism as the official state religion of Japan but abandoned the idea in 1945 when, post-Second World War and following Japan's surrender, the Americans forced a separation of church and state and Emperor Hirohito announced that he was not a living god.

Since the Second World War, the Japanese have become more secular, ascribing to a western style of living and social behaviour and although Shintoism lives on, it's more in the form of private beliefs than public attestations.

The roots of Abrahamic religions

We turn now to the roots of the three major Abrahamic religions; Judaism, Christianity and Islam, based on the teachings of holy books - the Hebrew Bible, the Christian Bible, and the Islamic Qur'an. The Hebrew Bible, known by Judaists as the *Tanakh*, is divided into the *Torah*, the *Prophets* and the *Writings*. The *Torah* contains the five books of Genesis, Exodus, Leviticus, Numbers, and Deuteronomy. The beliefs of the early Abrahamic religions, particularly Judaism, are based, in part, on the literal or symbolic interpretations of the *Torah*. The five books are a collection of old Hebrew Scriptures that tell of the creation of the world and all therein followed by the trials and tribulations of a semi-nomadic tribe of wandering shepherds in an area referred to as Canaan.[65]

Genesis, the first book of the *Torah*, relates the story of God's creation of the world and its first human inhabitants, Adam and Eve. At that time, God was known as YHWH written as Yahweh. As told in the book, the creation took just six days. This was followed not long after by the expulsion of Adam and Eve from the Garden of Eden because of Eve's original sin of persuading Adam to eat from the Tree of Knowledge of Good and Evil. Under the influence of Satan disguised as a Serpent, Eve had already eaten from the tree.

After the expulsion, Adam and Eve go on and have various children - Cain, Abel and Seth - plus further sons and daughters and, presumably because sibling incest was acceptable, they in turn produced further progeny and so the human population of earth commenced.[66]

Somewhere down the generations, Noah was born (tenth generation after Adam) and, subsequently, Abram (twentieth generation) later to be renamed as Abraham, literally 'father of a multitude', by the Jews and as Ibrahim by Islamists. Noah became famous for constructing the Ark and saving the world's animal population from extinction following Yahweh's summoning of a flood as punishment for all the wickedness that prevailed at the time. Noah was 600 years old when he embarked on his voyage!

Abraham, so the story goes, consulted Yahweh about the future of his nomadic tribe and Yahweh made an agreement with him, promising him and his descendants (but not others) a land 'flowing

---

[65] These days corresponding to the region encompassing modern-day Israel, Palestinian territories, Lebanon, and the western parts of Syria.
[66] Adam is reputed to have lived for 930 years so he had plenty of opportunity to mate with his descendants in order to expand the human race!

with milk and honey' in return for undying love and devotion and propagation of Yahweh as the 'one true god'.[67] The land was defined thus:

> *'In that same day, the Lord made a covenant with Abram saying unto thy seed have I given this land, from the river of Egypt to the great river, the Euphrates, the land of the Kenites, Kenizzites, Kadmonites, Hittites, Perizzites, Rephaites, Amorites, Canaanites, Girgashites and Jebusites.'*
>
> Genesis 15:18-21

This area is now known as Israel. The Kenites ... Jebusites seem to be long gone!

At some point in Abraham's search for the Promised Land his faith was tested by Yahweh. Yahweh commanded Abraham to take his second-born son, Isaac, up the mountain and sacrifice him.[68] Just at the point when Abraham was about to set fire to the sacrificial bonfire, Yahweh ordered him to stop and supplied a wild ram instead. Thus was Abraham favoured with greater prosperity and numerous descendants! In addition, Abraham and his son ate well that night.

Sometime later, Jacob (twenty-second generation), one of Abraham's grandsons, fell asleep and dreamt of a ladder. When he climbed the ladder, he encountered Yahweh and was told that the land he was on was, finally, the Promised Land. In this way, Jacob, who was later renamed Israel (possibly meaning 'God Rules' or 'Prince of God') by an angel, found the Promised Land and named the location Bethel.[69] Although he did not settle there at the time, he did return in later life but, ultimately he died in Egypt. His body was taken back to Hebron and buried in the Cave of Machpela, a cave purchased by Abraham and also Abraham's burial place.

Two other characters in this long-running saga of ancient times deserve mention: Moses and King David. Moses (twenty-seventh generation), a descendant of Jacob, was the prophet who led the Children of Israel out of Egypt, assisted by Yahweh parting the Red Sea for him and his Israelite tribe. Moses and his tribe settled on

---

[67] Part of this covenant included Abraham's promise to have every male child circumcised at birth, a distinguishing physical feature that was used with devastating effect by the Nazis in their identification of male Jews during the Holocaust.
[68] Or was it Abraham's first-born son, Ishmael? Interpretations of parts of the Qu'ran (37:99 – 109) suggest it may have been so.
[69] About 12 miles/20 kilometres north of Jerusalem.

Mount Sinai where, within sight of the Promised Land, he received the Ten Commandments, inscribed in stone.

King David (thirty-first generation), second king of the United Kingdom of Israel, composer of many psalms, slayer of Goliath the giant, and Michelangelo's muse, is credited with capturing a Jebusite[70] fortress at Jerusalem and making Jerusalem the capital of the kingdom of Israel. His son, Solomon, built a holy temple that was destroyed by the Babylonians in the sixth century BCE, rebuilt in the fifth century BCE, enhanced by King Herod the Great in the first century BCE, and finally destroyed in the eighth century CE by the Romans. Only the western wall, known as the Wailing Wall, remains, and is now a major place of pilgrimage. Modern Israelis consider Jerusalem to be the capital of Israel and the city is holy to all three Abrahamic religions: Judaists, Christians and Islamists.

Judaism

Judaists, more commonly called Jews, developed their religion from the teachings and stories of the *Tanakh*, and especially the covenant made between Yahweh and Abraham and, later, with Moses. In addition, they pay service to the *Talmud*, an ancillary religious text created by well-known Jewish rabbis and dealing with questions of interpretation, ethics, customs, history and philosophy. There is also a third source of Judaist knowledge, called the *Kabbalah*. Originally transferred by word of mouth, the *Kabbalah* contains mystical knowledge that is only imparted to those who are ready to receive it.

Jews base their approach to life on the commandments declared in the *Torah*, there being 613 in all covering rituals, hygiene and morality. Their belief that they are the Chosen People often causes conflict and contributed to the Nazi view that Jews were, in effect, not superior but rather inferior to others.[71]

The Ten Commandments are central to the covenant. Rather than reproduce the original words, of which there are at least two sets

---

[70] A pre-Israelite Canaanite tribe who founded Jerusalem, originally known as Jebus.

[71] The 'chosen people' label has created much discussion and disagreement. Most Jews will refute that 'chosen people' implies superiority. They argue that it means that they must carry additional burdens and that they have an obligation to God to teach his ways to non-Jewish people. Others see the label as a mark of religious superiority and they react accordingly depending on their own religious views and the prevailing circumstances.

written down in the Old Testament,[72] here is my personal interpretation:

1. There's only one god – me (Yahweh)!
2. Worship only me. Don't worship any false images either of me or any other gods.
3. Don't use my name for any purpose other than reverence.
4. Keep one day a week free in order to rest and to have the opportunity to worship me.
5. Honour your parents.
6. Don't murder any other human.
7. Don't commit adultery.
8. Don't steal material things or ideas from any other human.
9. Don't create false stories about any other human.
10. Don't lust after anything that doesn't belong to you.

These laws, plus many others defined in the Hebrew Bible, form the basis for Judaism rituals, practices and behaviour even though there are difficulties with their interpretation in modern life. For example, does #6 – encompass abortion or capital punishment? And what about war? Does #7 condemn or condone pre-marital sex?

Jews also believe that, one day, a Messiah ('anointed one') will arrive who will become their king and establish God's covenant on earth by killing the wicked people (despite Commandment #6) and promoting the righteous people to places in God's kingdom on earth. Jews do not consider Jesus Christ to be the Messiah because he did not fulfil their expectations of the Messiah. He is considered to be 'just another prophet' by Jews; similarly by Islamists (Muslims). This is a fundamental difference between Jews and Muslims on the one hand, and Christians on the other. For some Jews, however, the founding of the modern State of Israel in 1948 is seen to be a substitute for the Messiah. Others still cherish the belief that a Messiah will arrive one day, 'meek and riding on an ass'.

Central to the Jewish faith is loyalty to the family, loyalty to the synagogue (the traditional place of worship), and loyalty to the religion. Marriage of a Jew to a non-Jewish[73] partner is frowned upon and even forbidden by some Jewish sects. Among the many Jewish rituals are those that relate to:

---

[72] Exodus 20:2–17 and Deuteronomy 5:6–21.
[73] Commonly called a Gentile, defined to be anyone who is not of the Israelite tribe and therefore not a Jew.

- food (kosher versus non-kosher food, the ban on eating anything that contains blood, and the separation of meat and dairy products into separate dishes);
- hygiene (many are commonsense like washing hands before preparing and eating food or after urinating or defecating); and
- spiritual requirements (the lighting of candles to indicate God's constant presence).

The expulsion of the Jews from their homeland by the Babylonians between the eighth and sixth centuries BCE, called the Jewish diaspora,[74] created many different Jewish communities around the world. The scattering resulted in diverse versions of Orthodox Judaism including the more extreme forms known as Haredi and Hasadic Judaism. Haredi Jews maintain that the original laws handed down by God to Abraham and Moses cannot be changed or in any way updated to accommodate changes to social, sexual or material forces in society. Hasadic Jews are deeply spiritual. They originated and flourished in Eastern Europe but they were almost wiped out by the Bolsheviks following the 1917 Bolshevik Revolution in Russia and the subsequent expansion of the USSR. Their number is now thought to be around one million worldwide.[75] Hasidic Jews are recognised by their traditional dark clothing including a long black jacket *(rekel)*, black shoes, various types of black hats and long ringlets of uncut side hair *(payot)*.

An alternative to Orthodox Judaism is Reform Judaism, emerging in Western Europe in the nineteenth century CE. Its proponents accepted that civilization had changed since the days of Abraham and Moses and they suggested many modifications to bring the religion into line with modern thinking. Examples are a call for full equality for women including ordainment as rabbis; a rejection of commandments that were perceived as offensive such as animal sacrifice; and recognition that homosexuality is a natural inclination and not an abomination. Reform Judaists also produced new versions of the Jewish services to be performed in easier-to-understand English, not archaic Hebrew. Currently, Orthodox Jews reject the modernisations of Reform Judaism.

As with other religions, there are a number of Jewish festivals, examples being:

---

[74] Diaspora: literally, a scattering and resettlement of a nation or race or religious group into different parts of the world.
[75] http://en.wikipedia.org/wiki/Hasidic_Judaism#Post_War_rebuilding_of_Hasidic_life

- *Sabbath*, as per Commandment #4;
- *Passover* to celebrate the exodus of the Israelites from Egypt under the leadership of Moses;
- *Shavuot*, to commemorate God's delivery of the Ten Commandments to Moses on Mount Sinai in the Sinai Peninsula;
- *Yom Kippur*, a day of atonement for personal sins committed;
- *Hanukkah*, the festival of lights to commemorate the rededication of the Holy Temple in Jerusalem following its recapture from the Syrians in the second century BCE.

Zionism

A comment about Zionism. Zionism is not a religion as such. It's a term used in the Old Testament to mean the final gathering of all twelve tribes of Israel back in the Promised Land. As the Jewish diaspora took place, Jews originally thought that they would easily integrate into their new homelands. As it turned out, certain countries, political parties and ethnic races rejected the Jews with a hatred that developed into persecution. Anti-Semitism, so called, is still prevalent today.

In 1897, a Viennese journalist, Theodor Herzl, convened the first Zionist Congress and proposed that a Jewish State be formed to provide a homeland for diasporic Jews. And so was born the Zionist movement, a political movement that supports the State of Israel and encourages Jews outside of Israel to return to the Promised Land. Zionism has many opponents, particularly in the Arabic countries bordering or close to Israel and Israel is a country that is always prepared to go to war.[76] Such is the legacy of a set of stories written many years ago and in circumstances very different to today's society. I will continue this discussion in Chapter 8.

Christianity

One way to think about Christianity is that it is a post-Messiah update of Judaism. It is what happened when the Messiah Jesus Christ, the 'Christ' in Christianity, was born and lived on earth, come to atone for

---

[76] I first saw this when I visited Tel Aviv on business in the early 1980s. I observed the increased levels of security both when I boarded the flight in London and when I landed in Tel Aviv. After admission into the country, I was struck by the high number of people, male and female, in the towns I visited who were wearing military uniforms and carrying weapons. These days, security applies to us all, not just travellers to Israel, and it's not uncommon to see military or police personnel carrying guns.

the sins of mankind and restore faith in God. Atonement, defined to be the reconciliation of man and God through the ultimate sacrifice of his son Jesus Christ, is a central doctrine of Christianity and is explained as follows:

> Adam and Eve committed the original sin when they disobeyed God's instruction not to eat the fruit of the Tree of Knowledge of Good and Evil.
>
> This original sin was and still is transferred from one generation to the next. Therefore we're all burdened with the original sin as soon as we're born.
>
> The slate will only be wiped clean when Jesus Christ, the Son of God, lives on earth as a human and is put to death. On death, he will absorb the original sins of all those who confess or believe that they are carriers of this sin.

This happened two thousand years ago but some say it needs to happen again – the Second Coming of the Messiah. There are a lot of new sins to absolve!

The story of Jesus is told in the New Testament, a collection of writings by four of his disciples, Matthew, Mark, Luke and John, supplemented by a fifth disciple, a Roman citizen called Paul of Tarsus,[77] and then by many other disciples who came after Jesus was crucified by the Romans. Jesus was a Jew, born to a Galilean woman called Mary and whom Christians believe was a virgin made pregnant by the Holy Ghost[78] and not by her husband Joseph – the Immaculate Conception.[79] This belief is central to the Christian faith because it allows the follow-on claim to be made that Jesus was truly the Son of God, given that the Holy Ghost was a manifestation, an *avatar*, of God. Consequently, when Jesus was crucified by the Romans with the tacit approval of the Jews, an additional claim could be made that three days later he was reclaimed by God and taken back into God's care – the Resurrection.

In between the Immaculate Conception and the Resurrection, a number of other things took place, as chronicled by the disciples.

---

[77] Credited with being the founder of Christianity following the death of Jesus Christ.
[78] Also known as the Holy Spirit.
[79] We can ponder on what Joseph might have thought when he discovered that Mary was pregnant, not by him, but by a Holy Ghost! Matthew 1: 18 – 19 states that Joseph 'not willing to make her (Mary) a public example, was minded to put her away privily (secretively)' suggesting shame and even that the Holy Ghost was a cover up for some more mortal misdemeanour by Mary!

Jesus healed the sick, raised the dead, fed the poor, absolved sins, spoke many wise words, performed all sorts of miracles and generally did many things that an ordinary mortal of that era, or any era come to that, would find difficult without resorting to trickery, illusion and magic. And, in so doing, Jesus brought God back into the lives of humans and re-established his authority on earth: the Atonement.

All this happened during the time of the Roman occupation of the middle-east countries. Gradually, the Romans became convinced that Christianity was a better religion than their polytheistic pantheon. They adopted its beliefs and created the Roman Catholic Church, a multi-layered bureaucracy with a hierarchy of human officers starting with the laity (those who belong to the faith but are not part of the clergy) and spiralling up to the Pope via a chain of command that included monks, nuns, priests, bishops and cardinals. Beyond that, the hierarchy continued through saints, martyrs (believers who died for their faith) and angels up to God, the ultimate head of the chain. The Pope was, and still is, elected from the cardinals and is regarded to be the spiritual head of the church possessing the property of papal infallibility (an inability to get it wrong because it comes directly from God) when pronouncing on matters of faith or morals. Such dogmatic statements must be made *ex cathedra*, that is, when the Pope is speaking in his (there has never been a female Pope) capacity as the head of the Roman Catholic Church.

The Roman Catholic Church was not the only form of Christianity. Other forms developed, particularly during the sixteenth century European Protestant Reformation, leading to today's many variants: Anglican, Baptists, Congregational, Eastern Orthodox, Lutherans, Methodists, Oriental Orthodox, Presbyterian and many more. The list is almost endless. The splits (called schisms) that caused these branches to develop were usually based on articles of faith. Is the Holy Ghost truly part of the Trinity, or just an *avatar* of God? Does the wafer and the wine truly become the body and blood of Jesus Christ, or are they just symbolic tokens? Are sins forgiven simply by confessing them to a priest followed by the chanting of mystical mantras and possibly some financial contribution to the church? And so on.

I will say more on this in Chapter 7.

In general, Christians of any denomination believe that the word of God is contained in a holy book called the Bible: a combination of the Old Testament (the basis for the Judaist Hebrew *Tanakh*) and the New

Testament containing works created post-Christ. This book is full of prophecies (some fulfilled, some unfulfilled), ambiguities, contradictions, creeds (a statement of beliefs), unsubstantiated stories of magic and trickery, savagery and downright hatred in places. And yet it is revered as the basis for a way of life, defining how we should behave both in ourselves and to others, and based on a belief in God that cannot be proved. In this respect, Christianity in all its multi-hued forms is just like any other religion – the product of many fertile minds creating a mass of stories, myths, sagas based on a population of imaginary beings in imaginary worlds.

As an example of a creed, here are the twelve beliefs expressed in the Apostles' Creed, although not written by the Apostles, and used by the Roman Catholic Church. Other variants exist to suit other forms of Christian denominations.

1. I believe in God, the Father Almighty, creator of heaven and earth.
2. I believe in Jesus Christ, his only Son, our Lord.
3. He was conceived by the power of the Holy Spirit and born of the Virgin Mary.
4. He suffered under Pontius Pilate, was crucified, died, and was buried.
5. He descended to the dead. On the third day he rose again.
6. He ascended into heaven and is seated at the right hand of the Father.
7. He will come again to judge the living and the dead.
8. I believe in the Holy Spirit,
9. The holy Catholic Church, the communion of saints,
10. The forgiveness of sins,
11. The resurrection of the body,
12. And life everlasting.

Note that all items except possibly item 4, cannot be substantiated. This set of beliefs, called the Catechism of the Catholic Church, is a faith system on which is built a massive structure of management, morality, legality, judgment and punishment or reward. I will have more to say about this, and other aspects of modern Christianity, in Chapter 7.

Islam

Islam started some six hundred years after the life and death of Jesus and is based on the teachings of a prophet called Muhammad (variously spelt as Muhammed, Mohammed, Mohammad at least). At the time, many Jews had rejected the claim that Jesus was the son of God, born of a virgin made pregnant by the Holy Ghost and they continued worshipping God in the traditional Judaic way.

Muhammad was born in the Arabian city of Mecca in 570 CE and at age 40, disenchanted with his life as a merchant and a shepherd, he retired to a cave in Mount Hira in the hills around Mecca. There, he meditated on life, the universe and associated mystical subjects. When he returned, Muhammad claimed to have had conversations with God (*Allah* in Arabic, 'the one who is God') via God's emissary the angel Gabriel and he started preaching about the revelations. In this way are prophets created and new religions formed.

As is usual with new prophets, Muhammad met with hostility and it took him some years to gather enough support to start a new version of Judaism. He called this new version Islam, literally, 'one who submits to the one God to the exclusion of all other gods' and a follower of Islam is called a Muslim meaning the same thing.

During the years that followed, Muhammad regularly retired to the hills to meditate and refresh his acquaintance with God, each time returning with yet more revelations. In between all this, Muhammad had thirteen wives/concubines, one alleged to have been just six years old (Aisha),[80] and various sons and daughters. Opinions differ as to the exact number of offspring and how many survived childbirth. Muhammad also amassed a number of followers who started writing down the revelations he was receiving from God via Gabriel. These writings eventually became the Qur'an, the holy book of Islam, also written as Quran, Kuran, Koran, Coran or al-Qur'ān. The literal meaning of the word Qur'an is 'the recitation'. The contents of the book are considered to be the direct words of God and are non-

---

[80] There are several opinions about the age of Aisha bint Abu Bakr. The most informed opinion is that she was only six years old when she was married to Muhammad and that full consummation of the marriage (penetrative sexual intercourse) took place before she had her first menstruation when she was still a prepubescent nine-year old. These ages are backed up with many quotations from the Hadith (companion volumes to the Qur'an). Others say that the marriage and consummation ages were slightly later at nine- and twelve-years old respectively, again backed up by alternative Hadith statements. And yet others say that she was much older, at least 24, before consummation took place. Whatever the truth, Aisha's age, and presumed virgin status at marriage have stoked many fires of discussion on websites. If the six- and nine-year old ages are indeed true, we should not judge Muhammad by today's standards but more by the prevailing social mores among Bedouin tribes fifteen hundred years ago. But, in the minds of many the stigma of paedophilia hangs over Muhammad's head and taints his image.

negotiable, a point to which I will return in Chapter 8. The Qur'an replaced all earlier holy books such as the Hebrew Bible, the extended Christian Bible and, these days, is the holiest book in the Islamic faith.

Years later, the Qur'an was supplemented by the Hadith, literally 'conveyed information' or 'traditions'; a collection of sayings, teachings, aphorisms, stories and interpretations of Muhammad's words and deeds and regarded as companion volumes to the Qur'an. The laws of Islam, called the Sharia (literally, 'the path to a watering hole'), are derived from interpretations of the contents of the Qur'an and the Hadith.

There are several Hadith collections coming from different sources and at different times following Muhammad's death and they don't all agree on basic points of principle and belief. The two main collections, called Sunni and Shi'a Hadith, became the basis for the two main Islamic factions of Sunni ('one who follows the traditions of the Prophet') and Shi'a ('people of the household') and created differences in practices of worship and interpretations of law and punishment. Essentially, Sunni Muslims believe that the leadership of the religious movement should be elected and based on best fit for the job, whereas Shi'a Muslims believe that the leadership should always be a direct descendant of Muhammad. This fundamental schism has given rise to two very different Muslim organisations and has often resulted in conflict and death, notably in what is now Pakistan and in Iraq, Syria and several other middle-east Arab countries. Sunni Muslims represent about 85% of the Muslims in the world but Shi'a Muslims are very prevalent in the hard-line theocracy of the Republic of Iran and in Hezbollah, the Islamic guerrilla organisation that opposes the State of Israel. Saudi Arabia, another hard-line theocracy, is largely controlled by Sunni Muslims with interpretation of Sharia law based on the extremist Wahhabi rulings.

Some of the important differences between Shi'a and Sunni beliefs are listed below.

- Shi'as believe that their religious leaders, the twelve Shi'a Imams, are without sin and are infallible (similar to the Pope's infallibility). This can lead to dead imams being venerated as saints. Sunnis do not believe this, especially the Wahhabi faction of Sunnis. They believe that imams are not a privileged class of spiritual leaders and that they do not become saints after death.
- The Sunni world view of religion is two-fold: you either believe (in which case you are a Muslim) or you do not believe (in which case you are anything but a Muslim such as an apostate, infidel, or a

believer in some other faith). The Shi'a world view is three-fold: true believers and adherents of the Hadith of the twelve revered Shi'a Imams; common believers who don't accept the Hadith of the Shi'a Imams but are Muslims otherwise; and the anything-but-a-Muslim class.
- Shi'as have animosity towards some of the early authors and collectors of the Hadith - Abu Bakr, Umar, and Aisha[81] - and have rejected the contents of the Hadith written by these people. Sunnis accept these Hadith. Given that all three authors knew Muhammad well, the principles that have been rejected are fundamental to Islam and have caused major differences, notably in techniques for praying and in the interpretation of Sharia law.
- Shi'as allow fixed-term temporary marriages; Sunnis do not.
- Shi'as believe that, one day, a redeemer of Islam, called *al-Mahdi* ('the guided one' and last of the twelve Shi'a Imams) will return and rid the world of tyranny, sin and injustice. This will happen on the Day of Judgment, known also as Armageddon. Some Sunnis have this belief but point out that *al-Mahdi* is not mentioned in the Qur'an.

Muslims adhere to the Five Pillars of Islam, defined thus:

1. *Shahadah*: sincerely reciting the Muslim profession of faith – 'There is no god but *Allah*, and Muhammad is the messenger of *Allah*'. A single sincere recitation of the *Shahadah* is all that's required to become a Muslim.
2. *Salat*: performing ritual prayers in the proper way five times a day while facing in the direction of the sacred shrine Ka'ba, a large cube-shaped building in Mecca.[82] Muslims are called to prayer by a *muezzin*, a person selected for his good character and strong voice and who issues the call from minarets on a mosque.
3. *Zakat*: paying an alms (or charity) tax to benefit the poor and the needy. One fortieth of annual income is recommended. *Zakat* is considered to be an act of purification rather than a charitable gift.
4. *Sawm*: fasting, by which is meant no food, no drink and no sexual contact in the hours of daylight during the ninth Islamic month,

---

[81] Abu Bakr was a senior companion and father-in-law to Muhammad; Aisha, Muhammad's young bride, was his daughter. Umar was an admirer and friend of Muhammad.
[82] It's claimed that the Ka'ba was built by Abraham and his first son Ishmael, following orders from God. It stands on a site thought by many to be a sanctuary founded by Adam.

Ramadan – the month in which the Qur'an was first revealed to Muhammad – in order to experience and thus appreciate the deprivations of the poor.

5. *Hajj*: pilgrimage to Mecca, the spiritual centre of the world-wide Muslim community. The pilgrimage should be undertaken at least once in a Muslim's lifetime and during the twelfth Islamic month, *Dhu al-Hijja*.[83] (In 2010, an estimated three million people made the pilgrimage.)

The Five Pillars of Faith are designed to make sure that devout Muslims never subjugate their beliefs to matters related to their secular existence. Their religion comes first – always! More on this in Chapter 8.

Finally, a word about Sufis (literally, 'a wearer of wool' after the coarse garment worn by early Sufis). Sufis, also known as Dervishes, are ascetic Muslims who dedicate their lives to God, attempting to gain intense experiences by means of fasting and dancing to achieve ecstasy. In a way, they are like Hindu *sadhus* looking for *moksha*, or mendicants in Christianity. Sufis exploit the mysticism of Islam to achieve similar results. Although music is generally avoided by Muslims (it excites the senses!), Sufis use repetitive hypnotic chants accompanied by tambourines and pipes and engage in whirling dances to achieve a trance-like state – the whirling dervishes.

Sufis practice the Five Pillars of Islam but from a different perspective:

- *Shahadah* (profession of faith): same as Sunni and Shi'a belief.
- *Salat* (prayer): aids closeness to *Allah*.
- *Zakat* (giving of alms): is received by a Sufi, not because he needs it but because it helps another Muslim fulfil his obligation to give (a neat twist of logic).
- *Sawm* (fasting): weakens the body and in so doing strengthens the obedience to *Allah*.
- *Hajj* (pilgrimage): is an act of self-mortification whose true objective is to contemplate *Allah*, not visit Mecca.

---

[83] The Islamic Hijri calendar is lunar based and lasts either 354 or 355 days. This puts it slightly out-of-step with the Gregorian 365/366 day calendar and isn't synchronised with the seasons. The calendar re-cycles every 33 years.

The various orders of Sufis trace their origins back to associates of Muhammad, such as Abu Bakr and Ali,[84] who have subsequently become saints. Sufism is still very much alive and can be found in the Middle East, North and West Africa, Turkey, Pakistan, India, Caucasus, America and South-East Asia.

Middle Age development of Islam

In its early days, Islam was very involved in advancing the arts and the sciences. Although the invention of algebraic mathematics can be traced back to Babylonian times (around 2,000 BCE) followed by Greek mathematicians, the concepts were further developed by medieval Muslim mathematicians. In the so-called *Islamic Golden Age*, between the eighth and fourteenth centuries CE, Muslim scientists made contributions to many branches of science and engineering including mathematics, chemistry, metaphysics, medicine, psychology, and astronomy. And then it ground to a halt. Muslim clerics argued that the development of scientific concepts and applications by reasoning and logic went against the fundamental *knowledge-by-revelation* nature of Islam. They said that the ideas and applications had not come about by revelations from God and so should not be pursued. Effectively, this stifled invention and innovation by Muslim scholars and Islam became very introspective and reflective. This is an extreme view, of course. Islamic scholars have contributed to our scientific knowledge since the fourteenth century but very little in proportion to their non-Muslim counterparts. Using a search engine with the words 'Muslim inventions since the fourteenth century' yields virtually nothing of major significance.

Nowadays, the need for reform has been recognised by some leading Muslim jurists (scholars who pronounce Sharia law based on their interpretations of the Qur'an and the Hadith) and there are now some jurists who have said that Islamic law could be and should be modified by changes in society rather than always be based on the interpretations of the holy books. These are dangerous ideas for Muslim scholars to contemplate but necessary if Islam is to co-exist with non-Islamic societies, especially the secular societies of Western Europe and North America. I will explore further the development of modern Islam in Chapter 8.

---

[84] Ali was both a cousin and a son-in-law of Muhammad and regarded by Shi'as to be the first Imam. See earlier footnote on Abu Bakr.

Native religions

Native religions, also known as *shamanic* religions, are loosely characterized as being a set of beliefs, rituals and myths that arise naturally in primitive tribes that have had very little contact with the world as we know it today – tribes hidden away in the depths of the Amazon rain forest, or found in the jungles of Africa or Borneo. Typically, native religions arise from the basic requirements for survival: food and water, shelter, procreation, health and fire. A gods-of-nature pantheon is created – Sun god, Rain god, Fertility god, Hunting god – and *shamans* use a mix of knowledge, folklore and magic to cast good spells, foretell the future, heal the sick and act as conduits to the deities. *Shamans* rise to prominence and become revered by their tribal community if their forecasts and ritual acts produce favourable results. Those *shamans* who are capable of causing bad things to happen, either to you or to your enemies, are called *witch doctors* and are more feared than revered. Both *shamans* and *witch doctors* act through spirits, some good and some bad. The concepts of good and bad are well understood in native religions, along with their impact on the day-to-day lives of the members of the tribe.

Nobody knows how many native religions still exist in the world today. Missionaries, plus other contacts from the civilised world, have eroded away at these primitive belief systems but those that have been found and unobtrusively studied have revealed some fascinating facts about how primitive religions evolve. Here are some major characteristics of native religions:

- They are usually polytheistic with the deities either co-sharing the natural world with humans or occupying their own cosmological space – a sort of heaven. The pantheon, while not huge in number, represents a set of interlinked deities whose job is to provide the basic needs. There's usually a head god, considered to be the creator. The deities may, or may not, require gifts to encourage them to be kind and bountiful, or sacrifices to appease them in the event of some catastrophe. Gifts are usually of the form that has some value to the tribe members, typically food, whereas sacrifices may take the form of animals and, as we saw in the case of the Inca and Aztec religions, humans.
- Spirituality is often endowed to things that do not make godhood – trees, rivers, mountains – along the lines of Shintoism. One can postulate that living close to nature with a high dependence on

natural events creates an affinity far closer than that of the city dweller and one's sense of wonder and even awe at, say, the majesty of a large redwood tree or a cascading waterfall, is enhanced accordingly.
- Belief in a spiritual essence, a soul, and an afterlife is intrinsic to native religions. Burial of the dead is a solemn ritual with gifts added to the funeral pyre or grave to help the passage into the next world and as gifts for the welcoming deities. Even in graves that date back to the dawn of mankind, grave goods have been found. The eschatology of primitive native religions is just as sophisticated in concept as it is in modern religions. Even in native religions, although people die that's not the end of their existence. Some part of them continues into another world.
- Myths and legends play a major part in native religions. Stories of great events in the past – a hunt, a tribal migration, a feat of great strength and skill, a natural disaster - are told and retold, usually with embellishments depending on the skill of the story-teller, the attention of the audience and the environmental ambience. And so great sagas develop and become a part of the religious views of the tribe. The ancient Greek, Roman and Norse religions took these stories to unprecedented heights of imagination and seemingly impossible tasks of endurance and one can argue that similar things have happened with the biblical stories.
- The use of symbols is prevalent in native religions. *Shamans*, and *witch doctors*, attire themselves in outfits full of symbols – animal skins, feather head dress, amulets, bells and rattles and drums, face and body paint, dangling bones, metal ornaments and decorated clothing. Similarly, certain places and objects become sacred – waterfalls, outcrops of rocks, forest glades, caves, and burial grounds – as do man-made items such as totem poles, other wooden carvings, and stone statues.
- It's common to find rites-of-passage rituals, especially with boys about to achieve manhood – the native religion version of the Jewish *bar mitzvah*.[85] Often, there is some ritualistic ceremony that involves the boy becoming the centerpiece of a manly-pursuit dance, or the boy has to go forth and demonstrate his prowess as a hunter. Girls similarly may become the centre of attention when they reach puberty with ceremonies designed to acknowledge that they are now capable of childbirth.

---

[85] A Jewish ceremony carried out when a boy reaches his thirteenth year and designed to mark his attainment of religious duty and responsibility.

It's rare to find untouched primitive native religions but if discovered they offer anthropologists and others valuable insights into the evolution of a religious system and provide a base from which to study the development of more sophisticated religions.

New Religious Movements (NRMs)

Finally, I'll take a brief look at what are called New Religious Movements (NRMs), also known as religious cults. Although there's no precise definition of an NRM, the term is generally assigned to any religious movement founded in the last 200 years.

Wikipedia's entry on NRMs[86] lists over 250 movements. Here are some of the more esoteric and exotic entries:

- Assemblies of Yahweh: Adventists.
- Assembly of Christian Soldiers: founded by the Ku Klux Klan in the 1970s to use tax-exempt donations to fund segregated white-only schools in Alabama, Georgia and Mississippi.
- Aum Shinrikyo: responsible for the sarin gas attack on the Tokyo subway in 1995, killing 12 commuters and seriously injuring another 54.
- Baha'i Faith: linking Buddhism, Christianity and Islam.
- Branch Davidian: David Koresh's version of the Seventh Day Adventists.
- Cargo cults: primitive native religions based on first encounters with cargo transporters such as ships and airplanes. One example is the *John Frum* cult that sprung up in 1940 on the island of Tanna in Vanuatu following the arrival of American troops and their cargo supply ships on the island.
- God Saves The Earth Flying Saucer Foundation: a mix of Buddhism, Taoism and UFOlogy.
- Church of Aphrodite: monotheistic neopagan religion based on Aphrodite as the one true Goddess.
- Church of Satan: dedicated to satanic rituals and carnal pleasures.
- Cyberchurch: a Christian church based on the use of the internet to hold meetings.
- Dances of Universal Peace: based on Sufism but uses mantras from different religions.
- Dianic Wicca: female only witchcraft, focusing on feminist issues in religion.

---

[86] http://en.wikipedia.org/wiki/List_of_new_religious_movements

A Summary Of World Religions: Modern Religions 87

- Esoteric Nazism: race-specific pre-Christian Nazi beliefs.
- Falun Gong: Chinese fusion of Buddhism, Taoism and martial arts.
- Flying Spaghetti Monster Church: based on a dogma of 'there is no dogma' and designed originally to challenge Kansas State Board of Education's 2005 ruling that Intelligent Design (see Chapter 6) could be taught in schools as an alternative to Darwinian evolution.
- Ghost Dance: a religion based on native American Paiute beliefs.
- Jedi Church: based on the 'guardians of peace and justice' in the Star Wars films.
- Jehovah's Witnesses: Christian in origin, believers in Armageddon, and well-known for their door-to-door proselytizing and life-threatening views on blood transfusion.
- Mormonism: derived from the Latter Day Saint movement and notorious for its early-days advocacy of polygamy, allegedly with underage girls involved.
- Nation of Yahweh: a religion specifically for black Hebrew Israelites based on the claim that the original Jews were black Africans and not Arabs.
- Opus Dei: a secretive organisation of the Roman Catholic Church, featured in Dan Brown's 2003 novel, *The Da Vinci Code*.
- Raëlism: another UFO religion with additional emphasis on sensuality and sexual pleasure!
- Salvation Army: an evangelical Christian church, well known for its charitable work.
- Scientology: founded by the science-fiction author, L Ron Hubbard, and notorious as a business masquerading as a religion. More later.
- Shakers: known as the Shaking Quakers with emphasis on social equality and the rejection of sexual relations which has contributed to their decline!
- Transcendental Meditation: an Indian neo-Hindu cult introduced by the Maharishi Mahesh Yogi and made famous by the patronage of the Beatles pop group in the 1960s.

It seems invidious to select just one of these New Religious Movements for closer examination but that's exactly what I'll do: the Church of Scientology.

Church of Scientology

> *'You don't get rich writing science fiction. If you want to get rich, you start a religion.'*
> Attributed to L Ron Hubbard, the founder of Scientology, in response to a question from the audience during a meeting of the Eastern Science Fiction Association on 7 November 1948, as quoted in a 1994 affidavit by Sam Moskowitz[87]

Scientology was created by L Ron Hubbard (1911 – 1986) to further his theories of dianetics. Hubbard was an American pulp fiction[88] science-fiction author who developed *dianetics* as a self-help system. Dianetics considered the mind to be in three parts: the analytical, the subconscious or reactive, and the somatic (physical). Hubbard proposed an auditing process for identifying and removing past painful events from the reactive mind. He claimed that the process would reduce or even eliminate the effect of the subconscious reactive elements and so create a mind that was happier, more ethical and more aware. The auditing process was carried out by questions asked by a trained dianetic practitioner. It was claimed the process would remove memories of pain, shock or trauma. These memories were called *engrams*.

After *engram* removal, Hubbard claimed that intelligence would be increased, emotions eliminated and many illnesses of the mind would be alleviated or even cured. Such illnesses included 'arthritis, allergies, asthma, some coronary difficulties, eye trouble, ulcers, migraine headaches, sex deviations and even death'. Hubbard claimed these illnesses to be psychosomatic – bodily symptoms caused by mental or emotional disturbances.

Hubbard published a summary of dianetics in the pulp fiction magazine *Astounding Science Fiction* in 1950 and followed it up with a book entitled *Dianetics: The Modern Science of Mental Health* in the same year. The book was an instant success despite scepticism from the more orthodox scientific and medical communities and Hubbard went on to found Dianetic Foundations in six American cities.

---

[87] http://en.wikipedia.org/wiki/Scientology_controversies#L._Ron_Hubbard_and_starting_a_religion_for_money

[88] Pulp fiction refers to inexpensive fiction magazines printed on cheap paper with ragged, untrimmed edges and published between the 1890s and 1950s. They were devoted to many literature genres such as westerns, gangsters, romance, war, soft porn (early twentieth-century style) and science fiction/fantasy.

Following complaints that he was teaching and practicing medical techniques without a licence and faced with the closure of his Foundations, Hubbard decided to extend the concept into a non-medical domain. He called this extension *scientology* and said the goal was 'to rehabilitate the individual's spiritual nature so that he may reach his full potential'. In 1978, Hubbard published a series of courses called New Era Dianetics, designed to 'find the problem in the past that's causing the current problem and then remove the past problem, or memory of the past problem, thereby solving the current problem'.[89]

Needless to say, Hubbard's ideas were attacked by scientific and medical practitioners.[90] His approach was labelled pseudoscience (information that is presented as scientific but which fails to meet scientific standards of reputable evidence and fact), and 'a blend of science fiction and the occult, possibly assisted by hypnosis'. Despite these criticisms, Hubbard continued to grow his organisation. By introducing the concept of the *thetan* – 'the true self of a person, an immortal, omniscient and potentially omnipotent entity that had forgotten its full capabilities and was trapped in a *meat body*' – he managed to claim that scientology was a religious movement, thereby qualifying for tax reliefs. Although not a religious concept (that was to come later), the *thetan* enabled Hubbard to move dianetics away from mainstream medical practice and more into a spiritual environment. He claimed that the entrapped *thetans* were the result of events that occurred millions of years ago and that the aim of scientology was to rehabilitate the *thetan* in the human body so as to allow the body to achieve its full potential. He developed an instrument called the E-meter[91] that would reveal the innermost thoughts in the subconscious/reactive mind and allow a release of the memories that were stopping the mind from using the *thetan* to full effect.

The Church of Scientology was organised differently than the Dianetic Foundations. There was one central Scientology organisation,

---

[89] These are my words based on my interpretation of Hubbard's postulate. Hubbard dressed up the ideas behind scientology in a load of pseudoscientific mumbo jumbo designed, one suspects, to confuse the recipient and impress the non-cognoscenti.

[90] And even by fellow science-fiction authors. The great sci-fi author Isaac Asimov is said to have proclaimed Hubbard's book on dianetics as 'gibberish'!

[91] The E-meter is a variation of the well-known Wheatstone Bridge electrical instrument which passes a current through an unknown resistive media, in this case the skin, to measure electrical conductance (the opposite of resistance). The Church of Scientology presented it as 'a religious artefact used to measure the state of electrical characteristics of the static field surrounding the body thereby revealing the individual's innermost thoughts'. Hmm.

headed by Hubbard, responsible for designing training courses and 'training the trainers'. Branches were set up as franchises, similar to popular fast-food chains, with franchise holders paying a percentage income royalty back to the central organisation. As the *thetan* concept matured, so too did the religious flavour of the organisation with franchise holders becoming clerics of the 'church'. Stories began to circulate about the levels of control placed on franchise holders, preventing them from breaking away, and about the amounts of money that were being extracted by the scientologists. It seemed also that everyone was having a go at scientology, masterminded, according to Hubbard, by the US Government: the FBI, the US Internal Revenue Service (withdrawal of tax exemption), the US Food and Drug Administration (false medical claims for 'radiation cure' pills and the E-Meter), the Australian State of Victoria (with accusations of blackmail, extortion, brainwashing and causing mental health problems), British Minister of Health (scientologists were barred from entering the UK because they were undesirable aliens), and further accusations in Canada, New Zealand and South Africa.

Hubbard went on the offensive with three tactics: total disconnection and isolation of scientologists from any other organisation including family members; an encouragement for scientologists to produce sneak reports on fellow scientologists containing knowledge of any transgressions or misapplication of scientology techniques; and a mandate that said that it was fair game to injure and/or deprive anyone of property who was deemed to be an enemy of scientology. The tactics might have been vicious, but they were no worse than has been applied by Christians, Jews and Islamists in the names of their religions.

In the face of all this opposition, Hubbard, now a very rich man, acquired three ocean-going ships and moved his organisation, renamed the Sea Org, onto the high seas. He was accompanied by scantily clad young girls – members of the Commodore's Messenger Organisation – although allegedly just as personal servants, not for sexual purposes save maybe visual titillation. While he was constantly on the move, he spun yet more stories onto the church. In particular, he repackaged some of the higher-level courses as secret, only to be revealed when the trainee scientologist had reached a certain level of competence and had parted with a large sum of money. These levels were dubbed Operating Thetan, OT, levels.

He then released new and higher OT-level courses based on a mythical disaster that had occurred 'on this planet, and on another seventy-five planets which formed a Confederacy, 75 million years ago' (OT-3, the Wall of Fire). Budding scientologists had to complete the first two OT levels before learning how *Xenu*, the leader of the Galactic Confederacy, shipped billions of people to Earth in a Douglas DC-8-like spacecraft, stacked them around volcanoes and blew them up with hydrogen bombs. The victims' traumatised spirits, their *thetans*, were stuck together at 'implant stations', brainwashed with false memories and then contained within new human 'meat bodies'. Thus was explained the origin of how the *thetans* had become entrapped within the human bodies.[92]

Hubbard was to go on and release a further five OT courses up to OT-8, the Truth Revealed, a scientologist's version of *nirvana*.

In the end, Hubbard's behaviour became erratic and irrational, his persecution mania mammoth sized and he was vilified everywhere he tried to settle. He spent his final years in deep hiding living in a luxury motor home on a ranch in California and eventually dying from a stroke in 1986. Nobody has ever revealed how much money either he or the organisation made from scientology but Forbes Magazine estimated that he personally accrued over $200 million in 1982. On his death, the organisation declared that he had 'dropped' his human body and gone off to another planet to continue his work but that he would return one day as a political leader.

Hubbard's name is kept alive by the modern version of scientology. He is referred to as The Source and there are many signs that he is being turned into yet another prophet similar to Jesus and Muhammad. Nowadays (2011), scientology www.scientology.org, presents itself as 'helping man improve his lot through understanding'. The question 'Does scientology admit to a God?' is answered by 'the concept of God is expressed as the Eighth Dynamic—the urge toward existence and survival as infinity. This is also identified as the Supreme Being.' Basically, 'the concept of God rests at the apex of universal survival'.

Stop awhile and consider what these words mean – *the urge towards existence and survival as infinity; apex of universal survival*? Out of context, they mean nothing. After I've paid a lot of money, they may have some mystical meaning in the context of the previous seven Dynamics but I am not motivated to pay the money to find out. The

---

[92] This, of course, is classic science fiction fodder. The Scientology Church tried hard to keep this story secret, only to be revealed to those who (a) were ready for its dangerous knowledge and (b) had lots of money. The story was leaked however, by court documents and Hubbard's notes, and is now widely available on the Web. Google 'Xenu' and see where it takes you, but don't waste too much time!

story of L Ron Hubbard and the development of his so-called church based on a series of ever-expanding concepts reads like a sprawling science fiction novel. Looked at in the cold light of day, stripped of its pseudoscience mumbo jumbo and meaningless sound bite phrases, scientology is just a money-making machine.

What amazes me about organisations like the Scientology Church is how people fall for this kind of stuff? What is it that attracts well-known and seemingly intelligent people to join, such as actors and entertainers Tom Cruise, Chick Corea, John Travolta, Lisa Maria Presley, Juliette Lewis, Isaac Hayes, Sonny Bono, and, in the past but now withdrawn, author William S Burroughs, singer-songwriter Leonard Cohen, murderer Charles Manson, actresses Nicole Kidman, Sharon Stone and Demi Moore, actor Patrick Swayze, and comedian Jerry Seinfeld?[93] The short answer is, I don't know. Maybe they have too much money? Maybe they don't think it through? Maybe they have an innate affiliation with science fiction dressed up as a religion? Or maybe they are gullible or, in some other way, susceptible to smooth-talking salesmen? Whatever the reason, the Church of Scientology is probably the most fabricated (made up for the purpose of deception) religion I have looked at in these two chapters.

(^_^)

---

[93]http://en.wikipedia.org/wiki/List_of_Scientologists, http://www.adherents.com/largecom/fam_scientologist.html

Chapter 6
Evolution Versus Creationism

'The things that you're li'ble / To read in the Bible / It ain't necessarily so.'
Ira Gershwin, American lyricist

'If we are going to teach creation science as an alternative to evolution, then we should also teach the stork theory as an alternative to biological reproduction.'
Judith Hayes, The Happy Heretic
http://www.thehappyheretic.com/

'Successful genes are genes that, in the environment influenced by all the other genes in a shared embryo, have beneficial effects on the embryo. ... Natural selection favours some genes rather than others not because of the nature of the genes themselves, but because of their consequences – their phenotypic effects.'
Richard Dawkins, The Selfish Gene, 1976/2006, p. 235

Origins of life as per Genesis

In the beginning, God created the earth and all its contents. By the end of the sixth day, he'd even created a fully-developed, fully-functioning man and woman. That done, he took a well-earned rest.

Things have moved on since then, of course. Lots of new things have been created, but everything that exists on our planet does so because of the power and creativity of God.

Or at least that is how the story goes. The first book of Genesis tells the story in the following way – actually, in two ways. If you are familiar with the sequence of events, you can skip to the next section.

Genesis 1:1-2:3 (Bible, New International Version)

[1.1] In the beginning God created the heaven and the earth.
[1.2] And the earth was without form, and void; and darkness was upon the face of the deep. And the Spirit of God moved upon the face of the waters.
[1.3] And God said, "Let there be light," and there was light.
[1.4] God saw that the light was good, and he separated the light from the darkness.

1.5 God called the light "day," and the darkness he called "night." And there was evening, and there was morning—the first day.

1.6 And God said, "Let there be a vault between the waters to separate water from water."

1.7 So God made the vault and separated the water under the vault from the water above it. And it was so.

1.8 God called the vault "sky." And there was evening, and there was morning—the second day.

1.9 And God said, "Let the water under the sky be gathered to one place, and let dry ground appear." And it was so.

1.10 God called the dry ground "land," and the gathered waters he called "seas." And God saw that it was good.

1.11 Then God said, "Let the land produce vegetation: seed-bearing plants and trees on the land that bear fruit with seed in it, according to their various kinds." And it was so.

1.12 The land produced vegetation: plants bearing seed according to their kinds and trees bearing fruit with seed in it according to their kinds. And God saw that it was good.

1.13 And there was evening, and there was morning—the third day.

1.14 And God said, "Let there be lights in the vault of the sky to separate the day from the night, and let them serve as signs to mark sacred times, and days and years,

1.15 and let them be lights in the vault of the sky to give light on the earth." And it was so.

1.16 God made two great lights—the greater light to govern the day and the lesser light to govern the night. He also made the stars.

1.17 God set them in the vault of the sky to give light on the earth,

1.18 And to govern the day and the night, and to separate light from darkness. And God saw that it was good.

1.19 And there was evening, and there was morning—the fourth day.

1.20 And God said, "Let the water teem with living creatures, and let birds fly above the earth across the vault of the sky."

1.21 So God created the great creatures of the sea and every living thing with which the water teems and that moves about in it, according to their kinds, and every winged bird according to its kind. And God saw that it was good.

1.22 God blessed them and said, "Be fruitful and increase in number and fill the water in the seas, and let the birds increase on the earth."

1.23 And there was evening, and there was morning—the fifth day.

1.24 And God said, "Let the land produce living creatures according to their kinds: the livestock, the creatures that move along the ground, and the wild animals, each according to its kind." And it was so.

1.25 God made the wild animals according to their kinds, the livestock according to their kinds, and all the creatures that move along the ground according to their kinds. And God saw that it was good.
1.26 Then God said, "Let us make mankind in our image, in our likeness, so that they may rule over the fish in the sea and the birds in the sky, over the livestock and all the wild animals, and over all the creatures that move along the ground."
1.27 So God created mankind in his own image, in the image of God he created them; male and female he created them.
1.28 God blessed them and said to them, "Be fruitful and increase in number; fill the earth and subdue it. Rule over the fish in the sea and the birds in the sky and over every living creature that moves on the ground."
1.29 Then God said, "I give you every seed-bearing plant on the face of the whole earth and every tree that has fruit with seed in it. They will be yours for food.
1.30 And to all the beasts of the earth and all the birds in the sky and all the creatures that move along the ground—everything that has the breath of life in it—I give every green plant for food." And it was so.
1.31 God saw all that he had made, and it was very good. And there was evening, and there was morning—the sixth day.
2.1 Thus the heavens and the earth were completed in all their vast array.
2.2 By the seventh day God had finished the work he had been doing; so on the seventh day he rested from all his work.
2.3 Then God blessed the seventh day and made it holy, because on it he rested from all the work of creating that he had done.

Genesis 2:4-2:25 (Bible, New International Version)

2.4 This is the account of the heavens and the earth when they were created, when the LORD God made the earth and the heavens.
2.5 Now no shrub had yet appeared on the earth and no plant had yet sprung up, for the LORD God had not sent rain on the earth and there was no one to work the ground,
2.6 But streams came up from the earth and watered the whole surface of the ground.
2.7 Then the LORD God formed a man from the dust of the ground and breathed into his nostrils the breath of life, and the man became a living being.
2.8 Now the LORD God had planted a garden in the east, in Eden; and there he put the man he had formed.

2.9 The LORD God made all kinds of trees grow out of the ground — trees that were pleasing to the eye and good for food. In the middle of the garden were the tree of life and the tree of the knowledge of good and evil.

2.10 A river watering the garden flowed from Eden; from there it was separated into four headwaters.

2.11 The name of the first is the Pishon; it winds through the entire land of Havilah, where there is gold.

2.12 (The gold of that land is good; aromatic resin and onyx are also there.)

2.13 The name of the second river is the Gihon; it winds through the entire land of Cush.

2.14 The name of the third river is the Tigris; it runs along the east side of Ashur. And the fourth river is the Euphrates.

2.15 The LORD God took the man and put him in the Garden of Eden to work it and take care of it.

2.16 And the LORD God commanded the man, "You are free to eat from any tree in the garden;

2.17 but you must not eat from the tree of the knowledge of good and evil, for when you eat from it you will certainly die."

2.18 The LORD God said, "It is not good for the man to be alone. I will make a helper suitable for him."

2.19 Now the LORD God had formed out of the ground all the wild animals and all the birds in the sky. He brought them to the man to see what he would name them; and whatever the man called each living creature, that was its name.

2.20 So the man gave names to all the livestock, the birds in the sky and all the wild animals. But for Adam no suitable helper was found.

2.21 So the LORD God caused the man to fall into a deep sleep; and while he was sleeping, he took one of the man's ribs and then closed up the place with flesh.

2.22 Then the LORD God made a woman from the rib he had taken out of the man, and he brought her to the man.

2.23 The man said, "This is now bone of my bones and flesh of my flesh; she shall be called 'woman,' for she was taken out of man."

2.24 That is why a man leaves his father and mother and is united to his wife, and they become one flesh.

2.25 Adam and his wife were both naked, and they felt no shame.

So, what is the difference between the two stories? In the first version, God created the planet, then the livestock, then Adam and, finally, Eve. In the second version, the order in which the livestock and Adam were created is reversed. Eve still came last. Why the reversal and why two versions? Scholars have argued about it for years but, for me, it's crystal clear – the story was handed down word-of-mouth over many generations and somewhere along the way, just like all word-of-mouth stories, it got changed. And then, because there was doubt as whose story was correct, two written versions evolved – more if you take the one in the Qur'an into account. In fact, as you'll see, an evolutionary split to form a second species applies just as much to folklore stories as it does to life forms. I call it the Evolution of Stories. Darwin's theory of evolution is alive and well and, far from being contradicted by the Book of Genesis, is supported by it!

Prior to 1859, just about everyone who professed to worship this particular God – Judaists, Christians, Muslims – believed this story, although there were some who said it wasn't true. It was more an allegory, they claimed – a symbolic telling of God's role in the creation of the earth and its contents. But, these interpretations did not find wide acceptance, particularly among the faithful, so life went on secure in the belief that God was indeed the Supreme Creator and that he could complete huge feats of engineering in astonishingly short amounts of time.

And then along came Charles Darwin – well, Charles Darwin and Alfred Russel Wallace to be exact. I assume that most readers have some familiarity with the story of Charles Darwin (we will come to Wallace later) but, for those who don't, here it is in a nutshell.

Charles Darwin

> *'Darwin's Theory states that complex biological systems arise from the gradual accumulation over generations of random genetic mutations that enhance reproductive success.'*
> Steven Pinker, *The Language Instinct*, p. 333.

Charles Darwin was born in Shrewsbury, Shropshire, in 1809. One of his grandfathers was Josiah Wedgewood – the man who made his name, and wealth, manufacturing chinaware. Darwin's other grandfather was Erasmus Darwin, an eighteenth century intellectual.[94]

---

[94] Erasmus Darwin was a physician (he once turned down an invitation to become King George III's personal physician), philosopher, physiologist, abolitionist (of slavery), inventor (including a lift for canal barges, and a horse-drawn carriage that would not tip over), poet, and friend of Benjamin Franklin. No slouch then!

So, Charles was born into a wealthy family and blessed with high-quality ancestry – good genes, as we might say!

The young Charles attended Edinburgh University, bent on pursuing a career in medicine. Under the influence of his father, he was persuaded to switch to Christ's College, Cambridge, to study divinity so that he could join the Anglican clergy. While at Cambridge, his interest in medicine morphed into an interest in natural sciences, the first evidence being a craze for collecting and categorising beetles.

In 1831, Darwin joined *HMS Beagle's* round-the-world scientific expedition, visiting many foreign lands including the Galapagos Islands in the Pacific Ocean. En route, he made copious notes on all the variations of animals and geology he encountered. In particular, he recorded the variations in the size and shape of the beaks of the finches that lived on different Galapagos Islands. He worked out that variations supported the species' survival in the varied environments of the different islands. Some finches had developed long beaks to puncture the fruit of a cactus plant; others had developed short beaks more suitable for ground feeding.

Of interest to me when I visited the Galapagos Islands in the late 1990s was the evolution of iguanas. Iguanas are a land animal endemic to the South Americas and to the Caribbean but not to the Galapagos islands. The first iguanas in the Galapagos Islands came from South America, crossing the 600 miles (960 km) of ocean on some sort of floating object, probably a large tree trunk – a process called *rafting*. There are now several species of land iguanas in the Galapagos Islands but there's also a marine iguana – the only marine version of the species known and clearly evolved from the land iguana. The marine iguana feeds on algae and seaweed in the sea and can dive down to 30 feet (~ 10 meters) and stay down for up to 30 minutes before it needs to surface to breathe and regain body temperature.

The marine iguana has developed a laterally flattened tail and a spiky dorsal fin to assist swimming. It has a flattened snout to assist underwater foraging on the sea bed. When marine iguanas emerge from the sea, they bask on rocks to warm up. Salt absorbed into the blood stream while eating underwater is filtered out of the blood and expelled through nasal glands. I recall being amused by a colony of basking marine iguanas lying next to and on top of one another. Every now and again, an iguana would raise its head and expel some salt, usually over a neighbour. As a result, many had white patches of dried salt on their faces and bodies. Darwin is on record as saying that he did not like the animals because of this habit. In fact, he referred to them as 'disgusting clumsy lizards' and called them 'imps of darkness'.

Galapagos iguanas, both land and marine, are now under threat from predatory feral cats and dogs. These predators were not indigenous to the Galapagos Islands – they were introduced by early settlers - and, unfortunately, young iguanas are unable to protect themselves when attacked. They need sharper teeth and longer claws. Sometimes, it seems, the pace of evolution could do with an artificial boost!

When Darwin returned from his five-year round-the-world voyage, he continued his study of animal variations. He was puzzled by their development. What had caused the variations, for example? Did other animals exhibit similar characteristics in order to survive in a hostile environment? Thinking these questions through, he began composing a hypothesis. Random mutations must have occurred over time. Those that assisted survival had been retained in the species. Those that did not contributed to the eventual demise of the species. Later, the process became known as the 'survival of the fittest'.

In 1859, Darwin published his now famous and, at the time, highly-controversial book, *On the Origin of Species by Means of Natural Selection*. It caused uproar. It just wasn't acceptable to challenge the stories of creation as told in the first book of Genesis.

We will come back to Darwin's main conclusions in a little while. First, though, let's talk a little about his contemporary and, potentially, arch rival – a Welsh naturalist called Alfred Russel Wallace.

While Darwin was girding his loins, so to speak, and gearing up to write and publish his book, other researchers in natural science were coming to the same conclusions. Wallace was among them.

Born in 1823 in Llanbadoc, Wales, Wallace was a land surveyor who strayed into natural sciences. His travels took him to the Amazon forest in South America and then on to Indonesia via the Malayan Archipelago. His observations of both plants and animals had led him to a similar conclusion as Darwin. In 1858, one year before *On the Origin of Species* was published, Wallace wrote to Darwin outlining his thoughts on the nature of evolution and including the concept of survival of the fittest. Later that year, Darwin and Wallace collaborated, submitting a scientific paper on their joint conclusions. Darwin was named as the first author.[95]

Darwin and Wallace's paper *On the Tendency of Species to form Varieties; and on the Perpetuation of Varieties and Species by Natural Means of Selection* was presented to the London-based Linnean Society, a society for the study and dissemination of taxonomy and natural history, on 30th June, 1858, by Charles Lyell and Joseph Hooker. In their introduction to the paper, Lyell and Hooker said:

> 'These gentlemen having, independently and unknown to one another, conceived the same very ingenious theory to account for the appearance and perpetuation of varieties and of specific forms on our planet, may both fairly claim the merit of being original thinkers in this important line of inquiry; but neither of them having published his views, though Mr. Darwin has for many years past been repeatedly urged by us to do so, and both authors having now unreservedly placed their papers in our hands, we think it would best promote the interests of science that a selection from them should be laid before the Linnean Society.'

The paper was well received by the scientific community but had very little impact on religious leaders and philosophers.

Darwin, by now probably more than rattled that Wallace was about to steal his thunder, hastened the completion of his book. One year later it was published.

Wallace went on to publish his own books and scientific papers, but it was Darwin who took all the glory and who is now considered to be the father of modern evolutionary theory. He died in 1882 and is buried in Westminster Abbey, very close to Isaac Newton, the illustrious member of my school's alumni.

What did Darwin and Wallace say?

As if the full title - *On the Origin of Species By Means of Natural Selection* – wasn't enough, Darwin's book is subtitled *The Preservation of Favoured Races in the Struggle for Life*. It runs to 155,000 words/620 pages. That's a lot of words on a lot of pages – a work that's virtually impossible to summarise in a few terse words, but I'll try.

---

[95] Conventionally, in scientific papers, the first author is considered to be the person who did most of the work. Co-authors are named if they contributed to the work in some way that merits recognition. As you might imagine, the order of the authors can cause all sorts of disagreement.

Basically, Darwin's observations of variations of various plants and animals led him to two major conclusions. Here they are with a few explanatory additions.

1. Theory of Evolution.
All life forms change (evolve) over time because of mutations in the fundamental cells that make up the life form.

(These mutations are not caused by the environment. They are caused by random variations in the life form's cells when reproduction occurs. I'll elaborate when I talk about chromosomes, genes, DNA and human reproduction.)

2. Theory of Survival of the Fittest.
Some of these cell mutations work to ensure that only the fittest life forms will reproduce and multiply, and that these 'survival of the fittest' traits are passed down from one generation to the next to strengthen the successors.

(We can question 'Only the fittest what?' Ethnic group? Tribe? Family unit? Individual? Richard Dawkins argues that the correct answer is either the fittest gene or its host, what he calls the *survival machine* or *gene vehicle*. As humans, each of us is a gene survival machine. Thus we are the candidates for evolutionary fitness.)

In simple words, the net result of the Theories of Evolution and Survival of the Fittest is that today's *homo sapiens* is the product of random mutations and natural selection from earlier life forms.

Darwin's first conclusion implied that all life forms had evolved from earlier life forms and that, as a result, the ancestry of any given life form could be traced back to ancestors that, almost certainly, looked nothing like the plant or creature does today. *Homo sapiens*, for example, may have descended from some earlier life form that spawned both humans and similar-looking species such as monkeys, apes and chimpanzees. The earlier common ancestor will, in turn, have descended from an even earlier ancestor, and so on until we reach right back to the very first ancestor – the origin of life. From this very first ancestor, all life forms as we know them have developed. He, she or more likely it is the root of the so-called Tree of Life.

As a simple explanation, assume that a primitive life form species A started the process and, at some point and after some development based on random mutations, split to form two evolved species A_1 – a better version of A, and a new species, A_2. ('New' here means that A_2

cannot mate successfully with A_1 to produce offspring.) Later on, A_1 splits to form A_{11} and A_{12}, A_2 splits to form A_{21} and A_{22} and so on. While all this was, and still is, happening (witness the evolution of the marine iguana from the land iguana), each individual species is itself improving by means of the survival of those whose behaviour or characteristics are best-suited to their environment. The initial and final forms of species A, and its derivatives, differ in that the final form is stronger and healthier. As in the story of the doubling of grains of rice, or wheat, on each successive square of a chess board, so life forms evolved and split, creating the huge diversity of species that now exists on this planet.[96]

In the case of *homo sapiens*, if you trace the process back, it seems we shared a common ancestor with chimpanzees about five to six million years ago. Human development followed an evolutionary path that took us to our most recent ancestor, *homo sapiens neanderthalensis* (30,000 to 200,000 years ago)[97] and, finally to what we might call *homo sapiens modern* - us. It's a dazzling theory and one that is now supported by a wealth of factual evidence ranging from fossil records, radio-active carbon-dating procedures and, more recently, an understanding of the genetic blueprint impressed in each and every one of all members of the animal and plant kingdom – genes defined by coded sequences of DNA.

Of course, we know a huge amount now compared to what scientists had discovered in 1859 and we are tantalisingly close to identifying, and even demonstrating, the origin of life (of which more later), but the contents of Darwin's book were considered heresy by the religious leaders when they were published. The theory of evolution challenged the accounts of creation described in Genesis. Evolution assumed no creationist God, no Garden of Eden and most importantly, no Adam and Eve created from 'the dust of the ground'. Evolution said that the earliest forms of life probably originated from minute organisms that self-created in ponds. God, it seemed, had little to do with it.

---

[96] Nobody really knows how many different species exist on our planet and, like your bank balance, the number is constantly changing. Some species evolve (marine iguanas from land iguanas); some die out naturally (mammoths, sabre-toothed tigers); some are artificially rendered extinct (dodos, 'Lonesome George'); and some remain fairly constant (Komodo dragons, thought to have not changed for at least four million years; and alligators, thought to be extant for over two hundred million years).

[97] Contrary to popular belief, primitive man didn't wander the earth at the same time as dinosaurs. Fred Flintstone and Raquel Welch have a lot to answer for!

Evolution Versus Creationism

And so battle commenced, and is still raging as the war between Evolutionary Science and Creationism. But, before we get to Creationism and its spin-off, Intelligent Design, let's explore where we are now in our understanding of the origins of life.

Cells, chromosomes, genes, DNA and genomes

We have long known about genes and the role they play in passing characteristics of parents down to their offspring. How often have you looked at a new-born baby and said, or heard others say, 'she has your colour eyes/shape mouth/shape nose/colour hair ...'? More visibly, dark-skinned parents usually create dark-skinned babies. Light-skinned parents usually create light-skinned babies. Two parents with blue eyes are likely to create a baby that also has blue eyes. All types of domestic dogs, currently numbering around two hundred, have evolved from wolves using techniques of forced evolution, called breeding, perfected by humans. The many varieties of roses have evolved from the genus *rosa*, which dates back to prehistoric times and has since been subjected to intense hybridization, probably started in China some five thousand years ago. Kangaroo, wallaby and koala marsupials live only in Australia.[98] Lemurs live only in Madagascar and have evolved into nearly one hundred separately-identified sub-species. And so it continues.

The evidence for evolution is all around us and in the 1950s, Crick and Watson broke down the structure and very nature of DNA, the chemical substance that contains the genes, to show how everything we inherit has come not just from our parents but also from their parents and so on all the way back to the origin of life. DNA analysis can pinpoint our ancestors, and the perpetrators of crimes, with amazing accuracy. A tenth-generation American Negro can identify not only his or her country of origin in, say, Africa, but possibly the region and even the village from which his or her ancestors were snatched by slave traders in the seventeenth century.

DNA, the chemical substance that encapsulates our genes, is now at the centre of modern theories of evolution and, because of its importance, deserves more attention in this book. If you are put off by technical discussion of cells, chromosomes, genes, DNA and genomes, just read the following bullet-pointed summary. Those who are not afraid to tackle something a little more complex can read the human biology primer appended to this chapter.

---

[98] Although other marsupials, notably the opossums, live in North America.

Summary of human reproduction biology

- There are approximately 10^{15} (one thousand million million) cells in the human body. Each cell is comprised of a jelly-like substance called *cytoplasm* which contains *organelles* – 'little organs' in the cells performing different jobs such as the production of energy or removal of waste products - and a control centre called the *nucleus*.
- Every nucleus contains 46 *chromosomes* which, in turn, house the *genes* that determine the development of our bodies. Two of the chromosomes, named X and Y, contain genes that dictate our female (X) or male (Y) sexual characteristics. The remaining 44 non-sex-determining chromosomes are called *autosomal chromosomes*, shortened to *autosomes*, and house all our remaining genes. Half the 46 chromosomes come from the sperm donor (father) and the other half from the egg donor (mother). In this way, we inherit the genes of our parents.
- The *chromosomes* are constructed from an acid called *deoxyribonucleic acid*, DNA.
- DNA has a complex structure resembling the side struts and cross rungs of a twisted ladder – the *double helix* structure. Segments of chromosomes are uniquely coded by the sequence and type of chemical 'rungs' that bond the 'struts' of the twisted ladder. These coded segments are called *genes* and, if expressed, represent a particular feature in the human body (called the gene's phenotype). There are 400 to 4,000 genes in any particular chromosome.
- The various types of genes control our growth and collectively represent a set of instructions for how our body develops and functions. Some genes determine the colour of our eyes, some the colour of our hair, some the way muscles develop to control motion such as walking, running, and lifting, and so on. Basically, the genes are the recipes for making different types of proteins for the body's use in all its various locations.
- DNA sequences, and hence the genes and chromosomes based on the sequences, have two important properties: they self-replicate producing exact copies of themselves, and they control the manufacture and use of a range of protein molecules for use by various parts of the body. Protein molecules are what make us.

Evolution Versus Creationism

- The complete set of all different human genes, currently estimated to be somewhere between 20,000 and 25,000,[99] and their associated DNA codes is called the human *genome*. The *genome* is a complete instruction manual for how proteins are to be used to develop and maintain our bodies from initial conception into full adulthood and subsequent maintenance.
- During human reproduction, a special chromosome separation and cell division process takes place. Sperm cells produced by the male testes contain only 23 chromosomes, not 46 (the full set of chromosomes present in all other cells). Similarly with the egg cell(s) matured in and released by the female ovaries. During the creation of the sperm and egg cells, a gene shuffling process takes place that ensures that the chromosomes passed on to the offspring contain a random mix of the parental genes. This process, called *crossing over*, supports the transfer of parental genes but ensures that we are each unique.
- If a sperm cell succeeds in penetrating a mature egg cell, a process called *fertilization*, the resulting fusion produces a single cell called a *zygote* that now contains the full complement of 46 chromosomes – 23 from the father's sperm and 23 from the mother's egg. Cells in the *zygote* then start dividing and so a new life begins.
- Genes can be altered (become mutated) either during chromosome replication (random mutation) or by eternal agents such as ultraviolet light, carcinogenic chemicals, viruses, or radiation. Many mutations have a negative impact on the organism (life form) and weaken it, even to the point of natural extinction. But, some mutations serve to strengthen the host survival machine to the point where further reproduction takes place and the mutated gene is passed to the next generation, and the next , ... Such mutations ensure both evolution and survival of the fittest.

Impact on evolution

An egg is the chicken's way of making another chicken!
                                                Schoolboy aphorism.

Genes work individually or as members of a group[100] to benefit their host – Darwin's survival of the fittest theory – but we should question

---

[99] Some reputable websites claim that the number of separately-identified genes in our chromosomes is more like 35,000. I've yet to get at the truth.
[100] Dawkins argues very strongly for the latter – member of a group. Although we talk about an 'eye-colour' gene, or a 'hair-colour' gene, it's very unlikely that a single gene

what is meant by *host* and *fittest*. Dawkins uses the term *survival machine* to identify the host. In the case of human evolution, our bodies are the survival machines. Each and every one of us is a vehicle for the collection of genes within our body cells. Darwin's 'survival of the fittest' theory is all about the genes creating machines that increase the genes' chance of long-term survival – that is, across multiple generations. In other words, genes have to create life forms that survive long enough to reproduce, thereby transmitting the genes into a new survival machine. The theory is not about increasing a life form's longevity - survival machines only have to remain alive long enough to become sexually mature and reproduce. Once a successor has been created, the genes don't care anymore.

(This is a highly simplistic view of genes' actions – one that endows them with human characteristics such as selfishness, altruism, generosity, and greed. Genes are not like this, of course, but it sometimes helps to assume they are – dangerous ground, perhaps, but one adopted by Dawkins in his ground-breaking book *The Selfish Gene*. For those interested in how genes work to support their existence through cooperation and beneficial evolution, I recommend this book to you. By the time I got round to reading it, sales had passed the one million mark[101] – a rare thing in a technical book and a testament to Dawkins's ability to write clearly and authoritatively about an intensely scientific and even philosophical subject.)

Evolution scientists are interested in the effects of gene mutations and how species evolve.[102] If genes did not mutate, a species would remain static. Mutations do occur however, and are mostly random. They do not occur because DNA has self-consciously changed its form - DNA has no intelligence as such.

Not all mutations affect the animal or plant carrier, but some do. Some help the carrier adapt more easily to its environment by strengthening its ability to find and absorb food, escape from predators, and so on. I have already talked about one mutation that assisted survival – the one that spawned the marine iguana.

---

controls such a characteristic. He asserts that groups of genes, what he calls a gene complex, work together to produce their phenotype (the physical manifestation of a gene, such as eye colour). He also suggests that an individual gene could easily be a member of more than one gene complex. It's a fascinating topic.

[101] According to the front cover of the 30th Anniversary edition of the book.

[102] It's currently estimated that we humans share 99% of our DNA base-pairs (the 'rungs' of the twisted ladder structure) with our immediate ancestor, *homo neanderthalensis* and 98.6% of our DNA base-pairs with our closest living evolutionary relative, the chimpanzee.

Other mutations can have a negative effect on a life form's ability to survive and may, in extreme cases, cause all copies of the life form to die – that is, become extinct. Examples of such happenings are found in fossil records. They include trilobites, ammonites,[103] dinosaurs, many forms of plant life, and earlier versions of *homo sapiens*.

Although Darwin did not know about the role or even the existence of DNA and genes, he postulated that random mutations could occur in a species and that when they did they either strengthened or weakened the life form's ability to survive. Those life forms that were strengthened would then pass the survival factor down to their off-spring and thus strengthen their off-spring's ability to survive. Those mutations that weakened the ability to survive were likewise passed down, but the population of each new generation was smaller than its predecessor, so the species could eventually die out. On this basis, 'survival of the fittest' became Darwin's mantra. And as we now know, Darwin's theory inevitably leads to a fundamental series of questions about the origin of life and the existence and role of a Grand Creator.

One final thought ...

There are some evolutionists who claim that human evolution is slowing down. We are able to control our environment to the extent that we no longer need natural selection to help us adapt to environmental changes. If we're cold, we don more clothes. If we're warm, we shed them. If we don't want babies, we use birth control techniques. If we're hungry, we develop genetically-modified foods that produce a higher yield. If we need to travel vast distances, we develop high-speed modes of transportation, or we develop electronic communication systems that we can use from our armchairs with very little physical effort. We nurture and protect our old and weak through health-care programs, hospitals and the benefits society.

Basically, mutations that would once have helped our species survive no longer have any impact. They are simply added to the gene pool, in some cases perpetuating characteristics that have very little value – characteristics that would once have died out.

---

[103] In 2009, while trekking in the Upper Mustang Valley of Nepal, I picked up an ammonite fossil from the bed of the Kaligandaki River. It's a sobering experience to hold the remains of a once-living organism that existed somewhere between 65 and 240 million years ago.

In the meantime, 'superbugs', such as MRSA,[104] continue to prove that survival of the fittest still works, even in species that we would prefer to become extinct.

Evolution based on the transfer of heredity units called genes is a fascinating topic and one that nearly hijacked this chapter and even the whole book. So, let me close this section and move back to the main theme of the chapter – evolution versus creationism. There are excellent books on the various processes of evolution – Dawkins *The Selfish Gene* (1976/2006, OUP) is a good place to start – and I will come back to the question of 'How did it all begin?' in the next section.

Reaction to Darwin's theories and the rise of Creationism

First, we have to consider the most basic question about Darwin's theories: who or what created the first living cells some three to four billion years ago? That is, the *origin of life* question.

Fundamentally, there are only two answers:

- Spontaneous creation: a random chemical combination of oxygen, nitrogen, carbon and hydrogen that created the first self-replicating DNA cells, or a simpler pre-cursor.
- Supernatural creation: God, or some other supernatural being, created the first living cells and then left the rest to evolution by the process of random mutation and natural selection plus supernatural interventions where necessary.

Atheists believe in the former; Creationists in the latter. It really is as simple as that. However, as we will see, there are schisms in the Creationist camp.

Charles Darwin addressed the question in a letter to a colleague, Joseph Hooker,[105] in 1871:

> '*It is often said that all the conditions for the first production of a living organism are now present, which could ever have been present. But if (and oh! what a big if!) we could conceive in some warm little pond, with all sorts of ammonia and phosphoric salts, light, heat,*

---

[104] *Methicillin-Resistant Staphylococcus Aureus*, MRSA, is a bacterium that has evolved a resistance to conventional antibiotics. MRSA can cause septicemia (a blood infection), pneumonia and endocarditis (inflammation of the inside lining of the heart). There are thought to be as many as 17 strains of the evolved bacterium with strains 15 and 16 being the most resistant to antibiotics.
[105] The same Joseph Hooker who co-presented the Darwin-Wallace paper in 1858.

electricity, &c., present, that a proteine (sic) compound was chemically formed ready to undergo still more complex changes, at the present day such matter would be instantly absorbed, which would not have been the case before living creatures were found.'

In his 2009 book, *The Greatest Show on Earth*, Dawkins says that we are tantalisingly close to understanding and replicating the origins of life but that it will be research chemists who'll make the breakthrough, not evolutionary biologists. His argument is based on mathematical probability – what is the probability that, among a very large number of universes, there was just one planet where conditions were exactly right for basic chemical elements to combine spontaneously and randomly to form a primitive version of DNA that had the ability to replicate and so create something more complex – a life form? The chemicals required would be hydrogen (contained in water, H_2O, and the natural gas methane, CH_4), nitrogen (contained in ammonia, NH_3, and in the atmosphere), carbon (contained in methane, CH_4, and carbon dioxide, CO_2), and oxygen (also contained in water, H_2O, and in the atmosphere). All these chemical elements are abundant on our planet.

Dawkins argues that this event would only have to happen once and then evolution would take over. Statistically, it was a one-off event – something that could have happened anywhere, but actually happened here on Earth. It's an interesting and compelling argument but it cuts very little ice with theists. In contrast to their blind belief in something that cannot be proved – that is, in the existence of God – they demand cast-iron proof of something that is still beyond the reach of scientists.

Even more recently, in his 2010 book *The Grand Design*, the fundamental physicist, Stephen Hawking, advanced the theory that the creation of the universe followed inevitably from the laws of nature as expressed by M-Theory, a combination of classical and quantum mechanics. M-Theory is way beyond me, but I am told that it may account for the birth of our universe, and possibly of an infinite number of other universes (called the multiverse), during the Big Bang. Experiments are under way at the Large Hadron Collider at CERN near Geneva to duplicate the conditions just after the Big Bang (much to the dismay of doomsayers who fear the consequences). One interesting observation arises. Hawking and his colleagues are out to prove that the creation of the universe, or multiverse, can be explained by the laws of nature and expressed in concise and precise mathematical terms. Even if he is correct, this doesn't disprove the existence of God. It just proves that God had no part in the creation of the universe.

That should put the cat among the philosophical and theological pigeons!

Whatever or whoever is right, evolutionists will continue to believe that, eventually, biological science combined with chemistry will reveal the answer to 'life, the universe and everything', as Douglas Adams put it, and that it will not involve any supernatural creator. They argue that we have made tremendous strides in our understanding of hereditary evolution through gene transfer and that there's no reason to think that evolutionary scientists, biologists and others involved in studying the mystery of the human body and its origins will hit a brick wall containing a small door marked 'God, this way'.

Faced with all this, Creationists have been fighting back, especially in the USA since the 1920s. There have always been Creationists,[106] not only among Christians but also in other religions.

The publication of Darwin's book and its implications for the origins of humanity caused a serious re-assessment of how Creationism should be promulgated, especially among the malleable minds of young children still in education.

From the 1920s to the 1960s, several US states passed laws that required Creationism to be taught and the teaching of Darwinian evolution banned, creating a clear conflict between science and religion. The process was driven by American Christian fundamentalist groups and, in particular, by a Presbyterian Democratic politician William Jennings Bryan.

Allegedly a charismatic man, Bryan was well travelled, with a deep commanding voice and an orator of great skill and persuasion.[107]

Bryan's fight against evolution was based on two premises:

- Darwinian evolution undermined the whole basis for a belief in God, religion in general, and the moral laws governing modern civilization and its future development.
- Evolution and its drive for survival of the fittest was what had caused the First World War and, in particular, the war crimes

---

[106] Martin Luther, a key player in the European Protestant Reformation in the sixteenth century, was a strong advocate for the belief that the creation of the earth and all its life-form contents, including man, took just six days and was conducted by God; in other words, a literal truth based on the stories in Genesis.

[107] http://en.wikipedia.org/wiki/William_Jennings_Bryan

supposedly perpetuated by Germany's Armed Forces on the citizens of Belgium.[108]

Perceiving religion as the basis for laws of right and wrong, Bryan asserted that Darwinism had destroyed the moral base of the German people and thus motivated their belief that only the fittest should survive. As a result, he started to wage war against evolution. He considered it to be 'the most paralyzing influence which civilization has had to deal with in the last century' and that the theory of evolution when carried to its logical conclusion 'promulgated a philosophy that condemned democracy, ... denounced Christianity, ... denied the existence of God, overturned all concepts of morality, ... and endeavored to substitute the worship of the superhuman for the worship of Jehovah.' (1920 speech at the World Brotherhood Congress.)

The upshot of all this preaching against evolution was that Darwin's theories were banned from numerous classrooms and replaced with deeply-religious explanations of the origins of the universe, the earth, and humanity. The consequences of these misplaced views are still prevalent in the United States – witness the 2010 statistic that shows that between 40% and 50% of Americans still believe that everything on earth was created somewhere between 6,000 to 10,000 years ago by a Supreme Creator called God.[109]

Later, these laws were rescinded and Creationism, if taught at all, was taught as a religious subject and not a scientific subject.[110] But the Creationists responded in the late 1980s by inventing Intelligent Design as a scientific replacement for evolution. Intelligent Design holds that certain parts of the human body – eyes are often cited as an example - could not have evolved under Darwinian influences. Intelligent Designers (IDers) say that it is not possible for any complex organ to evolve to its final level of complexity without supernatural

---

[108] There is still controversy as to what was fact and what was manufactured propaganda designed to encourage male Britons to join the British Army and also enlist American moral support. Google *German War Crimes* and *The Rape of Belgium* to read more.
[109] http://en.wikipedia.org/wiki/Creationism#Views_in_the_United_States
[110] This occurred after a famous court case known as the Scopes Trial, in 1925. Bryan was taken to task by the lawyer Clarence Darrow who demolished Bryan's literal interpretation of the Bible and demonstrated the weakness of the creationist arguments. Bryan died five days after the trial, some say because of the cross-examination. The case has been fictionalised in the play *Inherit the Wind* by Jerome Lawrence and Robert Edwin Lee and turned into a film on three separate occasions.

help. How did it happen unaided? It could not have happened in a series of small steps. These organs must have appeared as a full-featured working part in one fell swoop created by an intelligent designer, God.

Let's stay with the eye for a minute. Based on irreducible complexity, the IDers' argument goes like this.

What use would a transparent protective cornea be without a pupil to pass the received light rays through to the focusing lens? What good is a lens without the vitreous humour to transfer the light rays to the rods and cones of the retina? Or what is the value of a light-sensitive retina without the optic nerve to transmit the coded light signals to the brain? And so on.

There are more than a billion cells in the human eye, all working in incredible harmony and synchronisation. How could such an organ evolve in a seemingly infinite number of small evolutionary steps over a long period of time assuming that on their own, the various components had no value?

The IDers' argument is based on 'the whole is greater than the sum of the parts so what value does each part have in isolation to the whole? You cannot reduce the complexity and still have something of value.' This is the crux of the irreducible complexity argument.

To quote from Steven Pinker's book, *The Language Instinct*, p. 349: 'It (the eye) can begin in an eyeless organism with a patch of skin whose cells are sensitive to light. The patch can deepen into a pit, cinch up into a sphere with a hole in front, grow a translucent cover over the hole, and so on, each step allowing the owner to detect events better.' And on p. 361, 'The ability of *many* ancestors to see a *bit* better in the *past* causes a *single* organism to see *extremely well* now.' (Pinker's italics.)

In his 1986 book, *The Blind Watchmaker*, Dawkins looks at irreducible complexity another way – he says that even though there's no immediate explanation, that doesn't mean that one will not be forthcoming in the future based on the uncovering of new evidence and scientific facts that yield a scientific explanation. Simply because such an explanation is missing is no justification for considering that some divine entity created the complex object. He cites the example of someone from ancient times finding a modern watch in a field and marvelling at its creation.

I will return to my own assessment of the irreducible complexity argument later on.

IDers say that the eye must have been created instantaneously by an Intelligent Designer called God. They point to a lack of evidence in the fossil records that shows that at some point in some earlier life form, half an eye had developed, whatever 'half an eye' means. These gaps in the fossil records are called just that – gaps – and, boy oh boy, do IDers love gaps! If a bridging fossil is discovered that, say, demonstrates that a nascent eye did in fact exist with a plausible scientific explanation for the function of those parts of the eye that are present in the fossil, the IDers simply state that this breaks a big gap down into two smaller gaps but the gaps are still there. In fact the number of gaps will have increased!

Of course, the fallacy in the IDers' theory is that if all gaps are subsequently reduced to such small differences that they are to all intents and purposes a continuous spectrum of minute changes, the need for a supernatural gap-filler goes away.

Intelligent Design was originally offered as an evolutionary science and as a replacement for Darwinian evolution as taught in US school science classes. But, in a 2005 landmark court case in Dover, Pennsylvania, Intelligent Design was judged to be a religious belief – Creationism in disguise – and, as such, the enforcement of its teaching contravened the US constitutional separation of church and state – the Establishment Clause of the First Amendment of the Constitution of the United States. But, Intelligent Design is still being promulgated as a *bona fide* scientific subject on a par with evolutionary biology, allegedly even in a UK faith school.[111] A scary thought!

As I mentioned earlier, Creationism has split into various schools of thought. Here's a somewhat coarse taxonomy of Creationism as it exists today.

---

[111] Dawkins, *The God Delusion*, p. 372 et seq., asserted that Intelligent Design was being taught at Emmanuel College in Gateshead in the early 2000s. The ensuing row peaked in 2005. I've studied Emmanuel College's website, http://www.emmanuelctc.org.uk/emmanuelcollege/emmanuelcollege/ and can find no mention of ID or Creationism as a substitute for Darwinian Evolution. Emmanuel College teaches religion according to the Assessment and Qualifications Alliance, the largest A-level and GCSE awarding body In the UK. I've scoured their website also, looking for favouritism towards creationist concepts over evolutionary concepts and can find nothing. So, it's probable that the accusation against Emmanuel College, even if it were true in 2005 is no longer valid.

Name	Who created man?	Who created all the other species?	How old is the earth?	How old is the Universe?
Young Earth Creationism	God, in six consecutive 24-hour days as per Genesis.	God, during the same six 24-hour creation periods.	Less than 10,000 years, some say 6000 years; reshaped and restocked by the Biblical flood (called Flood Geology)	Less than 10,000 years, same as the earth.
Old Earth Creationism: Gap Creationism, aka Day-Age Creationism	God, in six consecutive 'age' periods where 'age' > 24 hours.	God, during the same six 'age' periods.	Billions of years, as determined by science and Flood Geology.	Billions of years, as determined by science.
Old earth Creationism: Progressive Creationism	God, not created in man's present form but in the form of some earlier primate ancestor.	God created the initial life form. Darwinian evolution created the rest but guided by God.	Billions of years, as determined by science. No Flood Geology.	Billions of years, as determined by science.
Old Age Creationism: Intelligent Design (also known as Neo Creationism and Creationist Science)	Various beliefs. God, plus evolution from primates with gaps explained by yet more intervention from God to explain irreducible complexity.	God, with intelligent design where irreducible complexity exists.	Opinions vary. Some accept scientific estimates and explanations. Some claim that God created the earth less than 10,000 years ago + Flood Geology.	Billions of years, as determined by science.
Theistic Evolutionism	Darwinian evolution from a single common ancestor created by God.	Darwinian evolution from a single common ancestor.	Billions of years, as determined by science. No Flood Geology.	Billions of years, as determined by science.

Within these variations of definition, there are some interesting assertions.

Young Earth Creationists say that the earth was created within the last 10,000 years but with the appearance of old age. This is why carbon dating, fossil and rock dating techniques suggest that the earth is older than it really is!

Gap Creationists claim that the earth was created on a pre-existing old Earth. The words 'without form, and void' in Genesis 1.2 mean that the Earth existed for billions of years with no living creatures. Then, 10,000 or 6,000 years ago, God fulfilled the rest of the story and populated the earth. Thus gap theorists can agree with modern science about the age of the Earth but still claim a literal interpretation of the story told in Genesis.

Progressive Creationists believe that a creation day was not a 24-hour earthly day but more likely a period (an age) equal to thousands or possibly millions of years: a compromise between a full allegoric and a full literal interpretation of the Genesis story.[112]

Some Young Earth Creationists have very precise ideas about the date of the creation, adhering to a belief first postulated by James Ussher, Archbishop of Armagh, in 1654 that the date was exactly at nightfall preceding October 23rd , 4004 BCE – that is, 6,000 years ago! If you are interested to know how he arrived at this date, take a look at http://en.wikipedia.org/wiki/Ussher_chronology.

While we are on the topic of the exact date of creation, here are some other pronouncements snagged from a Wikipedia website on Creation dates.[113] On the basis of their source alone, they may or may not be accurate!

- Maya civilization (precursor to the Incas) - August 11th 3,114 BCE
- Judaism - September 22nd or March 29th 3,760 BCE – take your choice.
- James Ussher (1654) - October 23rd 4,004 BCE.
- Byzantine Church calculation - September 1st 5,509 BCE.
- María de Ágreda (a seventeenth century Spanish Abbess) – 5,199 BCE.

---

[112] Progressive Creationist scholars suggest that the original Hebrew word in Genesis, *yôm*, should have been translated as age, not day, and that we are now living in the seventh age corresponding to the seventh day of rest.
[113] http://en.wikipedia.org/wiki/Dating_Creation

- Harold Camping (an American religious radio broadcaster) – 11,013 BCE.[114]
- Puranic Hinduism, 158.7 trillion years ago.
- Eternity - Postulate made by a number of groups including historical and contemporary scientists and certain New Age idealizations that the universe has always existed, so there's no beginning of the universe (though the Earth and other celestial objects may have come into being closer to the current day). One such scientific theory is the steady state theory. Hindus believe in a Cyclic Universe consisting of endless cycles of the Universe expanding, contracting and subsequently reforming: what we might call 'a cosmic *samsara*'!
- The philosopher Immanuel Kant believed the question of when the universe began presupposed transcendental realism (an understanding of the limits of the human mind) and was therefore unanswerable. According to him the universe exists without reference to cause and effect.

For reference, according to radiometric dating, the Big Bang Theory has the Universe starting to expand 13.7 (± 0.2) billion years ago and the planet Earth forming 4.55 (± 1%) billion years ago. So, the exact date of the Creation is still up for grabs!

For those interested in statistics, here are the results of a 2010 UK YouGov poll.

2010 YouGov Poll
(Based on 2,651 British adults over 18.)

The question 'What do you think is most likely to be the correct explanation for the origin of humans?'

The answers, based on four tick-the-box solutions:

Creationists. 9% think that the Bible's account of creation is most likely to be the true explanation.
IDers. 12% are most convinced of evolution by intelligent design.

---

[114] Harold Camping predicted the end of the world on 21st May, 2011, a date that came and went as I was writing this book. When it didn't happen, Camping went into hiding for a few days and then emerged saying that it started on the 21st May but will conclude on 21st October 2011. Again, it didn't! The man's an idiot, albeit a rich one!

Evolutionists. 65% believe that Darwinian evolution is most likely to be the correct explanation for the origin of humans.
Not sure. 13% just 'don't know'.

Out of interest, I conducted my own impromptu poll among around twenty or so adult family and friends. The results I obtained were: Creationists 0%, IDers 0%, Evolutionists 100% And that was before I wrote this book!

How do other religions view Creationism?

Protestants are largely theistic evolutionaries: first God created the universe and the earth – probably even the first life form, but not in the form of Adam. Then evolution took over. As far as they are concerned, the Genesis stories are allegorical.

Roman Catholics have no corporate opinion on evolution. They believe God created the universe and the earth but say evolution is a science, not a religion. Science deals with scientific things (the whys, whats and wherefores of physical and natural things) while religion deals with spiritual matters (God, soul, faith), so the two are not in conflict. (This is probably one of the biggest cop-outs formulated by a religion. Clearly, science overlaps religion insofar as science has a duty to explain the inexplicable, and the existence or otherwise of God certainly comes under the category of inexplicable.)

Hindus don't care. *Brahma* created the universe and earth, possibly during one of a number of endless cycles, but whether he also went on to create man and all other species of animals and plants isn't something that Hindus worry about.

Muslims take a different view. For them, the story of creation as told in the Qur'an is similar to but less exact than the Genesis accounts and, consequently, more open to alternative explanations to suit the context. Basically, Muslims will believe any explanation that sounds plausible and fits the context of the question but, in general, they are theistic evolutionaries – that is they believe that God (*Allah*) created the earth together with Adam and Eve, but are happy with the idea that Darwinian evolution created everything else. Contradicting this, the Web is full of Muslim rants that claim that Darwin and his successors have got it wrong – God did it all. Here are some excerpts snagged from various websites:

Allah alone is Master of Existence. He alone causes all that is to be and not to be. Causes are without effect in themselves, but rather both cause and effect are created by Him. The causes and the effects of all processes, including those through which plant and animal species are individuated, are His work alone. To ascribe efficacy to anything but His action, whether believing that causes (a) bring about effects in and of themselves; or (b) bring about effects in and of themselves through a capacity Allah has placed in them, is to ascribe associates to Allah (shirk – the sin of idolatry or polytheism). Such beliefs seem to be entailed in the literal understanding of 'natural selection' and 'random mutation', and other evolutionary concepts, unless we understand these processes as figurative causes, while realizing that Allah alone is the agent. This is apart from the consideration of whether they are true or not.

As for claim that man has evolved from a non-human species, this is unbelief (kufr – unbeliever or infidel) no matter if we ascribe the process to Allah or to 'nature', because it negates the truth of Adam's special creation that Allah has revealed in the Qur'an. Man is of special origin, attested to not only by revelation, but also by the divine secret within him, the capacity for ma'rifa or knowledge of the Divine that he alone of all things possesses. By his God-given nature, man stands before a door opening onto infinitude that no other creature in the universe can aspire to. Man is something else.

Sheikh Nuh Ha Mim Keller,
http://www.masud.co.uk/ISLAM/nuh/evolve.htm

Question
What is Islam's view on evolution? How do we explain the fossil bones of our ancestors? Does that mean that the prophet Adam also looked like them?

Answer
In your question, if 'evolution' implies that man is actually an evolved form of a certain other creature, then Islam does not affirm such a standpoint. According to the Qur'an, Adam (pbuh) - the first man - was a direct creation of God, as a man. The Qur'an does not support that Adam evolved from another species.

http://www.understanding-islam.com/q-and-a/overview-of-islam/does-islam-refute-evolution

Does Islam believe in Evolution?

For humans, no it doesn't. Humans were not evolved from anything. **But however, both the Noble Quran and Science claim that animals were sent down to earth from space, and then developed into many physical shapes**

and forms. The idea of Evolution came from Charles Darwin, an English atheist scientist who lived in the 1800's (sic) in London, England. His parents were Christians. He believed that humans were originally animals; more closer to monkeys and Apes, then we developed and became more intelligent and formed the 'human' race. He also had other theories that dealt with reproduction and other human-animal related topics.

I won't comment much on Darwin's theories, because I don't know enough about it. But it is quite clear that the theory of Evolution has no support in Islam.

http://www.answering-christianity.com/evolution.htm

'I won't comment much on Darwin's theories, because I don't know enough about it.' Unbelievable!

As I was writing this chapter, a report appeared on the BBC website[115] about a Muslim science lecturer, Dr Usama Hasan, who worked at Westminster University in London. He wrote an opinion piece in *The Guardian* in which he claimed that 'science can neither prove nor disprove God' and that 'many believers in God have no problem with an obvious solution: that God created man via evolution'. Hasan also wrote:

'One problem is that many Muslims retain the simple picture that God created Adam from clay, much as a potter makes a statue, and then breathed into the lifeless statue and, lo!, it became a living human. This is children's madrassa-level understanding and Muslims really have to move on as adults and intellectuals.'

As a result of these statements, Hasan was removed from his role as a respected imam at his local mosque, castigated by Islamic scholars on various websites (where he has been accused of apostasy – abandoning his faith), had death threats made against him, and was forced to retract his statements.

It's a sad world for thinking Islamists.

To return to the paradox of irreducible complexity, Dawkins used the watch to demolish the concept. I would like to use something closer to my heart as an ex-electronics engineer – the laptop computer.

Consider the desktop/laptop/netbook/iPad/Blackberry/Android or some other electronic gadget that, nowadays, never leaves your side. Imagine how Darwin would have reacted if presented with the latest super-go-fast multiple-bells-and-whistles apps-enabled always-

---

[115] http://www.bbc.co.uk/news/uk-12661477

internet-connected gizmo. Would he have seen it as an object of irreducible complexity? What good is a screen without an electronic device (a graphics processor) to control the display? What good is a mouse without an on-screen cursor? What good is a keyboard that is not connected to the central processor? What good is a processor without a built-in power supply? You get the picture?

If Darwin had opened the laptop to reveal the motherboard, and then opened the package housing one of the devices on the motherboard, the microprocessor perhaps, he would have observed complex blocks labelled processor, memory, high-speed bus, cache, arithmetic and logic unit, and so on. Had he dug deeper, he would have observed slightly simpler building blocks called AND gates, OR Gates, NAND gates, NOR gates, and flip-flops. Going deeper still, he would have got down to transistors of various types – Bipolar, CMOS. Going further down, he would have reached silicon molecules and their attendant impurities that turned them into useful inverters and amplifiers. And had he dug right to the bottom, he would have reached atoms complete with revolving electrons and holes (gaps that can be filled by moving electrons).

And then he might have sat down and said 'How on earth did all these layers of complexity become an instrument with a screen, keyboard and mouse and appropriate word-processing software that I could have used to write my book? The hand of God must've been involved somewhere along the line.' And he would have been wrong – absolutely drop-dead spellbindingly totally wrong – because all this technology evolved in the 60 years following the Second World War.

Irreducible complexity just doesn't wash as an argument for God.

I have wondered about the motivation of Creationists, especially when they wish to abolish the teaching of Darwinian evolution and replace it with Creationism/Intelligent Design dressed up as a science subject. Bryan's motives were clear – evolution undermined religion and sowed the seeds of evil throughout humanity. But, what are the motives of modern day Creationist evangelists? Power and control through indoctrination must be high on the list of answers. But why? What drives this need for control? A need for money? A need for something else? It's difficult to see how inculcating Creationism into young minds is going to generate wealth other than through the normal wealth-creating channels of any religion. So why Creationism? I have to confess that, at the moment, I'm at a loss to understand what drives Creationists to evangelize their beliefs.

But the battle still rages.

(^_^)

Appendix: A human biology primer

Glossary
In this short appendix on human biology, you may find it necessary to recall what is meant by a technical term. This set of definitions is to assist your recollection.

Alleles (allelic, adj.): A variant of a gene that codes for the same body characteristic, such as eye colour. Alleles often exist at the same locus (position) of an *homologous* pair of chromosomes.
Autosome: The general name given to any non-sex-determining chromosome. Humans have 44 autosomes grouped into 22 *homologous* pairs. The name autosome is a contraction of *auto*somal chromo*some*.
Cell: The basic building block of the human body comprised of a *membrane* enclosing a jelly-like substance called *cytoplasm* and a control centre called the *nucleus*.
Chromosome: A strand of DNA. Segments of DNA within a chromosome are known as *genes*. Human cells contain 46 chromosomes, 44 of which are *autosomes* and 2 of which are the X and Y *sex-determining* chromosomes.
Crossing over: A gene exchange process that occurs in Phase 1 of *meiosis* and ensures that the chromosomes in sperm, and egg, cells, although based on the parental chromosomes contain a different mix of genes thereby ensuring variety in the offspring.
Cytokinesis: the division of the *cytoplasm, organelles* and *membrane* of a cell into two separate daughter cells.
Cytoplasm: A jelly-like substance within a membrane that forms the bulk of a cell and encloses the cell's *nucleus*.
Diploid (2N) cell: In humans, a cell that has 46 chromosomes, 23 from the male sperm cell and 23 from the female egg cell. All human cells are diploid except the sperm and egg cells prior to fertilization. Diploid cells are often denoted as 2N cells.
Division: The general term applied to a cell when it divides into two daughter cells following a sequence of chromosome replication followed by chromosome separation (by *meiosis* or *mitosis*) and, finally, division of the cytoplasm, organelles and membrane (*cytokinesis*).
DNA: *deoxyribonucleic acid, the* chemical used to construct chromosomes. DNA has a double-helix (twisted ladder) structure and can be segmented into separately-identifiable sections called *genes*. The order of the bonds, the 'rungs' between the 'struts' of the twisted

ladder, form a code that identifies one gene from another. DNA has the important property that it is capable of *self-replication* – that is, an ability to create an exact copy of itself.

Embryo: What a *zygote* (fertilized egg) becomes once it contains more than 32 cells; a developing new human life.

Fertilization: The process of a male sperm cell penetrating a mature female egg cell to create a new human life called, at this stage, a *zygote*.

Gene: A DNA segment of a chromosome that is coded to produce a particular protein and consequently becomes associated with a human body characteristic such as eye colour, hair colour, skin colour, and so on.

Genome: The complete set of genes contained within a 46-chromosome *diploid* human body cell.

Haploid (N) cell: In humans, a cell that has 23 chromosomes. Sperm and egg cells are haploid. Haploid cells are often denoted as N cells.

Homologous: A matching pair of chromosomes inherited one from the male sperm and one from the female egg and having the same *allelic* genes in the same chromosomal locus (position). Homologous chromosomes are identified mostly by genetic content but also by shape and size.

Meiosis: A chromosome separation process whereby a set of 46 chromosomes in a sperm or egg diploid nucleus separates first into two sets of 46 chromosomes, Phase 1, and then into four sets of 23 chromosomes in four separate haploid nuclei, Phase 2. Meiosis is preceded by chromosome *replication*, based on DNA replication, and is followed by *cytokinesis* to produce four haploid daughter cells. Meiosis occurs only in the male testes to produce sperm cells and female ovaries to prepare the egg for fertilization.

Mitochondria: Specific types of cell *organelles* that produces energy from sugar.

Mitosis: A chromosome separation process whereby a set of 46 chromosomes in a diploid nucleus separate into two sets of 46 chromosomes in two separate diploid nuclei. Mitosis is preceded by chromosome *replication*, based on DNA replication, and is followed by *cytokinesis* to produce two identical daughter cells each containing one of the diploid nuclei.

Nucleus: The control centre of a cell; the place where most chromosomes are housed.

Organelles: Literally 'little organs'; membrane bound structures in a cell's cytoplasm that perform various functions such as the production of energy (*mitochondria* organelles) or the disposal of waste products.

Phenotype: A characteristic or physical manifestation of a human being that can be traced back to a particular gene or gene complex; hair colour, for example.

Protein: A complex chemical that is required for the structure, function and regulation of the body's cells, tissues and organs. There are several classes of protein but they are all created from one or more chains of amino acids based on oxygen, nitrogen, carbon and hydrogen.

Replication: Applies to the DNA in chromosomes and means that a set of chromosomes produce an exact replica of themselves. Compare with *division*.

Sex-determining chromosome: Two special chromosomes, the X (female determining) and Y (male determining) chromosomes. A human female body cell has two X chromosomes; a human male body cell has one X and one Y chromosome.

Zygote: The result of a sperm cell successfully fusing with an egg cell to form a fertilized egg cell, the *zygote*. On fusion, the fertilized egg cell acquires both the 23 chromosomes of the haploid sperm cell and the 23 chromosomes of the haploid egg cell. The resulting zygote cell now contains a full complement of 46 chromosomes and thus becomes a diploid cell.

Introduction

To understand evolution, we have to understand the physical nature of the hereditary units of the human body, our genes, and how their transfer from one generation to the next creates opportunities to change the host vehicle – that is, the human body itself. This is a vast topic – one that has been, and continues to be, researched by biologists, chemists, geneticists, evolutionists, embryologists and many other scientists and even by philosophers interested in how and why we have evolved and, ultimately, where we might finish up. My objective in this appendix is simply to explore the biological nature of the process as it applies to humans. I will leave the more speculative interpretations and predictions to those better equipped to reason them through.

While researching this topic, I noticed that some authors adopt a top-down approach – cell to nucleus to chromosome to gene to DNA – while others adopt the reverse bottom-up approach. I prefer the big-picture-to-detail approach, so I have opted for a top-down explanation.

I'll start at the cell level.

Cell to nucleus to chromosomes

The adult human body is a collection of approximately 10^{15} cells (one thousand million million cells) that congregate together to form various body parts such as limbs, heart, kidney, brain, eyes, ears, blood, nerves, muscles, and so on. Each cell is contained in a membrane and comprised of a jelly-like substance called *cytoplasm* which contains *organelles* – structures performing different jobs such as the production of energy or removal of waste products - and a control centre called the *nucleus*.

The nucleus contains chemical units called *chromosomes* which, as we'll see, are the containers of our genes. In human cells, there are 46

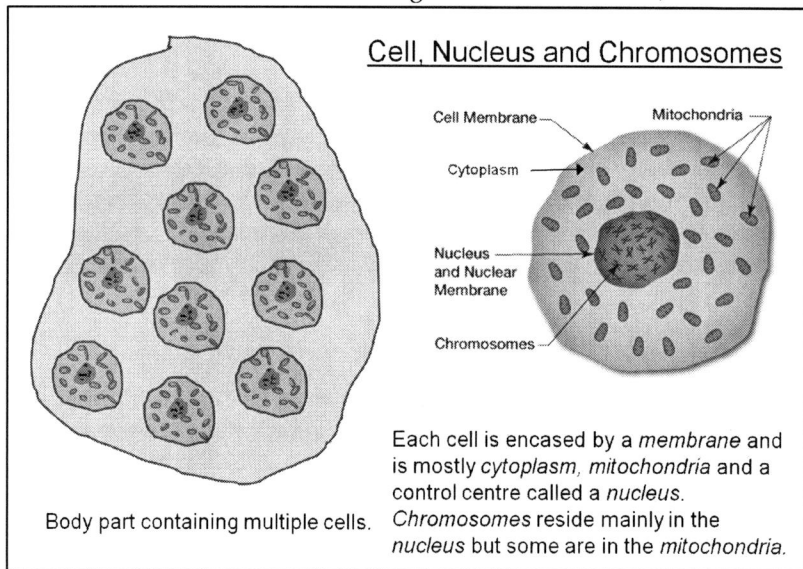

Body part containing multiple cells. Each cell is encased by a *membrane* and is mostly *cytoplasm*, *mitochondria* and a control centre called a *nucleus*. *Chromosomes* reside mainly in the *nucleus* but some are in the *mitochondria*.

different chromosomes. They come originally from our sperm and egg donor parents: 23 from one parent and 23 from the other. For convenience, I will use the letter 'A' to identify a chromosome from the father and 'B' to identify a chromosome from the mother.

Two of the chromosomes contain genes that control the determination of our sex. They are called the X (female orientation) and Y (male orientation) chromosomes. The remaining 44 chromosomes, 22 As and 22 Bs, are called autosomal chromosomes or *autosomes* for short. Each A chromosome, autosomal or sex-determining, is paired with its equivalent B chromosome based on shape, size and most importantly, genetic content – more later. Note that the word 'paired' does not mean that there is a physical

Evolution Versus Creationism

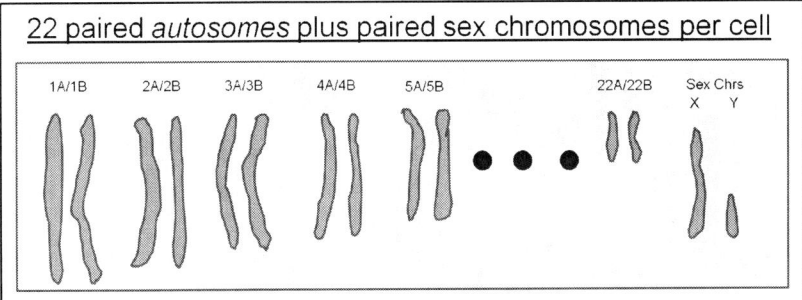

Each cell contains 22 paired sets of autosomal chromosomes (*autosomes*) - 1A/1B to 22A/22B - plus paired X and Y sex-determining chromosomes. Male cells contain one X and one Y chromosome, as shown. Female cells contain two X chromosomes.

connection between the A and B chromosomes in each pair. 'Paired' simply means that there is a correspondence between the genetic content of the A chromosome and that of the B chromosome. Chromosomes that are paired in this way are termed *homologous* pairs.

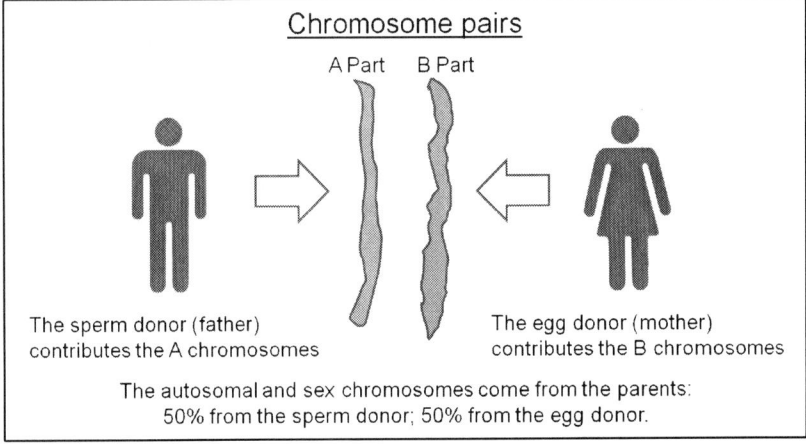

The autosomal and sex chromosomes come from the parents: 50% from the sperm donor; 50% from the egg donor.

The offspring's genes (the contents of the chromosomes) come only from its parents, half from the father and half from the mother. Similarly, the father has inherited half of his father's chromosomes (the offspring's paternal grandfather) and half of his mother's chromosomes (the offspring's paternal grandmother). Likewise, the mother of the offspring inherited chromosomes from her parents (the offspring's maternal grandparents). In this way, offspring inherit chromosomes from their ancestors, but the degree of inheritance per ancestor becomes diluted as we track back through ancestral generations. And, as we'll see, chromosomes passed by a parent to an offspring are not exact copies of the parental chromosomes. Their contents (genes) are mixed up by a gene-exchange process called *crossing over* during the production of sperm and egg cells. This ensures offspring are not clones of their parents, grandparents, great-grandparents, or anyone further back. We'll look at the mechanics of crossing over later.

Chromosomes to genes

Each autosome and the X and Y chromosomes is partitioned into chemical segments called *genes* with START and END codes that identify their boundaries. Each gene represents a set of instructions on how to make a particular protein. Proteins, in turn, determine how certain parts of our body develop and function – called the body's *phenotype*, its physical manifestation, or often the gene's *expression*. Some genes, for example, determine bone structure; others build organs; and so on. Basically, the set of all the genes in the 46 chromosomes dictates the body's manufacture and use of protein in all its various parts. They are like a massive instruction manual that sets out every stage of our development after conception. If the genes in corresponding locations in a pair of chromosomes contain either the same or different instructions for a particular body characteristic, such chromosome pairs are called *homologous*. In some cases, the genes in the same location (called the *locus*) of an homologous pair contain the same instruction for the characteristic: in other cases, alternative instructions for the same characteristic.

Let us assume that one of the genes that controls the iris pigmentation of eyes is located somewhere in the homologous pair of autosomes, 15A and 15B.[116] The gene in 15A, which comes from the father, may dictate blue eyes whereas the corresponding gene in 15B, which comes from the mother, may dictate brown eyes. One of the two eye-colour genes will win – say, the brown-eyes gene in 15B. The gene that wins is called the *dominant* gene. The gene that loses out – the blue-eyes gene in 15A – is still there but it's dormant and described as *recessive*. Such competing genes are called *alleles*, meaning rivals. Even though a gene is recessive in the current generation, it could well be passed on to an offspring or further down to the offspring's descendants. If two recessive genes are inherited, then the

---

[116] Eye colouring is complex and still being researched. The genes that influence iris pigmentation are located in the homologous autosomes 15 (brown/blue) and 19 (green/blue and brown) at least. See: http://en.wikipedia.org/wiki/Eye_color

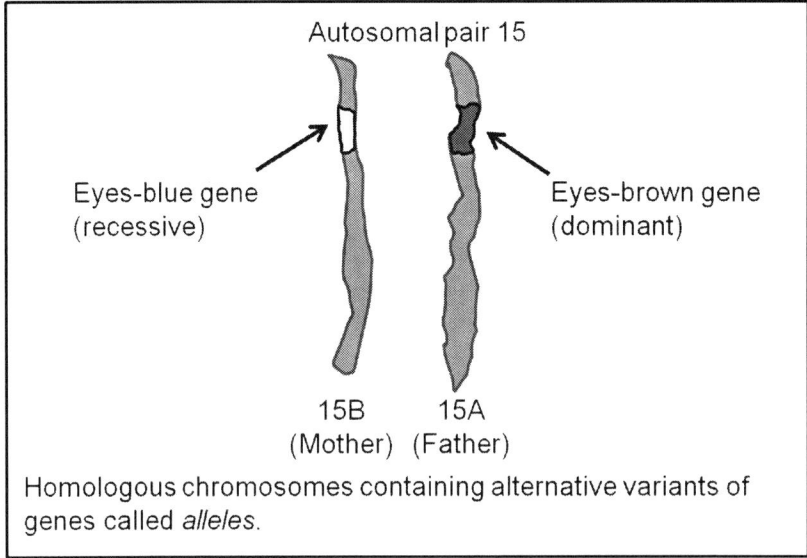

Homologous chromosomes containing alternative variants of genes called *alleles*.

genes will be expressed in a form of a physical characteristic possibly resulting in a re-emergence of an ancestral trait.

Alternatively, the two allelic genes may combine to form a compromise *co-dominance* solution – a human with one blue and one brown eye for example (a condition called *heterochromia iridum*). Or, if the genes are in a mischievous mood, purple eyes! Only kidding (about the purple eyes, that is).[117]

This is why body characteristics of grandparents and their ancestors sometime re-surface in grandchildren and their descendants. Basically, the 46 chromosomes contain a pool of genes, some dominant and some recessive but each capable of being handed down from one generation to the next to the next ...

It is important at this stage to remember that every cell in our body contains this complete set of alternative instructions – every cell, not just some cells. This may seem to be massive redundancy but, as it turns out, individual genes rarely work on their own. They work collaboratively with other genes to, for example, create an organ or develop a limb. Consequently, a massive replication of full

---

[117] Co-dominance occurs in the inheritance of blood groups. The blood-type genes A and B are dominant over type O. AO genes will be expressed as blood group A, for example. However, when both A and B genes are present they are both expressed and a person will have blood group AB. (Note: A and B used here to denote blood types is not to be confused with the A and B notation I have used to indicate the paternal or maternal origin of a chromosome.)

instructions turns out to be extremely beneficial for the gene collaboration program.

Genes to DNA

Genes are housed in a chemical structure based on an acid called *deoxyribonucleic acid*, DNA. A single DNA strand is a polymer[118] made of two strands of repeated units called *nucleotides*. Each nucleotide strand contains three parts: sugar, phosphate group, and a base. The sugar and the phosphate group are the same for all DNA nucleotides: the bases however have four variations - Adenine (A), Guanine (G),

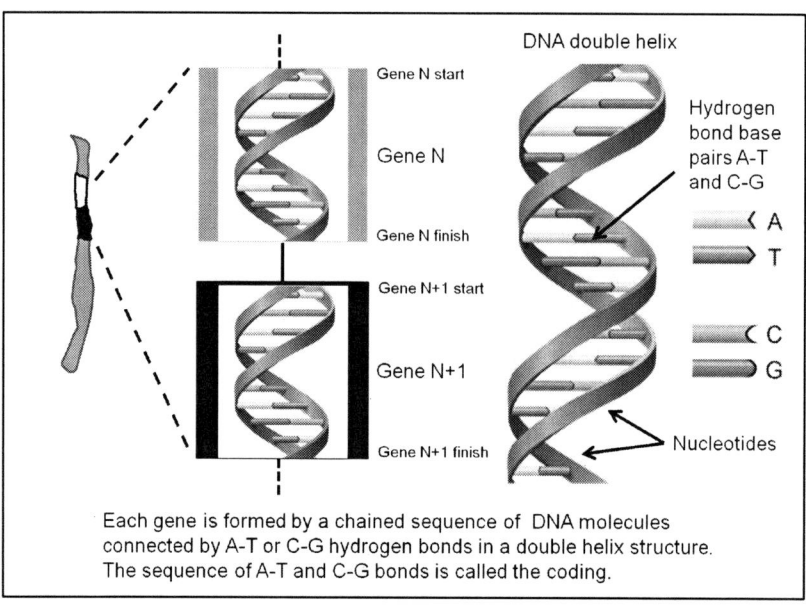

Each gene is formed by a chained sequence of DNA molecules connected by A-T or C-G hydrogen bonds in a double helix structure. The sequence of A-T and C-G bonds is called the coding.

Cytosine (C) and Thymine (T). These bases are built from various combinations of oxygen, carbon, hydrogen and nitrogen – the four chemical elements necessary to support life as we know it.

The first nucleotide strand contains a sequence of AGCT bases. The second strand is built using the base sequence of the first strand as a template. Within the DNA polymer, A always bonds with T on the opposite strand, and G always bonds with C on the opposite strand. This is referred to as *complimentary base pairing* and the bonds are

---

[118] A polymer is a chemical structure that consists of long chains of repeated structural units. Most plastics are constructed from polymer structures as is the child's plaything called *Silly Putty* or *Nutty Putty*.

called *hydrogen* bonds. The A-to-T, G-to-C bonding means that knowing the sequence of the bases of the first strand it is always possible to recreate the second strand and complete the DNA. This property of DNA is the key to DNA replication.

The exact order of each base-pair bond in the set of bonds represents the coded information in the DNA segment corresponding to a particular gene in a chromosome and determines the nature of the body part that will be made by that gene. Human DNA consists of around three billion base-pairs including some three million A-T/G-C different sequences packaged into the 46 chromosomes that are found in the cells of our bodies. The whole DNA structure looks like a twisted ladder with the *nucleotides* being the long struts up the sides of the ladder and the hydrogen bonds looking like rungs. The structure is often referred to as a *double helix* and was identified by two scientists, James Watson and Francis Crick, in 1953.[119]

The coding sequence within the double helix structure of DNA is based on just four letters: the sequence of AGCT bases along a nucleotide. The complete coding of all the genes, called the *genome*, is unique for every species of a living plant and animal, including us, and can be unravelled to reveal ancestry. DNA can also be extracted from organic remains at the scene of a crime – blood, saliva, semen, hair, skin, nails – and analysed to reveal the identity of those who were present at the time – a process called *DNA fingerprinting*.

Not all DNA is contained in the nucleus. Some DNA is found in the mitochondria units that exist in the cytoplasm area of the cell outside the nucleus (see earlier diagram). DNA in the mitochondria controls the use of protein in cells requiring a lot of energy, such as arm, leg and back muscles. Because mitochondrial DNA is not so well protected as nuclear DNA, it is more prone to damage and can result in mutations that cause a lack of resistance to diseases.[120] Also,

---

[119] Their discovery was a triumph for the scientific method for problem solving and hypothesis proving. They hypothesized a molecular model that would fit all available data about the structure of DNA – chemical, X-ray, and structural. Then they tested and modified the model until, finally, all data fitted and predicted behaviour was demonstrated. In 1962, Watson and Crick, plus Maurice Wilkins who had previously investigated the X-ray structure of DNA, received the Nobel Prize in Medicine for their pioneering work in identifying the structure of DNA. Their original paper, by the way, was just over one page long: a triumph for succinctness!

[120] Mutated mitochondrial DNA has been identified in cases of diabetes, deafness (a topic close to my heart; my mother went deaf and I am now also hard of hearing) and some heart diseases thought to have been inherited. There's also an unproven theory that an accumulation of mutated mitochondrial DNA is what drives the aging process and, with it, the onset of Parkinson's and Alzheimer's disease.

mitochondrial DNA is inherited only from the mother. It's present in the mother's egg but not in the father's sperm.[121]

In summary, DNA is the chemical building material for the variety of genes assembled into chromosomes, the carriers of the genes. Each gene's DNA coding carries with it not only instructions for how our own body develops and functions but, through the inheritance of genes from our parents, and their parents, and their parents before them ... a complete history of how we've evolved to the form we are today. Consequently, biologists and evolutionists have explored the structure, functioning and malfunctioning of DNA with a fervour comparable to that of medieval alchemists – the people who sought to convert lead and other base metals into gold.

DNA and gene replication

So far, so good. But what is the importance of DNA as a vehicle for coding genetic information? The key point is this: DNA replicates itself. A DNA molecule can create a copy of itself without external influence. The copy is usually but not always without error which, as it turns out, is why we evolve. In this way, the gene population is constantly changing, for better or for worse, and creating new protein as needed for development and maintenance of the human body – the gene's survival machine.

As a result, when we cut ourselves, the wound heals with new cells to replace the damaged cells. If we pull a muscle, the muscle repairs itself. If we lose blood through injury or donation, we simply create new blood cells. As we develop from childhood to adulthood, our milk teeth are rejected and replaced, our arms get bigger, our legs get longer, and breasts develop (even in some men, unfortunately!). Our finger and toe nails grow constantly, as does our hair. And so it continues ...

If new cells weren't created by a constant stream of replicating DNA followed by chromosome separation and cell division, none of these things would happen. And, as it turns out, the process of DNA replication leading to cell division helps to account for one highly-plausible hypothesis of the origin of life – the 'warm little pond' first postulated by Charles Darwin. (See the section entitled *Reaction to Darwin's Theories* in this chapter.)

---

[121] Mitochondrial DNA is present in the tail of the father's sperm but the tail falls off and isn't used once the sperm has penetrated and fertilized the mother's egg.

Evolution Versus Creationism 131

There is another reason why DNA replication is important. It's this: a gene (a segment of DNA) rarely works on its own. A gene needs help from other genes. Genes work in groups in ways that are still being understood. Put simply: the wider the variety of genes, the more likely some particular grouping will happen causing some new bodily manifestation to occur: a better eye to distinguish between friend or foe, a nascent nose with a sense of smell, a stronger muscle to assist escape from a predator. These are all things that will assist the survival machine (us) to survive longer or improve reproduction rates or in some other way ensure that the genes themselves survive. This is at the heart of Darwin's Survival of the Fittest Theory, but note that genes do not do this consciously – they have no emotions – but the greater the variety of genes, the more likely such survival-of-the-fittest events will occur.

As Francis Crick said, 'DNA makes RNA[122]; RNA makes protein; and protein makes us.'[123] All protein cell creation and use is controlled by various DNA-coded genes and, ultimately, is what makes our bodies tick. The source of the protein is the food and liquids we consume – we are what we eat and drink, literally. Enzyme proteins (chemical catalysts) speed up the processes of creating new molecules, including the identical DNA replicated from existing DNA, to make new cells to grow or repair organs or create new cells such as skin cells. Proteins also perform a number of other important functions such as:

- building blocks to shape cells to do their job, such as bone building and repair;
- hormones to transmit signals from organs (glands) to cells and tissues;
- antibodies to recognise and combat foreign and hostile pathogens such as allergens, bacteria and viruses; and
- transport molecules that deliver chemicals around the body such as oxygen in the blood.

---

[122] RNA – ribonucleic acid is similar to and transcribed (derived) from DNA, and is central to the synthesis of proteins and the expression of genes.
[123] This statement, known as the Central Dogma of Molecular Biology is variously ascribed to A Bolvin and R Vendrely (1947), James Watson (1952), Francis Crick (1958) and Marshall Nirenberg (date unknown). It seems many people want to claim credit!

Genomes

The full set of encoded DNA information specific to any animal or plant is called its *genome*. The international Human Genome Project was launched in 1990 to classify all our chromosomes and the genes contained therein. The Project's objective was to identify all sequences of hydrogen base-pairs for each and every gene type. This classification helps us understand what we are and where we've come from and, for scientific evolutionists, is a goldmine of data.

Current studies have estimated that there are somewhere between 20,000 and 25,000 different genes in the human genome.[124] The complete genome was published in April 2003, although the definition of the word 'complete' remains a matter of dispute. Many research groups are continuing with their investigations, particularly into the potential causes of diseases such as cancer, cystic fibrosis and diabetes, and how better to combat them.[125]

Gene transmission during human reproduction

Finally, we'll take a look at gene transmission during human reproduction through the eyes of cell division following self-replicating DNA that form the gene-containing chromosomes. In what follows, many details are glossed over so as not to obscure the principles. Note also that sexual reproduction is not the same as self-replication. We are each unique; not duplicates, copies or clones.

Cell division by DNA replication, mitosis and cytokinesis

This is the first clever bit.

First, the 46 chromosomes in a cell's nucleus employs DNA replication to create an exact copy of themselves. Then the nucleus containing the two sets of 46 chromosomes divides into two separate nuclei, each containing one of the sets. This separation process is called *mitosis*. And finally, the cell itself divides into two separate

---

[124] The exact number isn't yet known but it's variously reported to be in this range or, as other reputable websites have stated, around 35,000.
[125] The current 1000 Genomes Project aims to sequence and compare the DNA of 2,500 individuals from across the world. Specifically, the project is looking at the genetic variations. These base-pair variations are called Single Nucleotide Polymorphisms, SNPs. Results so far suggest that we each carry around 75 SNPs and that these variations may be responsible for a number of inherited diseases.

cells, each containing one of the nuclei. This last process is called *cytokinesis*.

Basically, each of the 46 chromosomes in the original nucleus produces an identical set of 46 chromosomes in a new nucleus and then the cell divides into two cells. In a nascent human *zygote* (a newly-fertilized egg), chromosome replication, separation and cell division starts once conception has taken place, and never really stops until death occurs. Conception occurs when a male sperm cell finds and penetrates a female egg cell, fusing into a new single cell called a *zygote*. At this point, the offspring is just one fused sperm-plus-egg

---

DNA replication, *mitosis* and cell division

Each of the 46 chromosomes in a 2N diploid cell self-replicates and then the cell divides to become two genetically identical 2N diploid cells. The process then continues again to produce four 2N cells, and so on ...

DNA replication

2N → 2N → 2N 2N

Mitosis
(Nuclei separation)

Cell division

2N, 2N, 2N, 2N, 2N, 2N, 2N

---

cell but replication, separation and division starts and continues over the years to reach the final approximate figure of one thousand million million cells, 10^{15}, cells. This is the number of cells in a fully-grown adult. From then on, new cell creation is more for maintenance mode than growth mode, unless we consume more food and drink than we need!

This is truly a remarkable feat, especially when you consider that (a) each set of 46 chromosomes in a cell contains a complete instruction manual and (b) when enough cells exist, the genes within the chromosomes can begin to work in unison to create more-complex parts of the body. The process puts me in mind of the technique for booting a laptop computer into action. The core of the booting process, the Binary Input Output System (BIOS), is hardwired into the computer and is automatically activated when power is applied to the computer – that is, when the computer, assumed female, is fertilized by an intrusive 18.5 volt DC supply, assumed male! The BIOS establishes a set of core actions that enable a more-sophisticated operating system, such as Microsoft's Windows or Apple's OS X, to be loaded and activated. Thus the computer bursts into life ready to run a variety of complex application programs. 'Booting' is short for bootstrapping – pulling yourself up by your boot straps. DNA self-replication followed by cell division followed by gene collaboration is genetic bootstrapping.

Gene mutation

Chromosome replication is not perfect. As chromosomes separate in *mitosis*, deviations in the replicated chromosomes can, and do, take place. Genes in a replicated chromosome can change as a result of three main mutation processes:

1. Omission. A gene in the original chromosome is not replicated in the new chromosome.
2. Duplication. A gene in the original chromosome is replicated twice in the new chromosome.
3. Inversion. The DNA strand of a gene in the original chromosome is inverted before addition to the new chromosome.

The evolutionary effects of such mutations on the functions of the human body survival machine can range from *disastrous* (extinction of the survival machine and possibly all survival machines carrying this mutant gene) to *no-effect* to *brilliant* (a strengthening of the survival machine's ability to survive in a hostile environment). Mutations are the key to evolution.

Cell division by DNA replication, meiosis and cytokinesis

Now we come to the next clever bit: cell division by chromosome replication followed by *meiosis* instead of *mitosis*. Consider the following problem.

If sperm cells were produced by *mitosis*, each sperm cell would contain a full complement of 46 chromosomes – that is, they would be

2N diploid cells. If the same thing happened in egg cells, the resulting fusion of a 2N diploid sperm cell with a 2N diploid egg cell would produce a 92-chromosome cell to start the new life. Consequently, the offspring's development would be controlled by all the genes inside the 92 chromosomes and almost certainly would not look anything like its parents!

If this was repeated, the next generation would be based on 184-chromosome cells – nature gone wild!

But, this doesn't happen. Why not?

The answer is that an alternative chromosome separation process, called *meiosis,* occurs only in the sperm-producing testes of the father and the egg-maturing-and-releasing ovaries of the mother.[126] At the cell level, the first part of meiosis divides the 2N diploid cell into two cells, each containing 23-chromosome sister pairs – that is 46 chromosomes linked together to look like 23 single units. These sister pairs are called *chromatids* and the link between them is called the *centromere.* Although the cells still contain 46 chromosomes, the linking together into 23 chromatids means that technically they are classed as haploid cells.

The second part of meiosis further divides the two haploid cells into four separate N cells, resulting in four sperm cells (male) or egg cells (female). In this way, the final sperm and egg cells contain 23 separate chromosomes each and the resulting fused sperm and egg cell contains the sum of the two sets of 23 chromosomes, thus regaining its requisite total of 46 chromosomes.

Okay, so far so good but the next question is what 23 chromosomes, and hence genes, are present in the N haploid sperm and egg cells? And, this is where we come to the really clever bit.

---

[126] It is a common misconception that ovaries produce eggs. They do not. All eggs in a female human are produced and stored in a yolk sac in the ovaries before she is a 9 week old embryo. Female babies are born with all the eggs they will ever have – millions of them – but the number is down to around 400,000 by the time the female reaches sexual maturity at puberty (from 12 years onwards). From then on, the ovaries mature and release one, sometimes more, fertile egg(s) a month during ovulation until she finally reaches the menopause in her late-40s/early-50s.

For sperm cell production, during the first phase of meiosis, the 23 chromosomes that make it to the initial two N haploid sperm cells are based on a random mix of genes from the father's original 46 chromosomes. Similarly, the 23 chromosomes in an N haploid egg cell are based on a random mix of the mother's original genes. For each homologous pair of chromosomes, each gene in the new *chromatid* pairs has originated from the genes in the original homologous chromosomes but the mix of genes is different. A gene exchange process called *crossing over* has taken place. Genes in one homologous chromosome swaps places with genes in the other homologous

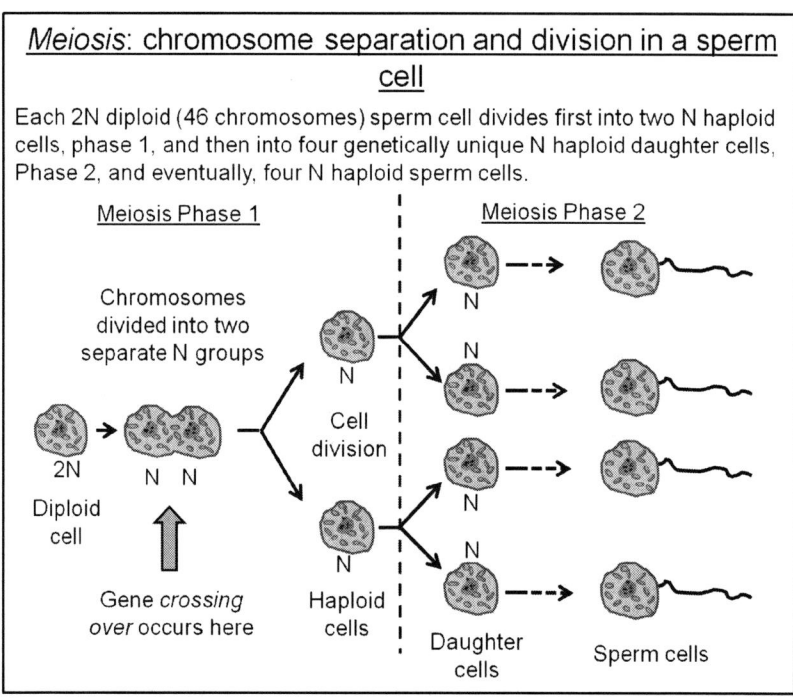

chromosome.

For sperm cells, once the genes have been shuffled around, the two N haploid cells divide further into four N haploid cells, eventually becoming four genetically unique sperm cells.

A similar process occurs during the maturation of egg cells in the ovaries but with some important differences. Unlike sperm which is manufactured on a daily or as-needed basis, egg cells go through the first stage of meiosis - crossing over followed by the diploid to haploid cell split - and are then held in an arrested state until ready to be released into the Fallopian tubes during the ovulation phase of the female monthly cycle. Just before release, the second stage of egg cell meiosis occurs - two haploids split into four daughter haploids - but only one of the four haploid cells becomes the final egg. Called the *ovum*, this cell grabs all the cytoplasm and mitochondria from the other three cells and goes on to develop into a new life if fertilized by a sperm cell. The other three cells, called *polar bodies*, die off.

Two types of aberrations can occur during meiosis crossing over: *inversion* (a part of one chromosome disconnects and joins another chromosome) and *translocation* (a part of one chromosome disconnects and joins another chromosome *and vice versa*). Inversion and translocation aberrations are other sources of *mutation.*

Crossing over ensures that the offspring does not inherit exactly the same genes as the parents, even though all the genes in the chromosomes have come from the parents. This is what makes us unique.

The crossing over mechanism within *meiosis* takes place in each sperm cell produced in the male testes and each mature egg cell released by the female ovaries. The resulting 23-chromosome sperm and egg cells are each essentially unique in their gene mix. This is because there are a vast number of possibilities for shuffling the genes in the 46 original chromosomes into a particular 23 chromosome result. It's a lottery.[127] When a particular sperm cell, out of upto 500 million per ejaculate, finds and penetrates the egg cell travelling through the Fallopian tubes on its way to the uterus (womb), the fusion of the two cells now contains the two new individual sets of 23 chromosomes, and a new life starts.

From then on, your whole life in terms of bodily development is fixed. Your eyes will be blue, your skin brown, your hair black, and so on. You will also be unique insofar as nobody else in the world will have exactly the same set of genes as you, except in the case of

---

[127] We can see this even at the chromosome level. Each N haploid sperm cell derived from the original 2N diploid sperm cell contains one of the two modified homologous chromosomes. There are two ways of selecting the chromosome from the first homologous pair, two from the second pair, two from the third pair, and so on upto the final twenty-third pair. This is 2 x 2 x 2 x... twenty-three times – that is, 2^{23} choices of chromosomes. Similarly with the chromosome selection process in the egg cell. Thus, the final fertilized egg contains one of 2^{23} male selections and one of 2^{23} female selections of 46 chromosomes – that is, one of a possible 2^{46} selection. This is roughly one in 70,000,000,000,000 choices. Now if you factor in all the various possible assortments of genes within the chromosomes, assumed to number somewhere between 20,000 and 25,000, you can begin to appreciate just how unique you are! As Billy Bunter's Greyfriars' friend, Hurree Jamset Ram Singh might have said, 'The degree of uniqueness is terrific.'

identical twins – see later. You may have some characteristics that are similar to one or both of your parents but you are definitely not a clone of either of them, nor of any siblings that may come along. Your genetic makeup is radically different to that of your parents' even though your genes have come from theirs. You will also contain genes from your parents' ancestors, as discussed, and it could be that genes that were recessive in the past are re-activated and become expressed in you. Thus, even if both your parents have brown hair, you could finish up with hair that's jet-black. Or, more startlingly, even if your parents' skin colour was classed as 'black', you could be classed as 'white'.

(Coincidently, a case of this happened about three weeks before I drafted the first version of this appendix. It appeared on the BBC website at http://www.bbc.co.uk/news/health-10697682 In brief, a white-skinned blond-haired blue-eyed baby was born to black Nigerian parents with no known white ancestry. The three possible causes were listed as

- dormant white genes which entered both of the baby's parents' families long ago,
- a genetic mutation unique to the baby, or
- albinism caused by a mutated pigmentation gene.)

Mutations (aberrations in the genes) occur at two points in the reproduction process: when the chromosomes in sperm cells and egg cells are created by DNA replication during *meiosis*– that is, before conception – and at conception, when a sperm cell penetrates the egg cell to create the *zygote* whose chromosomes then start to replicate. But even with mutations, each *embryo* (a *zygote* that possesses 32 or more cells) is unique unless it too splits on its way to the uterus or even in the uterus.[128]

---

[128] Sometimes, the developing multi-cell embryo divides as it is travelling towards the uterus thus creating an exact copy of itself – that is, a second embryo with exactly the same set of 46 cellular chromosomes. If this happens, the resulting babies are genetically identical and are called identical twins. This is quite different to the situation where two separate egg cells in the Fallopian tubes are each fertilized by different sperm (a sperm cell can only fertilize one egg cell) thereby creating two separate embryos with different sets of chromosomes. If this happens, the resulting babies are not genetically identical and are called fraternal twins – that is, they have shared the same uterus but they are as different as chalk and cheese, just like two time-spaced siblings.

The other way to produce an identical organism is by artificial cloning based on exact laboratory reproduction of an animal's genetic makeup including, potentially, a human – a scary science.

One last comment about genes …

Genes pass unaltered from one generation to the next. If they change, it is the result of mutations during the replicating processes, as discussed, or of damage caused by external agents such as exposure to ultraviolet light, radiation, viruses, or carcinogenic chemicals such as nicotine. The fact that we acquire knowledge, expertise and skills during our lifetime does not affect our genes, so the only way we can pass any of it on is through teaching. This fact is often misunderstood. We have all heard people say things like 'He has inherited his father's mathematical skills' or 'She has inherited her mother's piano-playing skills'. He or she may well have acquired the same skills, but not as a result of inheriting genes. But the presence of certain inherited genes may predispose us with the ability and talent to acquire such skills more readily than those without these particular genes. The jury is still deliberating on whether certain genes contribute to our ability to emulate and even surpass the skills of our parents.[129]

The structure of genes and the process of transmission during human reproduction is an amazing and fascinating process and seemingly far

---

[129] This theory of evolution, known as *inheritance of acquired characteristics* or, sometimes, *soft inheritance*, was prevalent before Darwin published his *On the Origin of Species* book in 1859. The theory is often attributed to Jean-Baptiste Lamarck and called *Lamarckism* although he was not the originator. Lamarck, 1744 – 1829, died before the publication of Darwin's book. An oft-cited example of Lamarckism is the evolution of the long necks of giraffes enabling them to reach the upper leaves in high trees. It's argued that each generation of giraffes grew slightly longer necks and this characteristic was passed down to offspring. In other words, the environment influenced the development of the neck. Darwin's theories explain this by saying that those with longer necks were able to satisfy their hunger easier and the genes that helped create the neck were then passed to offspring. Those without the long-neck genes died earlier, presumably of starvation. Put differently, survival of the fittest accounts for the long neck, not inheritance of acquired characteristics.

Another example that comes to mind is circumcision, removal of the foreskin that covers the glans of the male penis. Since Abraham's time, baby Jewish boys have been circumcised just after birth and yet the need to do this with today's Jewish boys (and non-Jewish boys) still exists. It seems it's going to take more than 3,750-ish years for foreskins to disappear!

Lamarckism still has its supporters and the theory isn't entirely dead. Read more at http://en.wikipedia.org/wiki/Lamarckism

more complex than the intricate electronic components I studied during my professional career.

(^_^)

Chapter 7
Christianity: Not What It Seems

'If you hear that in one of the towns which Yahweh your God has given you for a home there are men, scoundrels from your own stock who have led their fellow-citizens astray, saying 'Let us go and serve other gods', hitherto unknown to you, it is your duty to look into the matter, examine it, and inquire most carefully. If it is proved and confirmed that such a hateful thing has taken place among you, you must put the inhabitants of that town to the sword; you must lay it under the curse of destruction – the town and everything in it. You must pile up all its loot, offering it all to Yahweh your God. It is to be a ruin for all time and never rebuilt.'

Deuteronomy, 13:12-16

'The Bible, it seems certain, was the work of sand-strewn men and women who thought the earth was flat and for whom a wheelbarrow would have been a breathtaking example of emerging technology.'

Sam Harris, *The End of Faith*, p.45

Introduction

In this chapter, I will comment on some of the open questions I raised in Chapter 3: those about the possibility of virgin conception, miracles, and some of the less-acceptable teachings in the Bible. But first, a little bit of history to explain how Christianity exploded into its many different styles following the establishment of the Holy Inquisitions and their effects on the European Roman Catholic Church.

The Holy Inquisitions

After the Roman Empire's adoption of Christianity, not long after the death of Jesus Christ, the Roman Catholic Church spread throughout Europe consolidating into a strong and somewhat sinister organisation. By the twelfth century CE, most of Europe was Catholic and the Vatican had become both a religious and a political power base, influencing the development of society across large swathes of the continent – so much so that voices of dissent were growing.

To combat the rising tide of opposition, the Roman Catholic Church instigated a series of Inquisitions – the Medieval Inquisition (1148 – 1230s), the Spanish Inquisition (1478 – 1834), the Portuguese Inquisition (1536 – 1821) and, finally, the Roman Inquisition (1542 - ~1860).

Inquisitors were on the lookout for two things – heresy, defined to be any opinion or doctrine contrary to the dogma of the Roman Catholic Church, and blasphemy, defined to be the act of insulting or otherwise showing disrespect towards or contempt of God. Together, these ungodly actions were undermining the Catholic faith. The Inquisitions were designed to eliminate them and bring the populace back under the Church's control.

The Inquisitions became renowned for their use of many forms of torture to extract confessions. Set up by papal edict, they involved both local and papal religious leaders. Their purpose was to assess guilt, or otherwise. Once heresy had been determined – and it often was – cases were passed to a local non-religious court for trial and punishment. This way of working allowed Inquisitions to argue they were not responsible for whatever final punishment was meted out. And some of those punishments were brutal – death by burning at the stake or long-term imprisonment accompanied by confiscation of personal goods and property, for example.

The declared intention of the Inquisition punishments was spelled out in a 1578 handbook.

> '... for punishment does not take place primarily and per se for the correction and good of the person punished, but for the public good in order that others may become terrified and weaned away from the evils they would commit.'
> Jonathan Kirsch, *The Grand Inquisitors Manual, A History of Terror in the Name of God*. HarperOne, 2008

In other words, subservience to the Roman Catholic Church was to be achieved by means of terror.

But the Inquisitions were only part of the picture. They only 'tried' people who had been baptised Roman Catholics. Those accused of blasphemy or other offences were tried in secular courts. Thus, most witchcraft trials were conducted by the secular courts and not by the Inquisitions.

(Witchcraft is a topic in its own right. We won't consider it in depth, other than to note that it was mostly considered separate to religious heresy or blasphemy and that there was no common religious authority to form a base for guilt or innocence. Consequently, local authorities could decide their own trials and punishments. Typically, these were based on a mix of superstition and fear of the unknown. It could be argued that witchcraft accusations were really a result of earlier pagan beliefs: no rain = no crops = hunger; blame the old lady down the road who lives on her own, has a black cat, and mumbles to herself.)

Although each major Inquisition had its own horror stories, the Portuguese Inquisition deserves a special mention. Before the sixteenth century, Portugal had a large population of Muslims and Sephardic Jews, a Jewish sect originating from the Iberian Peninsula. The Portuguese state forced both Muslims and Sephardic Jews to convert to Catholicism or leave the country. Many professed to have converted but were suspected of following the doctrines of their earlier faiths in the privacy of their own homes. Consequently, persecution of Muslims and Sephardic Jews was rife.

As an aside, we can ask 'Why the Jews?' Anti-Semitism is intrinsic in both Christianity and Islam. Many followers of both religions believe the Jews to be bunglers of God's revelations. Additionally, Christians hold the Jews responsible for the crucifixion of Jesus Christ. Islamists are angry because the Jews never accepted Muhammad as a true Prophet. There is also anger at the Jewish belief that they are the 'chosen people': the bearers of a unique covenant with God.

Getting back to the Inquisitions, one of the more famous persecutions was that of Galileo Galilei, commonly known just as Galileo. Galileo, 1564 – 1642, was an Italian physicist, mathematician, astronomer and philosopher, famous for many discoveries and inventions and a founder of the scientific method for proving or disproving a hypothesis, described earlier in Chapter 3.

Until 1543, conventional religious (and astronomic) wisdom stated that the Earth, perceived to be God's finest creation, was at the centre of the universe and that the sun was in orbit around the Earth. This was called *geocentric* cosmology.

In 1543, the Polish astronomer Nicolaus Copernicus published a book in which he said this was all wrong: the sun was the centre of the universe and the earth revolved around it. This was called *heliocentric* cosmology and at the time the idea was postulated, it caused considerable dismay within the Vatican and among contemporary astronomers.

Galileo, then at the height of his fame, argued that Copernicus was correct. As a result, Galileo was brought to trial by the Roman

Inquisition in 1633. He was found guilty, branded a heretic, forced to recant, and kept under house arrest until he died nine years later.

Retrospectively, we see that the Roman Catholic Church, just like Islam at approximately the same time, was unable to reconcile scientific truths (Copernicus was right) with literal interpretations of passages in the Bible. It was this inability to adjust to irrefutable scientific evidence that contributed to the Protestant Reformation.

The European Protestant Reformation

The European Protestant Reformation, roughly attributed to the years 1517 to 1648, brought seismic change to Europe's religious landscape. Until 1517, the Roman Catholic Church had held the supreme and superior position as the religion of Europe. However, it was coming under increasing criticism – not just for financial corruption and greed, but for becoming self-serving, all controlling and shrouded by mumbo jumbo ceremonial mysticism. The various Inquisitions did nothing to reduce the unrest. In fact, they fuelled it.

In 1517, Martin Luther, a German Roman Catholic priest and Professor of Theology at Wittenberg University, published a book, the *Ninety-Five Theses*, that stated that a release from God's punishment for sins committed could not be purchased with money. This practice, called the *purchase of indulgences,* was widely advocated by the Church as a way of extracting money from the populace.[130] Luther also challenged the infallibility of the Pope, claiming that there was only one source of divine guidance – the Bible.

Luther was asked to retract his statements by Pope Leo X and, later, by the Diet (a deliberative assembly) of Worms (a town in Germany)[131] but he refused. This led to his excommunication from the Church.

At that point, Luther and others established an alternative Christian faith based on a modified Christian theology – the Protestant theology.

Luther was a fascinating character. He was responsible for translating the Bible from Latin into German, an act that opened up the contents to the lay public and which influenced the creation of Tyndale's English Bible, the forerunner of the 1611 King James Bible.

---

[130] You sin. You pay money to the Church. The greater the sin, the greater the payment. Your sins are forgiven. Done and dusted! A souped-up version of the modern confessional.
[131] Diet of Worms sounds like a new-age repulsive food regime. Hence the explanation in brackets!

In addition, Luther married a nun, Katherina von Bora, after he'd smuggled her hidden in a herring barrel out of her convent. The couple went on to break the mould of celibacy and non-marriage for Catholic priests by having six children. Luther was also a prolific hymn writer with many of his compositions surviving in the Lutheran hymnal. And finally, in his later life, he wrote several polemics condemning both Islam and Judaism, for which he was criticised by other members of the Lutheran Church. I guess modern-day Californians would call him 'a mover and a shaker'.

The Protestant Reformation was sparked by Luther's break from the Roman Catholic Church. As it spread across Europe, an array of variations was created: Adventist, Anabaptist, Anglican, Baptist, Calvinist,[132] Congregationalist, Lutheran, Methodist, Pentecostalism, Presbyterian, Reformed, and Puritan. The Roman Catholic Church counter-attacked with the Counter Reformation, also known as the Catholic Reformation. The legacy of this battle is, I'm afraid, still evident – in the sectarian divide between the inhabitants of the Irish Republic and Northern Ireland, for example.

I'll turn now to some of the articles of faith of Christianity – the genealogy of Jesus Christ linked to the virgin conception and birth (the Immaculate Conception), the possibility of miracles, and the teachings of the Bible.

First, the genealogy of Jesus Christ ...

Genealogy of Jesus Christ

A central tenet of Christianity is that Jesus Christ, although born of a woman, was, in fact, the Son of God. In other words, he was the Incarnation of God. Mary, his mother, was both a virgin at conception and remained so throughout the pregnancy to the final birth, which took place at what Christians now call Christmas – literally, Christ's Mass, a spiritual union with God.

The New Testament specifies Jesus's genealogy in two places: Matthew 1:1-16 and Luke 3:23-37. Each details the ancestors of Joseph, Mary's husband and supposed step-father of Jesus. Matthew starts

---

[132] John Calvin (1509 – 1564), a French Roman Catholic pastor and theologian, was also very influential in fostering the Protestant Reformation, albeit slightly later that Martin Luther. Calvin broke from the Roman Catholic Church in 1530 and following increased tensions against the new Protestant movement, he fled to Switzerland and eventually settled in Geneva where he preached and promulgated his new ideas on Christianity. Calvinism, Presbyterianism and Reformed owe allegiance to John Calvin's religious philosophies and teachings.

from Abraham and progresses forward to Joseph and hence Jesus through 41 generations. Luke starts from Jesus and progresses back to Adam and thence to God through 77 generations.

Here are the passages. First Matthew's lineage:

Matthew 1:1-16 (New International Version)

¹ This is the genealogy of Jesus the Messiah the son of David, the son of Abraham:
² Abraham was the father of Isaac, Isaac the father of Jacob, Jacob the father of Judah and his brothers,
³ Judah the father of Perez and Zerah, whose mother was Tamar, Perez the father of Hezron, Hezron the father of Ram,
⁴ Ram the father of Amminadab, Amminadab the father of Nahshon, Nahshon the father of Salmon,
⁵ Salmon the father of Boaz, whose mother was Rahab, Boaz the father of Obed, whose mother was Ruth, Obed the father of Jesse,
⁶ and Jesse the father of King David. David was the father of Solomon, whose mother had been Uriah's wife,
⁷ Solomon the father of Rehoboam, Rehoboam the father of Abijah, Abijah the father of Asa,
⁸ Asa the father of Jehoshaphat, Jehoshaphat the father of Jehoram, Jehoram the father of Uzziah,
⁹ Uzziah the father of Jotham, Jotham the father of Ahaz, Ahaz the father of Hezekiah,
¹⁰ Hezekiah the father of Manasseh, Manasseh the father of Amon, Amon the father of Josiah,
¹¹ and Josiah the father of Jeconiah and his brothers at the time of the exile to Babylon.
¹² After the exile to Babylon: Jeconiah was the father of Shealtiel, Shealtiel the father of Zerubbabel,
¹³ Zerubbabel the father of Abihud, Abihud the father of Eliakim, Eliakim the father of Azor,
¹⁴ Azor the father of Zadok, Zadok the father of Akim, Akim the father of Elihud,
¹⁵ Elihud the father of Eleazar, Eleazar the father of Matthan, Matthan the father of Jacob,
¹⁶ and Jacob the father of Joseph, the husband of Mary, and Mary was the mother of Jesus who is called the Messiah.

And now Luke's lineage:
Luke 3: 23-38 (New International Version)

[23] Now Jesus himself was about thirty years old when he began his ministry. He was the son, so it was thought, of Joseph, the son of Heli, [24] the son of Matthat, the son of Levi, the son of Melki, the son of Jannai, the son of Joseph, [25] the son of Mattathias, the son of Amos, the son of Nahum, the son of Esli, the son of Naggai, [26] the son of Maath, the son of Mattathias, the son of Semein, the son of Josek, the son of Joda, [27] the son of Joanan, the son of Rhesa, the son of Zerubbabel, the son of Shealtiel, the son of Neri, [28] the son of Melki, the son of Addi, the son of Cosam, the son of Elmadam, the son of Er, [29] the son of Joshua, the son of Eliezer, the son of Jorim, the son of Matthat, the son of Levi, [30] the son of Simeon, the son of Judah, the son of Joseph, the son of Jonam, the son of Eliakim, [31] the son of Melea, the son of Menna, the son of Mattatha, the son of Nathan, the son of David, [32] the son of Jesse, the son of Obed, the son of Boaz, the son of Salmon, the son of Nahshon, [33] the son of Amminadab, the son of Ram, the son of Hezron, the son of Perez, the son of Judah, [34] the son of Jacob, the son of Isaac, the son of Abraham, the son of Terah, the son of Nahor, [35] the son of Serug, the son of Reu, the son of Peleg, the son of Eber, the son of Shelah, [36] the son of Cainan, the son of Arphaxad, the son of Shem, the son of Noah, the son of Lamech, [37] the son of Methuselah, the son of Enoch, the son of Jared, the son of Mahalalel, the son of Kenan, [38] the son of Enosh, the son of Seth, the son of Adam, the son of God.

These listings are difficult to analyse so here's the same data restructured into a time-lined tabular form, starting from Jesus Christ (generation 0, the reference point) and working back in time (negative generations).

0. Jesus	-7. Zadok	-14. Josiah	-21. Jehoram	-28. Jesse	-35. Hezron
-1. Joseph/Mary	-8. Azor	-15. Amon	-22. Jehoshaphat	-29. Obed	-36. Perez
-2. Jacob	-9. Eliakim	-16. Manasseh	-23. Asa	-30. Boaz	-37. Judah
-3. Matthan	-10. Abihud	-17. Hezekiah	-24. Abijah	-31. Salmon	-38. Jacob
-4. Eleazar	-11. Zerubbabel	-18. Ahaz	-25. Rehoboam	-32. Nahshon	-39. Issac
-5. Elihud	-12. Shealtiel	-19. Jotham	-26. Solomon	-33. Amminadab	**-40. Abraham**
-6. Akim	-13. Jeconiah	-20. Uzziah	**-27. King David**	-34. Ram	

Matthew's Genealogy

0. Jesus	-13. Maath	-26. Elmadam	-39. Menna	-52. Judah	-65. Shem
-1. Joseph	-14. Mattathias	-27. Er	-40. Mattatha	-53. Jacob	-66. Noah
-2. Heli	-15. Semein	-28. Joshua	-41. Nathan	-54. Issac	-67. Lamech
-3. Matthat	-16. Josek	-29. Eliezer	**-42. King David**	**-55. Abraham**	-68. Methuselah
-4. Levi	-17. Joda	-30. Jorim	-43. Jesse	-56. Terah	-69. Enoch
-5. Melki	-18. Joanan	-31. Matthat	-44. Obed	-57. Nahor	-70. Jared
-6. Jannai	-19. Rhesa	-32. Levi	-45. Boaz	-58. Serug	-71. Mahalalel
-7. Joseph	-20. Zerubbabel	-33. Simeon	-46. Salmon	-59. Reu	-72. Kenan
-8. Mattathias	-21. Shealtiel	-34. Judah	-47. Nahshon	-60. Peleg	-73. Enosh
-9. Amos	-22. Neri	-35. Joseph	-48. Amminadab	-61. Eber	-74. Seth
-10. Nahum	-23. Melki	-36. Jonam	-49. Ram	-62. Shelah	-75. Adam
-11. Esli	-24. Addi	-37. Eliakim	-50. Hezron	-63. Cainan	-76. God
-12. Naggai	-25. Cosam	-38. Melea	-51. Perez	-64. Arphaxad	

Luke's genealogy

The most obvious point is that the two genealogies are glaringly different. The number of generations from Jesus back to King David varies (27 or 42), as does the number to Abraham (40 or 55). Differences even exist in closer generations. Was Joseph's father Jacob or Heli? And other than between David and Abraham, few of the names and generations match. So, what is the explanation?

A wealth of discussion has generated a host of differing viewpoints. Some scholars assert that Luke's genealogy is that of Mary whereas Matthew's genealogy is that of Joseph. Other scholars *vice versa* but not so commonly. Yet others assert that the genealogies differ because Joseph had two fathers – his natural father, Jacob, and his legal father, Heli (postulated to be Joseph's father's half-brother –same mother, different father - who became Joseph's legal guardian when Joseph's biological father died – keep up!). Others explain the discrepancies by saying that the genealogies were invented as post-rationalisations of the prophecy that the Messiah would be born from David's line. And so it goes on with scholarly essays, hypotheses, and impossible-to-check theories.

More basic questions are these. Who on earth remembered the names of all the ancestors, and why? Just think how hard people have to struggle to trace their families back more than a few generations today – even with the benefit of computer databases. The lists must have been created retrospectively following the birth of Jesus Christ. This either points to someone having a prodigious and remarkable memory, or to the existence of excellent records of births dating back to Adam!

More fundamentally, why even bother to list a genealogy if the father of Jesus Christ is the Holy Ghost and not a human? What does it prove if Joseph who, supposedly, is not the biological father can be shown to be descended from David and Abraham?

And finally, why did Matthew and Luke not list the genealogy as simply being Jesus to Mary to the Holy Ghost to God?

The genealogy of Jesus Christ may be just one of many inconsistencies in the Bible, but it's a vital one if we are to believe in divine Incarnation and subsequent Resurrection after death. Harris (*The End of Faith*, p. 244), references W H Burr's *Self-Contradictions in the Bible (1860)*. Burr lists 144 contradictions including many perfect contradictions: cases in which asserting one proposition invalidates another, such as human versus ghostly impregnation. And yet, we are asked to accept the content of the Bible as the Word of God handed down from generation to generation and supplied as a basis for a religion.

Continuing with the circumstances surrounding the birth of Jesus Christ, let's now examine the possibility of the Immaculate Conception: impregnation and birth without the act of human sexual intercourse.

Immaculate Conception and virgin birth

Did Mary conceive and give birth to Jesus while remaining a virgin?

Christians believe she gave birth to the Son of God after conceiving by the Holy Ghost. Islamists do not believe the 'Son of God' label. They agree that Jesus Christ was a prophet and that he was born of a virgin (*No man has touched me, nor am I an unchaste*, Qur'an 19:20 – 22) but this accorded him no special status *vis-a-vis* God. They point out that Adam was similarly created but was a human, not a divinity. For Muslims, the true and final prophet was Muhammad, who lived some 600 years after Jesus, but even he wasn't the Son of God.

So, what is the truth about the Immaculate Conception? It could all hinge on the translation of a Hebrew word – *almah* – present in the original Hebrew version of the New Testament Gospels. In Hebrew, *almah* means 'young woman' and does not imply a state of virginity. The Hebrew word for a female virgin is *betulah*, also present in the original Hebrew Old Testament (Isaiah 23:4; 23:12; 37:22; 47:1; 62:5). But, it would appear that when the Hebrew scriptures were translated into Greek in the third century by a panel of Hebrew scholars and Jewish rabbis, *almah* was translated into the Greek word *parthenos* meaning 'virgin' rather than *neanis* meaning 'young woman'. This created a range of different translations into English, for example:

> Old Testament: *virgin*, Genesis 24:43; *maid*, Exodus 2:8; *damsels*, Psalm 68:25; *maid*, Proverbs 30:19; *virgin*, Song of Solomon 1:3; 6:8; *virgin*, Isaiah 7:14
>
> New Testament: *virgin*, Matthew 1:22-23
>
> Bible, King James version

Thus was created one of the great cornerstones of Christian beliefs – that Mary, the mother of Jesus Christ, was *virgo intacta* at and after conception and thus both worthy and capable of bearing the Son of God via the Holy Ghost's impregnation.

Matthew and Luke are the only two disciples in the New Testament Gospels to claim that Jesus was conceived by a virgin. Mark and John make no such claim and even suggest that Jesus was illegitimate (an inference from the fact that Jesus is usually referred to as 'the son of Mary' rather than 'the son of Joseph'). Paul attributes Mary and Joseph as being Jesus's natural parents, *seed of David according to the flesh* (Romans 1:3), and that Jesus was *made of woman* (Galatians 4:4), what we might term the normal way.

What are the facts as we know them today? Self fertilization/asexual reproduction, called parthenogenesis from the Greek *parthenos*, does occur in some lower plants and invertebrate animals (animals with no spinal column), examples being water fleas and aphids. It also occurs in some vertebrates, examples being snakes and some species of scorpions, but self-fertilization is not considered possible in the female species of *homo sapiens*, nor in hermaphrodites.[133]

There is a terrible logic here. If Jesus was conceived normally, presumably as a result of intercourse between Mary and her husband Joseph, then he cannot be the Son of God. If this is true, it is highly unlikely that Jesus rose from the dead three days after his crucifixion and went to join God his Father in heaven. Thus, not one but two of the major beliefs of Christianity – the Incarnation (the belief that Jesus was the Son of God, immaculately conceived by Mary) and the Resurrection – tumble and fall into the dust of antique beliefs.

The Immaculate Conception also belies the Roman Catholic Church's teaching that sex is sinful. The original act of sex, expressed symbolically by Eve's seduction of Adam in the Garden of Eden, underlines the Roman Catholic's 'sex is bad, long live celibacy' doctrine and yet without reproductive sex, there would be no Roman Catholics! Where's the logic in condemning the very act that creates the followers of Catholicism? And why must Roman Catholic priests be celibate? We can but conjecture on why enforced celibacy (not married) came about and how it has contributed to or even been the major cause of the penchant for paedophilia among the clergy of the Roman Catholic Church.

---

[133] A human hermaphrodite may possess both fully-functioning male and female sexual reproduction organs but it's highly unlikely that the male organ can reach and penetrate the female organ and thus fertilize an egg. Consequently, human hermaphroditic self-fertilization is not considered possible. If it was however, where would the male-determining Y chromosome come from to cause the birth of a male offspring? Assuming the hermaphrodite to be predominantly female and capable of nurturing an embryo to full term over nine months, 'she' would presumably have two X chromosomes but no Y chromosome. If 'she' was predominantly a 'he', possessing an X and a Y chromosome, would 'he' have all the female bodily apparatus to conceive and carry an embryo to full term? The mind boggles!

Miracles: real or illusions?

The miracle of miracles - what is a miracle? I'll use the first of Merriam-Webster's definition: an extraordinary event manifesting divine intervention in human affairs. The key word is *divine*.

Recently, I watched a YouTube video in which a Taiwanese illusionist, Liu Qian, appeared to pass his hand through a transparent glass tabletop and retrieve some coins held under the table by a witness.[134] Prior to the hand-through-the-tabletop act, Qian passed coins through the table and caught them in a bowl underneath. How did he do it? Was it a miracle?

I know – I just know – that the answer to my question is 'No'. Qian is a magician, an illusionist, similar to the UK's Derren Brown and the USA's David Blaine. Most of us have no idea how they do what they do, despite so-called spoilers on various websites and forums. What we do know is that these performers do not perform miracles. They just perform tricks.

So, did Jesus walk on water, raise the dead (Lazarus), cure the leper, change water into wine, heal a withered hand, restore the sight of two blind men, catch a fish with a coin in its mouth – all in all, perform 37 miracles according to the books of the New Testament?

Many books have been written, both for and against the possibility of such miracles, but, as far as I'm concerned, all the supposed miracles remain to be proven to have been such. If there was a divine intervention, then I cannot argue with the veracity of the event. But, if there was no divine intervention, because such a divinity does not exist, then all the miracles prove is that people as clever as Liu Qian, Derren Brown and David Blaine existed some 2,000 years ago and that they were just as good as modern magicians, illusionists and even scam artists at fooling the crowds.[135]

---

[134] http://www.youtube.com/watch?v=uf_Bcsci-xI or if this link is no longer working, enter the YouTube website at www.youtube.com and search for Liu Qian.

[135] Even as I was finishing this chapter, a British magician called Dynamo, real name Steve Frayne, apparently walked halfway across the surface of the River Thames (27th June, 2011) with no visible means of staying on top of the water and in full view of many onlookers on a nearby bridge. He was picked up mid-river by what might have been a river-police boat. Did he walk on water? Apparently. Was it a miracle? No. What was it? An illusion. How did he do it? I don't know. It drives me nuts!

Creating saints

I wonder also about the Roman Catholic Church's desire to continue to create saints out of people who have recently died.

When Pope Benedict XVI visited the UK in 2010, one of his missions was to set Cardinal John Newman on the path to sainthood. Cardinal Newman was a nineteenth century Englishman who converted from the Anglican teachings to that of the Roman Catholic Church in 1845. For Newman to be canonized and thus become a saint, it's necessary to show that he had been responsible for two posthumous miracles. The Cardinal had performed only one so he could only be beatified (given the title *Blessed*).

The posthumous miracle is purported to have involved one Jack Sullivan and to have occurred in 2001. (Newman died in 1890, before Sullivan was born). Sullivan was suffering from intense postoperative pain following a surgical operation to relieve compression of the spinal cord and nerves. Sullivan, a pious man in training to become a deacon in the Catholic Church, prayed to Newman after he (Sullivan) had watched a program about Newman on television. Sullivan's exact words were 'Please Cardinal Newman, help me to walk so that I can return to classes and be ordained.'[136]

Following the prayer, Sullivan said 'Suddenly I felt an intense heat, like an oven blast, and a strong tingling sensation throughout my whole body. I felt an indescribable sense of joy and peace, and was totally transfixed by what I believed to be God's presence. When I became aware of what was happening around me I was standing upright and I exclaimed to the nurse that I felt no more pain.' The following morning, he woke up pain-free and was able to leave the hospital and complete his studies.

Sullivan is now a fully ordained deacon in the Roman Catholic Church, working in Boston, Massachusetts.

Cynics, including members of the medical profession, argued that what took place was just natural healing. Sullivan, however, is adamant that he was the recipient of a miracle and, after a further eight years of investigation by a Vatican-appointed panel of medical experts (what did they investigate and why did it take eight years?), the recovery was hailed a miracle by the Holy See (the Catholic Government).

---

[136] http://www.bbc.co.uk/news/uk-11186584

Now Newman is just one step away from full sainthood.[137] I assume that the hunt is on for a second posthumous miracle but my question is this – what's the point?

The beatification of Newman was conducted in an open-air park attended by around 50,000 people. Many others are said to have followed the ceremony on television. What did they or the Catholic Church gain from Newman's public beatification? The Catholic Church already has more than 10,000 *beatis* (those who have been blessed) and saints (those who have received full canonization). That's an average of five new beatis/saints per year since the birth of Jesus Christ! Why does the Catholic Church need more? What role do they fulfil? What does the Church do with the beatis and saints it already has? Assuming that a beati or a saint never loses his or her status, will the list just keep on growing or is there a natural limit?

I don't know the answers to these questions but any event that can attract 50,000 people to confirm or reconfirm their faith is no bad thing if you're one of the governors of this faith.

The Ten Commandments

There has been some discussion of the limitations of the Ten Commandments in Chapter 5. What I would like to do now is extend the list of directives based on other statements in the Bible.

The Ten Commandments are very limited. For example, they make no judgment of activities such as slavery, rape, child abuse, bestiality and many other things that would be listed as highly unacceptable in a modern society. However, other parts of the Bible either condemn or condone a variety of practices and in common with authors like Richard Dawkins and Sam Harris, I would like to highlight a few of the bad things that are approved. I accept that many good things are also recommended and approved but given the status of the Bible and the respect it is accorded by Christians world-wide, it behoves us to understand its teaching on a variety of bad practices.

---

[137] As is Mother Teresa of Calcutta. She was beatified in 2002 based on the miraculous healing of a cancerous tumour in an Indian woman, Monica Besra. Besra was receiving conventional medical treatment at the time and informed medical opinion was that the treatment had worked as expected, or that, retrospectively, the tumour was not cancerous. But Besra maintained that the tumour was cured by light emanating from a locket containing a picture of Mother Teresa. The medical records are not available for scrutiny. They are held by a Roman Catholic religious order called the Missions of Charities and all attempts to see these records have been refused. The Mission of Charities was founded by Mother Teresa. Enough said!

Christianity: Not What It Seems

Here's a sample of bad behaviour that's approved in the Bible, the second most influential book ever written.[138] Note that the following list is very male-dominated and ultra misogynistic.

- Infants of slain enemies can be dashed to pieces as acts of revenge. Hosea 13:16, Isaiah 13:16,
- Women pregnant with child, *fruit of the womb*, can be ripped open. Hosea 13:16, Isaiah 13:18, 2 Kings 15:16
- Male enemies can be circumcised after they've been slain. 1 Samuel 18:27
- Women can be donated as a reward to the perpetrators of wholesale slaughter in the name of God. 1 Samuel 18:27
- Dead enemies can be decapitated and their heads displayed at city entrances. 2 Kings 10:7-8
- In times of famine, cannibalism is approved. Your sons can be killed, cooked and eaten. 2 Kings 6:28-29
- The females of captured enemies can be ravished or killed, except *women children that have not known a man*, Isaiah 13:16, ... or they can be kept for sexual purposes. Numbers 31:17-18
- Polygamy on a grand scale is acceptable. 1 Kings 11:3 (King Solomon had 700 wives and a further 300 concubines), Matthew 25 (Parable of Ten Virgins)
- Females must be subservient to males. They must: live in fear, submit to sexual demands, keep silent (especially in a church), dress modestly, and be the property of the male. 1 Corinthians 14:34-35, 1 Timothy 2:11-12, 1 Peter 3:1-7
- Female pre-marital sex is condemned with death by stoning as the punishment. Similarly for men found guilty of adultery. Deuteronomy 22:20-21
- Female slaves can be used for sexual purposes. Exodus 21:7-11
- Homosexuals must be killed. Leviticus 20:13, Romans 1:24-32
- Virgins can be used to restore flagging male sexual powers. 1 Kings 1:1-3
- Gluttons and drunkards can be stoned to death. Deuteronomy 21:18-21
- Corporate punishment of children is approved – *beat with a rod*. Proverbs 23:13-14

No further comment is needed.

---

[138] *I Ching*, a fifth century BCE Chinese classic text, is listed as number one. http://en.wikipedia.org/wiki/The_100_Most_Influential_Books_Ever_Written

Conclusions

Christianity has come a long way in the last two thousand years. Its many variations and ornate trappings have been accompanied by a history of corruption, murder and mayhem plus excessive mind control based on unsubstantiated beliefs, but the basic tenets of virgin conception and birth plus resurrection after clinical death do not stand up to scientific scrutiny. Nor do supposed miracles. The Bible is riddled with inconsistencies, ambiguities, unethical advice and unsubstantiated historical statements. And yet the contents of the book are considered to be the foundation of a religion that encompasses 2.2 billion people and is rated as the world's number one religion.[139]

In my opinion, Christianity, like all other major religions, has become big business – a means of generating wealth by playing on the superstitions and ignorance of people who are seduced by its trappings and dogmas and are unaware of or unconcerned by its sinister past. Basically, cashing in on God. I will say more about this in the final chapter.

(^_^)

---

[139] http://en.wikipedia.org/wiki/Christianity#Demographics

Chapter 8
Islam And Armageddon

'Let those that would exchange the life of this world for the hereafter, fight for the cause of God; whoever fights for the cause of God, whether he dies or triumphs, We shall richly reward him ...The true believers fight for the cause of God, but the infidels fight for the devil.'

Qur'an 4:74 – 78

'Surely, if we could create the world anew, the practice of organizing our lives around untestable propositions found in ancient literature – to say nothing of killing and dying for them – would be impossible to justify.'

Sam Harris, The End of Faith, p. 24

Hard-Line Islam

This book, and especially this chapter, was motivated by my reading and re-reading of Sam Harris's provocative 2005 book, *The End of Faith*. As mentioned in Chapter 1, my reaction and response was originally intended to be a private essay to my granddaughters to be read when they reach an age when world affairs and the role of religion therein mattered to them. Harris paints a very black picture of Islam, arguing that the Muslims' total and unquestionable belief in God (*Allah*) and in the Qur'an as a basis for society is leading us inexorably towards Armageddon. Is this true?

In this chapter, I'll explore current (2011) general attitudes towards Islam and the impact the religion is having on non-Islamic societies. I will also comment on my own feelings about Islam and, as you'll see, they are somewhat different to those of Harris. I have tried to keep an open mind and to be as objective as I can given that I have an engineering and science background.

First, though, a personal anecdote ...

Several years ago, when I was still working as an electronics engineer, I flew from London to Dallas – a nine-hour non-stop flight. Once I had boarded the aircraft, I discovered that I was seated next to a Muslim woman clad head to foot in a *burqa*.[140] My heart sank at the

---

[140] Also spelt *burka*, *burkha* or *burqua* at least. The Arabic word *burqa* implies the combination of a *jilbab* (loose full-body covering), *hijab* (head covering) and *niqab* (face veil).

sight of the *burqa* but social etiquette and a full aircraft forbade any attempt to change my seat. So I followed my normal practice of settling in and opening a book.

Sometime into the flight, when the first meal had been served, the *burqa*-clad lady offered me some unwanted food on her tray. Or maybe it was a gambit to start a conversation? I will never know because I refused the offer, indicating that I was wearing hearing aids and would not be able to hear what she said. (There's partial truth here. By then, I had started to become hard of hearing and I was wearing aids, but I might still have been able to engage in conversation.) She acknowledged my excuse and we spent the rest of the flight in silence.

After the aircraft had landed and we had gone our separate ways, I felt guilty. I wondered why. Did I hate women? No. Did I hate Muslims? Also no. Did I hate what the *burqa* represented? Well, yes.

Much has been written about the suppression of women in hard-line Islamic societies. For many, myself included, the *burqa* is a visible and outrageous symbol of suppression, oppression and imprisonment of adult females. It flies in the face of enlightened societies' views on the equality of men and women and, as a symbol, suggests subservience and religious slavery. When I sat down on that aircraft, my whole body reacted with loathing towards the garment. Retrospectively, had the lady been willing, it might have given me a golden opportunity to ask why she wore such a garment, to further my own understanding of Islam and explore my own prejudices. But, courage failed me and the opportunity passed me by.

Many think that the *burqa* is an extreme manifestation of the Sharia, the sacred law of Islam. But is it? Sharia stems from two primary sources: the Qur'an and the Sunnah. The Sunnah is a record of Muhammad's personal sayings, habits and codes of conduct. Some consider the Sunnah to be part of the general body of interpretative works called the Hadith; others that the Sunnah is separate from the Hadith. But neither the Qur'an nor the Sunnah mandates complete covering of the female body. As a result, the *hijab* (headscarf accompanied by modest body clothing) is worn in most Muslim countries, with or without a *niqab* (face veil).

So where did the *burqa* come from? It is thought to have originated in either Persia or Afghanistan long before Islam was established. And why was it invented? Allegedly to stop men looking at the wives and concubines of the rich. Nothing to do with religion then; just rich men stopping poor men from ogling their women in the harem!

Nowadays, it isn't just non-Muslims who see the *burqa* as a prominent symbol of oppression – it is decried by most moderate Islamic clerics and societies. The governments of France and Belgium have banned its wearing in public and the Italian government looks set to follow suit. In the Muslim world, Turkey and Tunisia prohibit the wearing of the *burqa* in public buildings. But others have different ideas.

One of the most extreme cases was Afghanistan where, when the Taliban were in control, women had to wear the *burqa* in public. It was just one of the ways the group imposed its control on society. Take a look at the other laws it put in place ...

(The following list is reprinted with permission from pages 247-9 of Khaled Hosseini's excellent 2007 novel *A Thousand Splendid Suns*, Bloomsbury Publishing plc, about life for women in Afghanistan in the period 1960 – 2000. Although a work of fiction, the book is very factual about the laws imposed after the Taliban took control of most of Afghanistan in 1996.)

Our watan (nation, country) is now known as the Islamic Emirate of Afghanistan. These are the laws that we will enforce and you will obey.

- *All citizens must pray five times a day. If it is prayer time and you are caught doing something other, you will be beaten*
- *All men will grow their beards. The correct length is at least one clenched fist beneath the chin. If you do not abide by this, you will be beaten.*
- *All boys will wear turbans. Boys in grade one through six will wear black turbans, higher grades will wear white. All boys will wear Islamic clothes. Shirt collars will be buttoned.*
- *Singing is forbidden.*
- *Dancing is forbidden.*
- *Playing cards, playing chess, gambling and kite flying[141] are forbidden.*
- *Writing books, watching films and painting pictures are forbidden.*
- *If you keep parakeets, you will be beaten. Your birds will be killed.*
- *If you steal, your hand will be cut off at the wrist. If you steal again, your foot will be cut off.*
- *If you are not Muslim, do not worship where you can be seen by Muslims. If you do, you will be beaten and imprisoned. If you are caught trying to convert a Muslim to your faith, you will be executed.*

---

[141] A long-time tradition in Afghanistan, well described in Khaled Hosseini's first novel, *The Kite Runner*, published in 2003.

Attention women:
- *You will stay in your homes at all times. It is not proper for women to wander aimlessly about the streets. If you go outside, you must be accompanied by a mahram (male relative). If you are caught alone on the street you will be beaten and sent home.*
- *You will not in any circumstance, show your face. You will cover with a burqa when outside. If you do not, you will be severely beaten.*
- *Cosmetics are forbidden.*
- *Jewellery is forbidden.*
- *You will not wear charming clothes.*
- *You will not speak unless spoken to.*
- *You will not make eye contact with men.*
- *You will not laugh in public. If you do, you will be beaten.*
- *Girls are forbidden from attending school. All schools for girls will be closed immediately.*
- *Women are forbidden from working.*
- *If you are found guilty of adultery, you will be stoned to death.*[142]

Listen. Listen well. Obey. Allahu-Akbar (God is Great).

© Hosseini, 2007, *A Thousand Splendid Suns*, Bloomsbury Publishing Plc. Reprinted with permission.

Quite apart from the pettiness of some of these laws – 'don't keep parakeets' and 'no kite flying', for example – they go right to the heart of extreme Islam. The general aim is to subjugate and control the population, governing through fear and dogma. But for women, they go several steps further, advocating total subservience – no education, no job, no dressing up – and making no allowance for any who are not Muslim.

The Taliban Sharia represents the extreme of what must qualify to be the most controlling religion in the world today. Islam is based on a book recording the sayings of a man supposedly in contact with God via an angel called Gabriel. Muslims believe that the words are, literally, the words of God and therefore sacrosanct. This can lead to some cruel and, at times, barbaric interpretations. Every day, new stories come to light: honour killings (surely a macabre oxymoron?), yet another *fatwa*[143] against an aspiring author, outrage if someone

---

[142] Adulterers were publically stoned to death or otherwise executed in what was the football stadium in Kabul.
[143] Strictly speaking, a *fatwa* is an authoritative opinion on some question of religious interpretation but the term is also seen by some Muslims as permission to perform

threatens to burn a copy of the Qur'an, a flogging to death of a young girl who was first beaten and then raped by an older male relative (see Unfolding Events later in this chapter), calls to behead a Dutch politician (Geert Wilders) who spoke out against encroaching Islam in Europe, intolerance to all other religions and especially to atheists (seen to be infidels), and so on.

Sam Harris states 'We are at war with Islam' (*The End of Faith*, p. 109). It would probably be better to say that 'Islam is at war with apostates and infidels.' Islam, like Christianity in the past, is a religion of conquest and subjugation. The Qur'an is full of exhortations to seek out and kill those who do not believe in the rules, principles, dogmas and beliefs laid down in the 'book of God'. The very word *jihad* means a call to war – a Holy War. Merriam-Webster defines *jihad* to be:

1 : a holy war waged on behalf of Islam *as a religious duty* (My italics)
2 : a crusade for a principle or belief

According to those who interpret the Qur'an, it is the duty of every Muslim to wage *jihadic* war using whatever means is appropriate. Fortunately, most Muslims are moderate in their approach, preferring argument and persuasion to knives and guns. But every now and then, extremist methods come to the fore: suicide bombings, out-and-out warfare, honour killings (especially if a Muslim girl wants to marry a non-Muslim boy, but not as often in the opposite case), and executions by a variety of techniques including throat cutting, immolation, stoning, whipping or even gunshot. Moderate Muslims may not approve of such actions, but sometimes they are either slow to criticise or to condemn them.

This is the insidious problem of Islam: it neither shows mercy nor takes prisoners. Both the Qur'an and the Hadith are littered with calls to arms (take a look at Harris, *The End of Faith*, pp. 32-33, p.112) and a general hatred of infidels.

---

some deed: witness the *fatwa* issued by Ayatollah Ruhollah Khomeini in 1989 pronouncing a death sentence on author Salman Rushdie for writing his book *The Satanic Verses*. Witness also the two *fatwas* issued by Osama bin Laden, who said it was permissible for Muslims to kill US civilians and military personnel anywhere until the US withdrew support for Israel and pulled out all military forces from Islamic countries.

Islam and war

Harris (*The End of Faith*, pp. 117-123) devotes more than five pages of his book to a list of quotations from the Qur'an that vilify infidels. To get a flavour of the sentiments expressed, both in the Qur'an and in the Hadith, here are some quotations that I snagged from an, admittedly, anti-Islam website maintained by a Roman Catholic Church organisation.[144]

- *Muslims are encouraged to be wholly occupied with fighting for Allah's cause.* Hadith Sahih Bukhari 3:46: 694, Hadith Sahih Muslim 1:149
- *Allah will give a far richer recompense to those who fight for him.* Qur'an 4:95
- *Regarding infidels (unbelievers), they are the Muslim's inveterate enemies.* Qur'an 4:101.
- *Muslims are to seize them (infidels) and put them to death wherever you find them, kill them wherever you find them, seek out the enemies of Islam relentlessly.* Qur'an 4:89.
- *Kill the infidels wherever you find (them). Fight them until Islam reigns supreme.* Qur'an 2:191-193.
- *Cut off their heads, and cut off the tips of their fingers.* Qur'an 8:12
- *If a Muslim does not go to war, Allah will punish with a severe punishment.* Qur'an 9:39.
- *A Muslim is to be told the heat of war is fierce, but more fierce is the heat of Hell-fire.* Qur'an 9:81
- *A Muslim must strive for the cause of God.* Qur'an 22:78
- *Muslims must make war on the infidels (unbelievers) who live around them.* Qur'an 9:123
- *Muslims are to be harsh and stern against the disbelievers.* Qur'an 48:29
- *A Muslim should eat from the spoils you have earned (from fighting).* Qur'an 8:69
- *A Muslim can kill any person he wishes if it be a just cause.* Qur'an 17:33. (See later for more on this statement.)
- *Allah loves those who fight for his cause.* Qur'an 61:4
- *Anyone who fights against Allah or renounces Islam in favour of another religion shall be slain or crucified or have their hands and feet cut off alternative sides.* Qur'an 5:33

---

[144] http://www.catholic.org/international/international_story.php?id=31347 and reprinted with the permission of Catholic Online. Some of the referenced sources on this website are incorrect. I've corrected the sources, and sometimes the text, in the statements above.

- *Whoever changes his Islamic religion, kill him.* .Hadith Sahih Bukhari 9:57
- *So when the sacred months have passed away, then slay the idolaters wherever you find them, and take them captives and besiege them and lie in wait for them in every ambush, then if they repent and keep up prayer and pay the poor-rate, leave their way free to them; surely Allah is Forgiving, Merciful.* Qur'an 9:5
- *Take him and fetter him and expose him to hell fire.* Quran 69:30-37
- *Know that paradise is under the shades of swords.* Hadith Sahih Bukhari 4:52:73. In other words, those that would have peace must be ready for war although an alternative interpretation could be that the surest way to Paradise is by means of *jihad*.

Taken together, the quotations provide an undeniable link between Islam and the use of violence to achieve world dominance of the Islamic religion. But remember, the Qur'an is not alone in suggesting courses of action that, today, seem grossly inappropriate. The Old Testament lists death by stoning as the punishment for taking the Lord's name in vain (Leviticus, 24:16); working on the Sabbath (Exodus 31:15); cursing one's mother or father (Exodus 21:17); and adultery (Leviticus 20:10). If we obeyed any one of these directives literally, there would be no further need to worry about the world's exploding population – at least, not until we run out of stones!

Note also that the Islamic Holy War is aimed at apostates as well as infidels. Apostates are people who abandon or renounce their faith. If they used to be Muslim, the Hadith is firm on their fate – death, nothing less.[145] This means that if moderate or liberal-thinking Muslims attempt to modify their faith or make statements that might be considered unorthodox or in some way considered a threat to core Muslim beliefs, then they could be killed.

The implication of this is enormous. Attempts to modernise the tenets of the Islamic religion cannot be undertaken lightly or without due examination of the likely impact on modernisers. As a result, the religion has stagnated, some say for at least six hundred years, causing a massive mismatch between secular twenty-first century

---

[145] The Qur'an does not advocate death as such – see Qur'an 3:86-91 which promises 'Allah's curse and non-acceptance of a subsequent repentance unless the repentance is made quickly and honestly'. The Qur'an merely details the punishments that'll happen to the apostate in the next world. But given the fundamental belief in the next world as part of a continuation of existence beyond human life, the penalties for being an apostate are severe, if not extreme. The Hadith however, is explicit: 'Whoever changes his Islamic religion, kill him.' Hadith Sahih Al-Bukhari, 9:57

society and the beliefs of some Muslims. For example, it is acceptable for non-Muslim Western Europeans to consume alcoholic drinks, wear bikinis in public (especially if they are nubile females), eat the flesh of pigs, have sex before marriage (and usually without implying marriage!), use the left hand as well as the right for both eating and drinking, eat non-halal food, speak against God, and so on. For Muslims, each of these things is forbidden. As a result, it has proved difficult to integrate Muslims into West European societies. At best, they've been resented and feared by liberal westerners. At worst, their arrival has increased racist tensions, caused riots and, occasionally, led to deaths. Unless some major liberation of thought takes place within the central teachings of Islam, the situation could well get worse. As Harris points out:

> '... we will see that in our opposition to the worldview of Islam, we confront a civilization with an arrested history. It is as though a portal in time has opened and fourteenth-century hordes are pouring into our world. Unfortunately, they are armed with twenty-first-century weapons.'
> Sam Harris, *End of Faith*, p. 106-107.

Of course, I'm painting an extreme picture, as does Harris. Islam is not one coherent set of beliefs and associated societies. There are many Muslim scholars who have advocated major changes to the tenets of Islam, and are still doing so. There are also many different interpretations of Islam split along either dogmatic boundaries (Sunni, Shi'a, Sufi, Wahhabi ...) or country borders (Iran, Egypt, Afghanistan ...). In Egypt, for example, it's considered okay to watch the seductive and salacious weavings of belly dancers while drinking alcoholic beverages.[146] This gives us hope that, eventually, Islam will modernise to the point where it no longer sees world dominance as one of its main aims. But who is going to explain all this to the young male or, these days, female, suicide bomber strapped up with enough munitions to kill and maim many innocent men, women and children

---

[146] This might change. As I was writing this chapter (Spring/Summer 2011), the Middle East and North African Arab nations were in turmoil: Tunisia, Egypt, Syria, Libya, Bahrain, Yemen with maybe more countries to follow. Dubbed the *Arab Spring*, the fear among some political and theological commentators is that the Egyptian Muslim Brotherhood (slogan 'Islam is the solution') will take advantage of both the unrest and the calls for democracy to reassert its position and become a dominant Islamic force in the reshaping of the political structures of these countries. See the section entitled Unfolding Events later in this chapter for more comment.

in the name of a religious belief that cannot be proved or in any other way substantiated or justified?

Islam and God

> *'Allah! There is no God save Him, the Living, the External. Neither slumber nor sleep overtake Him; to Him belongs what is in the heavens and earth. Who will intercede with Him except by His leave? He knows what is before them and what is behind them, while they grasp nothing of His knowledge except what He wills. His throne encompasses the heavens and the earth, and He never wearies of keeping them. He is the Supreme, the Tremendous.'*
>
> Qur'an 2.255

Consider the significance of the Islamic name for God – *Allah*. Literally, it's a contraction of the Arabic *al-ilah*, The God. According to the Qur'an, there is only one God and no other God is permissible. There cannot be separate Gods for Jews or Christians. These would be false gods, so anyone worshipping them is *de facto* an infidel. Because Islam tolerates no other God, it tolerates no other religion.

This stance, coupled with Islam's call for followers to make war on all infidels, is what worries others about the religion. Those of other faiths rarely make calls for war in the name of their deities. Mostly, they show tolerance and respect to those that have different beliefs. Ironically, an unbiased outsider would say that Yahweh, God, *Allah*, Jehovah, Supreme Creator, *Brahma*, and so on are all different names for the same entity. So what's the problem? If each god claims to have created the earth and its contents, then all the gods must be the same god. There can only be one supernatural creator.

I have yet to find a rational explanation for why Muslims not only consider all other gods false but require them to be vilified and their followers killed.

Islam and censorship

Consider also the popular misconception, even among Muslims, that any image – statue, painting, cartoon – of Muhammad is forbidden. This isn't actually the case, but it is with respect to images of *Allah*. Nowhere in the Qur'an are images of Muhammad forbidden, although the document does forbid idolatry and the worshipping of statues or pictures. But the Hadith of Sunni Muslims – the majority of Muslims – does forbid 'images of animals or people to exist, especially in the home',[147] and says that those who make or display such images, be they Muslim or non-Muslim, will be punished on the Day of Resurrection (Judgment Day) unless they 'can breathe soul into their creations'. Consequently, although Muhammad's name is not expressly mentioned in the Hadith rulings, neither his image nor any other image of an animal or person is acceptable to Sunni Muslims. (What is not clear is how a devout Sunni Muslim can read an illustrated story book to a child, or read a magazine or newspaper without feeling that a basic Islamic law is being broken?)

When I searched the internet for images tagged 'Muhammad the Prophet', almost five million results were reported! Not all the images were of Muhammad but many were. So why was so much fuss made when the Danish newspaper *Jyllands-Posten* featured cartoons of Muhammad in September 2005? In the uproar that resulted five months later (why did it take five months?), Muslims demonstrated outside Danish Embassies (why? – the Danish government had nothing to do with the publication of the cartoons), Danish flags were burnt, *fatwas* were issued against the cartoonists, Christian churches were burned down (why Christian?), people died in Libya (in the Italian consulate – why the Italians?) and in Nigeria (black Christians – again, why Christians?).

If you search online for images tagged 'Muslim protesters', you will find photographs of demonstrators displaying banners in London following the publication of the *Jyllands-Posten* cartoons, and other supposedly anti-Islamic events. The placards feature slogans such as:

- Slay/behead/butcher/massacre/exterminate those who insult/mock Islam. (Pick your favourite frontend and backend verbs.)
- Europe will pay, demolition is on its way.
- Europe, take some lessons from 9/11
- Insult to the Prophet is an insult to Islam.
- Freedom of expression, go to hell. (My favourite. Does the banner holder realize the irony of his slogan?)
- Islam will dominate the world.
- Europe is the cancer. Islam is the answer.

And held by women (I assume!) wearing *burqas*:

- Be prepared for the real holocaust.
- The veil is womens (sic) liberation.

---

[147] http://en.wikipedia.org/wiki/Depictions_of_Muhammad

- Hajib liberates, France oppresses.

A more recent example of censorship, in this case self-imposed, was the planned publication of Sherry Jones's book *The Jewel in the Medina* by publisher Random House in 2008. The book gives a fictionalised account of the life of Aisha, Muhammad's alleged six-year old bride mentioned earlier in Chapter 5. The book wasn't especially salacious when describing Aisha's deflowering by Muhammad – in fact, Sherry Jones's writing style has been likened to that of a Mills and Boon author – but Random House decided to stop publication at the eleventh hour for fear that it would inspire violent reactions from Muslims on a par with those that followed publication of the *Jyllands-Posten* cartoons. Eventually published by Beaufort Books, the book proved far less contentious than had been expected. To date, there have been no violent reactions.[148] Perhaps those who incite such reactions have come to their senses?

Suicide bombers

Let's turn now to the phenomenon and psyche of the suicide bomber, the terrorist's ultimate weapon.

Suicide bombing came to prominence in the 1980s. The first to use it were the Lebanese Shi'a Hezbollah, but the Sri Lankan Liberation Tigers of Tamil Eelam (the Tamil Tigers) came a close second. Since then, the tactic has been used by extremist factions across the Middle East, Turkey, Indonesia, India, Afghanistan, Pakistan, Russia, USA, Spain and the UK.

What distinguishes extremist organisations like these from groups like the FARC (Colombia), ETA Basque Separatists (Spain) and even the IRA (Northern Ireland) is that, with one exception (the Tamil Tigers), their members are radicalised Muslims – people who have an extreme view of Islam, and are sometimes called fundamentalists or extremists as a result. (The Tamil Tigers brought together Hindu, Tamil and Marxist revolutionaries.)

But turning yourself into a bomb is an extreme step even for a fanatic, so why do radicalised Muslims do it? In short, they are driven by a combination of three motivating factors: religious zeal, in which traditional familial kinship has been replaced by a religious kinship;

---

[148] The book has been criticised by reviewers for historical inaccuracies, lightweight literary style and even anti-Islamic sentiments. Sherry Jones has now written a sequel called *The Sword of Medina* (Beaufort Books, 2009). I must confess that I've not read either of Jones's novels.

political gain; and ethnic grievances. But the thing that dominates their thoughts as they prepare to carry out their atrocities is their belief that they will be rewarded in Paradise by, to use the words of the Qur'an, *'72 pure companions, beautiful of eye'*, (both virgin maidens and sexually-available young boys), *'in the land of pure water, fresh milk, delectable wines'* (forbidden during earthly existence but non-intoxicating in Paradise!) *'and clear honey, dressed in fine green silk and rich brocades, and wearing silver bracelets'* (why not gold?).

The dark-eyed virgins available for intercourse (*'high-bosomed, chaste and fair as corals and rubies, bashful'*), or, if preferred, young boys available for sodomy (*'handsome as pearls well guarded, of perpetual freshness'*) are mentioned in several places in the Qur'an: verses 37:40-48, 44:51-55, 52:17-20, 55:56-58, 55:70-77, 56:7-40, 78:31 for the virgins, and verses 52:24, 56:17, 76:19 for the young boys.

No other religion offers such a guaranteed X-rated reward in return for what can only be described as pre-meditated murder.

Elements of this reward, sometimes disrespectfully referred to as *Allah's Brothel*, can be found in the Qur'an as above, and also in the Hadith:[149]

> Hadith reads literally as follows: *Sawda (Tirmidhi's grandfather) reported that he heard from Abdullah, who received from Rishdin b. Sa'd, who in turn learned from Amr b. al-Harith, from Darraj, from Abul-Haytham, from Abu Sa'id al-Khudri, who received it from the Apostle of God [Muhammad]: The least [reward] for the people of Heaven is 80,000 servants and 72 wives, over which stands a dome of pearls, aquamarine and ruby, as [wide as the distance] between al-Jaabiyya (a Damascus suburb) and San'a (Yemen).*
> Hadith Sunan al-Tirmidhi Hadith 2562 (Ch. 23)

Failed suicide bombers (an interesting concept!) have attested to their belief that they would have received 72 virgins plus all the food and wine they could consume had they succeeded. Surely a hedonistic but out-dated concept of Paradise? For this, they were prepared to disintegrate themselves and others close by in what Muslims refer to as sacred explosions. Why? With the exception of the *72 pure companions*, I have access to all the things on offer at my local supermarket, jewellery and department stores. There's even doubt about the promise of *72 pure companions*. The Arabic word used in the

---

[149] Visit http://sites.google.com/site/islamicscripturesunveiled/Home/paradise_lust and http://www.islam-watch.org/Brahmachari/Destination-Allah-Brothel.htm for a more-complete anthology of the origins of the rewards cited above.

Qur'an is *houri*, usually understood to mean 'a pure companion, beautiful of eye'. ('Virgin' seems to be an alternative translation of *houri* arising from its conversion into various European languages.) Christoph Luxenberg, in his 2007 book *Syro-Aramaic Reading of the Koran: A Contribution to the Decoding of the Language of the Koran*, said the word is derived from an earlier Syro-Aramaic word, *hur*, meaning 'white grape' or 'white raisins of crystal clarity'. If the intention was to reward a suicide bomber with 72 white grapes, then I can get them in my local supermarket as well![150]

So what is it that motivates a bomber to commit suicide in such a spectacular and devastating manner? And given the sexual repression of devoted followers of Islam, is this really what they crave as they activate the detonator? How can suicide bombers enjoy all these pleasures of the flesh if their body parts are disconnected and spread over a wide area back on earth? Even God, if he existed, would have a hard time re-assembling a disintegrated body!

Note as well that the Qur'an expressly forbids suicide, stating that those who commit it will be roasted in a Hell fire:

> *Do not kill yourselves, for Allah is compassionate towards you. Whoever does so, in transgression and wrongfully, We shall roast in a fire, and that is an easy matter for Allah.*
>
> Qur'an 4:29-30

Those who commit suicide will also be forbidden entry into Paradise:

> *A man was inflicted with wounds and he committed suicide, and so Allah said: My slave has caused death on himself hurriedly, so I forbid Paradise for him.*
>
> Hadith Sahih Bukhari 2.445

And they will be punished in Hell by whatever means they used for suicide.

> *He who commits suicide by throttling shall keep on throttling himself in the Hell Fire (forever) and he who commits suicide by stabbing himself shall keep on stabbing himself in the Hell-Fire.*
>
> Hadith Sahih Bukhari 2.445-6

---

[150] See http://www.guardian.co.uk/books/2002/jan/12/books.guardianreview5 for a review of the original 2002 German-language version of Luxenberg's book.

(As Hadith Sahih Bukhari 7:670 points out, this also applies to those who jump off cliffs, poison themselves, or use an iron weapon to end their lives.)

In fact, the very term 'suicide bomber' is a misnomer. No devout Muslim about to dismantle their body in the name of Islam would use the term – to do so would guarantee a one-way ticket to the fires of Hell. So, the outlook for a would-be suicide bomber looks bleak.

But here comes the twist - martyrdom is fine!

Strictly speaking, a religious martyr is someone who voluntarily or otherwise suffers death as a penalty for refusing to renounce or confess to a religious belief. Think Socrates, Joan of Arc, Martin Luther King Jr, and even Jesus Christ. But Islam redefines the word to mean someone who deliberately kills non-believers (the enemies of Islam) in the name of *Allah* and sacrifices their own life in the process. This twist in the meaning is supported by various verses in both the Qur'an and the Hadith, as we will see in a minute.

Dawkins has described the Qur'an as a 'pick 'n mix document'. It's a good description. The Qur'an, like the later Hadith, is full of omissions,[151] ambiguity and even contradictions,[152] In this respect, it is not unique – the Jewish and Christian Bibles are the same.

The problem is that ambiguities leave room for interpretative manoeuvring to suit other purposes – political, social engineering, manipulation of a population, or rabble-rousing and mischief-making.

There's an army of imams (those who lead prayers),[153] mullahs (Southeast Asian name for an imam), muftis (Islamic scholars who interpret or expound Islamic Sharia law), and Ayatollahs (chief muftis, similar to Anglican Bishops or Roman Catholic Cardinals) who make a living out of interpretations of Sharia based on the Qur'an and various Hadith. It's a business, like any other business, and the Web is bursting with sites that interpret questions of basic meaning, ambiguity and contradictions and reel off quotable references to argue points one way or the other.

---

[151] Is polygamy, widely practiced in Muhammad's time, permitted? Is slavery, also widely practiced at the time, condemned? The answers are not given in the Qur'an.

[152] For example, in various parts of the Qur'an, the first Muslim is cited to be either Muhammad [6:14, 6:163], Moses (Musa) [7:143], some Egyptians [26:51], Abraham (Ibrahim) [2:127-133, 3:67] or Adam [2:37]. The truth is out there somewhere!

[153] Sunni Muslims, comprising around 90% of the world's Muslim population, don't have a rigid clerical structure and their imams are just people who are deemed capable of leading worship and interpreting the Qur'an and Hadith. Shi'a imams are considered to be direct descendants of Muhammad and possessed of divine knowledge, authority and infallibility.

But, do not be misled by semantics. The suicide bomber is neither a martyr nor a hero. The suicide bomber is, quite simply, a murderer – someone condemned by most judicial systems known to civilised man, including some versions of Islamic Sharia law. But none of this seems to deter radicalised Muslim suicide bombers.

Here's what the Qur'an has to say about those who murder others in *Allah*'s name.

> *Do not consider those killed [while engaging] in God's cause dead. Rather, they live with their Lord, who sustains them!*
>
> Qur'an 3:169

> *Let those fight in the way of Allah who sell the life of this world for the other. Whoso fighteth in the way of Allah, be he slain or be he victorious, on him We shall bestow a vast reward.*
>
> Qur'an 4:74

> *Allah hath purchased of the believers their persons and their goods; for theirs (in return) is the garden (of Paradise): they fight in His cause, and slay and are slain: a promise binding on Him in truth, through the Law, the Gospel, and the Qur'an: and who is more faithful to his covenant than Allah? then rejoice in the bargain which ye have concluded: that is the achievement supreme.*
>
> Qur'an 9:111

> *And do not kill the soul which Allah has forbidden, except by right.*
>
> Qur'an 17:33

This last verse is used by suicide bombers to justify the deaths of innocent bystanders (called *witnesses*) who, for all the bombers know, might also be believers. Thirty-one Muslims, including a seven-month pregnant mother, died in the 9/11 attack on the Twin Towers.[154] Did they die happily knowing they would be rewarded in Paradise just as surely as Mohamed Atta and his fellow hijackers? Or did they die screaming at the sheer horror of the attack on their workplace and with no understanding of who perpetuated the attack, or why?

---

[154] http://islam.about.com/od/terrorism/a/Muslim-Victims-Of-9-11-Attack.htm

The danger of quoting from the Qur'an

While I was checking the textual correctness of the quotations from the Qur'an and Hadith in this chapter, I came across a variety of different wordings depending on who had done the translation from the original Arabic. For example, for Qur'an 17:33, an important verse noted above, I found the following four alternatives:

1. *And do not kill the soul which Allah has forbidden, except by right.*
2. *You shall not kill any person – for God has made life sacred – except in the course of justice.*
3. *Nor take life – which Allah has made sacred – except for just cause.*
4. *And slay not the life, which Allah hath forbidden, save by right.*

Do they all say the same thing? What's meant by 'except by right', 'in the course of justice', 'except for just cause', 'save by right'? The various versions of the Qur'an do not elaborate. Therein lays the danger!

In the Hadith, martyrdom is viewed as follows:

> *The words of Muhammad: 'I would love to be martyred in Allah's Cause and then get resurrected and then get martyred, and then get resurrected again and then get martyred and then get resurrected again and then get martyred.'*
>
> Hadith Sahih Bukhari 52:54

> *During the battle of Uhud, Muhammad was desperate to push men into battle. He promised paradise for those who would martyr themselves, prompting a young man who was eating dates to throw them away and rush to his death.*
>
> Hadith Sahih Muslim 20:4678

> *Nobody who enters Paradise will (ever like to) return to this world even if he were offered everything on the surface of the earth (as an inducement) except the martyr who will desire to return to this world and be killed ten times for the sake of the great honour that has been bestowed upon him.*
>
> Hadith Sahih Muslim 20.4635

> *If anyone fights in Allah's path as long as the time between two milkings of a she-camel, Paradise will be assured for him. If anyone*

sincerely asks Allah for being killed and then dies or is killed, there will be a reward of a martyr for him.
                                            Hadith Sunan Abu Dawud, 14:2535

It has been argued that there are many explanations for wanting or succumbing to the exhortations of others to become a suicide bomber:

- frustration or despair at the oppression and loss of freedom afforded by a prevailing political situation;
- a personal revenge for an attack that caused the loss of life of family members;
- a loss of purpose in life (linked to frustration and despair as above);
- loneliness;
- a desire to please God with the ultimate sacrifice (a deeply religious reason), and, above all;
- a profound belief that the ending of one's life is but one stage in the cycle of existence and that Paradise awaits complete with a surfeit of sex, food and drink.

How can this be? How can individuals get to the point where they willingly kill themselves with the sole objective of murdering other human beings? The answer for the Muslim suicide bomber has to be mind control, also known as brainwashing– the subversion of the mind[155] of an individual to control their thought processes, emotions and subsequent actions.[156]

Mind control is what induced more than 900 people to commit mass suicide in Jonestown in 1978. Mind control is what caused Aztec warriors to willingly (maybe?) submit to sacrificial death at the hands of an Aztec priest armed with an obsidian knife. Mind control is what motivated Japanese aircraft pilots, the *kamikaze*, to fly their aircraft into an enemy target during the Second World War. Mind control is insidious, life-threatening and the central force behind Islamic suicide bombers, and much more as we've seen in earlier chapters.

---

[155] Used here to mean that part of us that controls the ability to think rationally and make decisions that reflect personal ethics and morality and, normally, within accepted social behaviour.

[156] These ideas are explored in John Updike's 2006 novel, *Terrorist*, which tells the story of a New Jersey teenage Muslim boy, Ahmad, who is coerced into becoming a suicide bomber by his local imam, Shaikh Rashid. Simultaneously, Ahmad is struggling to suppress his feelings following the sexual offers of a promiscuous female admirer, Joryleen. I found the ending of the story to be contrived and unconvincing but the indoctrination episodes are well described and very plausible.

It is clear that recruitment and indoctrination during pre- and early-teen years have a major role to play in mind control. Some Islamic educational establishments in countries like Saudi Arabia, Pakistan and Afghanistan specialise in teaching the Qur'an and Hadith and are widely suspected of being training grounds for future suicide bombers. Known as *madrassas*,[157] they are usually funded by sources in Saudi Arabia, the birth place of Osama bin Laden, and they teach a particularly harsh and militant form of Islam called Wahhabism, a branch of Sunnism. Most leaders of the Afghanistan Taliban were educated in Saudi-financed *madrassas*.

Once the indoctrination is complete, would-be bombers are taught how to deliver bombs strapped to their torso; or concealed in cars, boats, or submarines; or by hijacking and using aircraft. Then, it is just a question of selecting targets and delivering the bombs.

Unfolding events (2011): The Arab Spring

As I was writing this book (February – July, 2011), dramatic events, dubbed the *Arab Spring*, were unfolding in Muslim countries across the Middle East and North Africa.

First, the Tunisian population used people-power to rid their country of President Zine al-Abidine Ben Ali, the dictator who'd ruled their country for more than 24 years.

Egyptians followed suit, staging mass demonstrations to remove President Hosni Mubarak, another dictator with 30 years of experience behind him.

Clearly rattled by what was happening in the Arab world, King Abdullah of Jordan sacked his entire cabinet and installed a new one with the express aim of speeding up reforms.

Libya erupted with calls for Muammar al-Gaddafi to relinquish his 42-year dictatorship. The rebels were supported by a NATO-led coalition that included the UK. At the time of writing, the National Transitional Council (the new Libyan government) has secured control and Gaddafi has been found and brutally executed.

Violent demonstrations occurred – first in Bahrain and later in Syria where many demonstrators have been killed by armed forces loyal to President Bashar al-Assad.

---

[157] A *madrassa* is simply the Arabic name for any educational establishment, religious or secular. Some *madrassas* teach religious fundamentalism but others don't. Unfortunately, the meaning of the word *madrassa* has been distorted to imply that all such establishments are teaching and churning out future suicide bombers. This is not the case.

Violence also erupted in Yemen, culminating in an assassination attempt on President Ali Abdullah Saleh that forced him go to Riyadh (Saudi Arabia) for hospital treatment. He returned after two months but, so far, has been unable to quell the demonstrations.

And so it continues.

Each of these incidents took place in what we might call a reasonably secular Arab country. The separation between church and state might be an uneasy one, but Islam does not play a significant role in their governments. The Muslim Brotherhood and its political arm, the Islamic Action Front, are banned in Tunisia. In Egypt and Jordan, they are tolerated but not in power.

Currently, the media is full of speculation about what will happen next in other Arabic countries, and whether the Muslim Brotherhood will gain political advantage from the turmoil and political vacuums that have arisen from the overthrows. Relations between Israel and the Palestinians are especially fraught and Iran is looking on with a very interested eye and almost-done ability to build a nuclear bomb.

These are macroscopic events. An array of microscopic events also occurred during the period. For example, the reported death of a fourteen-year-old Muslim girl, Hena Begum, in a somewhat remote village in Bangladesh.[158] Her crime? Allegedly, she was first beaten up and then raped by her 44-year-old married cousin with whom, it was said, she was conducting an affair. At fourteen?

Under Sharia law, Begum was as responsible as her cousin for the rape, so she was sentenced to be publicly whipped by the local village council of elders and Muslim clerics. The punishment of 100 lashes was carried out by council members, including an Islamic cleric. She collapsed after 80 lashes and died six days later. A post-mortem found that she had bled to death. The cousin is in custody awaiting trial.

What does Islam say about all this?

According to the Qur'an, the penalty for adultery (is rape adultery?)[159] is 100 lashes.

> *The adulteress and the adulterer, then flog each of them with hundred stripes, and you should not be compassionate for them in the religion*

---

[158] 2 February 2011, http://www.bbc.co.uk/news/world-south-asia-12344959
[159] Some translations of verse 2 in Surah 24 use the word 'fornication' instead of adultery. Fornication is generally defined as consensual sexual intercourse between a man and a woman who are not married to each other. Is rape consensual? But, a correct translation of the original Arabic word, *zina*, is 'any form of sexual intercourse outside marriage'. This includes rape and thus the woman is punished as well as the man.

of Allah if you believe in Allah and the Last Day. And let a party of the Muslims be present at the time of their punishment.

Qur'an 24:2

'One hundred stripes', 'Don't be compassionate' and 'Let a party of Muslims be present ...'! Unbelievable in the twenty-first century!

Preliminary conclusions

Based on the analyses of Harris, supplemented by the additional evidence of recent events, we can draw the following hard-line conclusions:

- Islam can be perceived to be a religion with no tolerance for other religions, or even those who have no religious beliefs.
- Islam is a religion that often advises death as a punishment for those who leave the faith either to convert to another faith or to become a non-believer.
- Islam is a religion that endorses fourteenth-century methods of execution – stoning, beheading, whipping, and throat-cutting.
- Islam is a religion that's controlled by uncontrollable and unaccountable imams who are free to interpret the content of the Qur'an and Hadith in almost any way that suits their purpose.
- The Qur'an is positioned as a book that purports to state the word of God as told by his agent, the angel Gabriel, to a man called Muhammad. There is no evidence whatsoever that either God or Gabriel actually existed or still exist. As a result, Islam is a religion that epitomises and demands blind belief with absolutely no questions asked and which rules by means of inculcated dogma that starts from birth.
- Islam is a religion that accepts very little of the understandings of modern science and consequently is stuck in a time warp with virtually no hope of extraction given the reaction to any suggestion for modernisation.
- Islam is a religion that's able to convince young men, and women, that the acquisition of 72 virgins plus unlimited food and wine is sufficient justification to commit voluntary suicide and, at the same time, cause the death of others including women and children and, possibly, fellow Muslims.
- Islam is a religion that condemns any Muslim who dares to advocate radical change based on non-Islamic tenets.

Because of all these limitations and restrictions, Islam has made very little contribution to music, art, poetry, literature, science, engineering or philosophy for at least 600 years. Instead, Islamists have concentrated on waging physical and mental war with just about every other religious and non-religious belief, and the social or ethnic groups who practice these religions.

The irony of all this is that West European and North American Governments have bent over backwards to 'be nice' to Muslims. This has created a situation in which the rest of the world's population – Christians, Hindus, Buddhists, Atheists ... – is now vulnerable to the extremist views of Islam. The risk is that our complacency and timidity could cost us our democratic, scientific and religious freedoms.

Here are some interesting statistics.

- In 2009, the world's population stood at 6.78 billion.[160]
- In 2009, the world's Muslim population stood at somewhere between 1.57 Billion and 1.82 billion,[161] 87% to 90% Sunni, the rest mostly Shi'a.

This means that roughly one quarter of humanity is Muslim. The rest are anything but.

Unlike other religious groups, Muslims think of themselves primarily as followers of Islam and members of the world-wide Islamic community, called the *ummah,* and secondarily as something else such as nationality (Iraqi, Iranian, ...), ethnic origin (Arab, Javanese, ...), or skin colour (dark skinned, fair skinned, ...). This is the opposite of the way that most citizens of, say, Western Europe countries and North America think of themselves. A native Frenchman/Englishman/American is first and foremost a Frenchman/Englishman/American. It is only after that that factors like religion and ethnic group come into play.

This alternative view of the nation-state as the donor of the prime identity fosters patriotism, healthy competition, innovation and progress and, as we've seen, encourages citizens to greater heights in developing the very fabric of their societies.

In contrast, Islam, controlled as it is by Sharia law based on a document that was written 1,400 years ago, has been held in a time

---

[160] http://www.google.com/publicdata?ds=wb-wdi&met=sp_pop_totl&tdim=true&dl=en&hl=en&q=world+population
[161] http://www.islamicpopulation.com/,
http://en.wikipedia.org/wiki/List_of_countries_by_Muslim_population

warp. Only now are Islamic scholars beginning to realize the stark choice they face. Harris paints a dark picture of the future, holding out little hope that one quarter of the world's population can be convinced of the reality of progress based on secularism and a massive updating of the interpretation of the contents of the Qur'an.

He contends that the world's non-Islamic citizens have to persuade Muslims to integrate with us, not *vice versa*. We have to help Muslims realize that God might not exist and that all they believe in could be but a house of cards built on a belief that may be false. We have to convince Muslims that it is acceptable to question and change their beliefs. Only in this way will we be able to persuade Muslims to contribute to the future of our civilization rather than cause its downfall. Until this happens, the next time an atrocity such as 9/11 or 7/7 occurs, people's instinctive reaction will be that it was caused by a radicalised Muslim in the name of an unprovable deity called God – and all for the reward of 72 virgins and unlimited food and wine.[162]

Further considerations

It was easy to write the preliminary conclusions above. They are along the lines of those reached by Harris and, to a lesser extent, Dawkins. They play on people's fear of a religion that allows no dissent and whose followers believe – truly believe – that there is an afterlife more enjoyable than their earthly existence. On that basis, they relish death and even invite it – it opens the gates to a future existence 'full of eastern promise'.

But ... there's always a but!

In researching the topic of Islam and how it might co-exist with modern secular governments and societies, I developed an alternative view. I will set it out below. First, though, two general observations.

Religions such as Islam are intricately linked with political and social developments. To expound on one while giving scant attention to the others is like trying to explain the nature of a fluid without referring to the container needed to hold it. It doesn't work.

---

[162] As I was reviewing this chapter, Anders Breivik set off a bomb in Oslo and went on the rampage on the nearby island of Utoeya, killing 77 people. I happened to be awake at 4 AM, listening to the news on the BBC's World Service. In both the 4 AM main bulletin and again in the 4:30 AM news summary, the statement was made that the gunman was thought to have links with an Islamic terrorist group. Later, this statement was rescinded as it became clear that Breivik was acting out of extreme anti-Islamic beliefs. But, the initial and default suspicion was that he was an Islamic extremist. See later in this section for more comment about the Oslo Massacre.

Islam And Armageddon

Second, the intricate relationships between religion and politics are so complex that simplification and paring down to a few thousand words is extremely difficult, if not impossible. I have almost certainly over-simplified some of the issues involved. Nevertheless, I am motivated to answer the question implicit in the title of the chapter: are we heading pell-mell towards Armageddon because of the unshakeable beliefs of the followers of Islam?

More history

In Chapter 5, I mentioned that the development of the theological aspects of Islam ground to a halt around the fourteenth century. I said that 'Muslim clerics argued that the development of scientific concepts and applications by reasoning and logic went against the fundamental *knowledge-by-revelation* nature of Islam. They said that the ideas and applications had not come about by revelations from God and so should not be pursued. '

It was only in the seventeenth and eighteenth centuries that western European countries began to separate church and state, creating what we now call secular nation-states. This followed on from the sixteenth century European Reformation. The yoke of the Roman Catholic Church was cast off and replaced by the more-liberal Protestant and Anglican Churches, accompanied by the liberalisation of art and education as part of the Renaissance that also swept across Europe at the time. Subsequently, the founding fathers of the newly-formed United States established a Constitution that allowed freedom of religion but excluded any constitutional dependence on or adherence to religious beliefs and dictates. In fact, there are only two references to religion in the US Constitution:

> *Congress shall make no law respecting an establishment of religion, or prohibiting the free exercise thereof; ...*
> Amendment 1 - Freedom of Religion, ...

> *No religious Test shall ever be required as a Qualification to any Office or public Trust under the United States.*
> Article 6. Debts, Supremacy and Oaths, US Constitution

Towards the end of the eighteenth century, various Islamic scholars, exposed to the workings of the new western European secular governments, became alarmed at what they saw as a diminishing role for Islam. Islamic power and influence was waning. Gone already was the vast Muslim Mughal Empire, centred in India. The Muslim Ottoman Empire, centred in Turkey and dominant throughout the Middle East, was on the wane. In its place came colonization by West European nations: the British in Australasia, India, Malaya, North America and parts of Africa; the Dutch in the East Indies (now Indonesia) and South Africa; the Portuguese in Goa, South America and parts of Africa; the Spanish in Central and South Americas; and so on.

Colonialization undermined an already weakened Muslim faith. In earlier centuries, the spread of Islam along the traditional trade routes into the Asian world had caused variations in the religion that were frowned upon by hard-line Islamic clerics. In India, Islam had been influenced by Hindu beliefs. In Java, now Indonesia, it had been influenced by Hindu, Buddhist and earlier native-religion beliefs. In North and West Africa, similar influences from earlier native religions had occurred. So, although Islam had spread, it had become diluted and polluted by other religions, a process called syncretism.

All this was made worse by the Muslim realization that European governments were not driven by laws extracted from ancient religious books. Rather, these governments were motivated by capitalism and the creation of wealth, and accompanied by a belief in the freedom of the individual, a desire to secure national welfare and, above all, the provision of education across a broad field of subjects including science, engineering, art, philosophy and business. In short, religion had ceased to be the prime driver of government and education.

The Islamic countries in the Middle East retrenched into their religion, hunkered down and did nothing until they entered the twentieth century. Then the First World War broke out and they became involved, probably unwittingly, because they were part of the declining Muslim Ottoman Empire.

Middle East developments in the twentieth century

There were, I believe, two major developments in the twentieth century that are the fundamental causes of the concern we have with Islam today – the perceived annexation of the Palestinian lands by the Jewish population and the invasion of Afghanistan, primarily by the United States and Britain. Both were strongly criticised by Muslims and caused an array of adverse reactions, but for different reasons.

The presence of Middle-Eastern oil reserves also became a factor, but I will comment on this in a little while.

After the First World War and the defeat of Germany and its Ottoman allies centred in Turkey, the League of Nations (later to become the United Nations in 1945) granted France a governing mandate over Syria and Lebanon, and Britain a governing mandate over Palestine and Iraq. As this was happening, Islamic reformers in various Muslim countries were wrestling with the nature of their recommendations for the further development of their religion and their states. Some reformers advocated loosening the grip of Sharia law on Islamic society in order to align more with the newer more-progressive European styles of secular government. Others advocated a return to the original and very strict interpretations of the Qur'an, the Hadith and the resulting set of Sharia laws. Basically, the options were either a move towards liberalisation or a return to the old school.

Between 1920 and the early 1960s, the Middle East countries that had been placed under the governance of Europeans gradually regained their independence. Most established internal governments that attempted to separate church and state. Iraq became independent in 1958, for example, renaming itself as The Republic of Iraq. Saddam Hussein came to power in 1979. As we know, he ruled the country as a dictator but he never imposed Sharia law on the population. He was a member of the Ba'ath party, which operated an Arabic form of socialism, although socialism didn't figure much in the way he ruled the country. Images of Napoleon the pig in George Orwell's *Animal Farm* spring more readily to mind!

Syria regained independence in 1946, establishing itself as a parliamentary republic controlled by the Ba'ath party. Although it has remained so ever since, it has a history of military coups – some successful, some not. Its citizens lived under Emergency Law between 1962 and 2011, when the law was lifted in response to the waves of internal strife that followed the Arab Spring.

But not every Muslim country was placed under the rule of European governments following the end of the First World War:

- Turkey became a republic in 1922 under a secular Turkish government and has remained so.
- Iran, initially a democracy with a Shah as the titular head of government, became a hard-line Islamic theocracy following the departure of the Shah in 1979 and the return of the exiled Ayatollah Khomeini.
- Afghanistan has always been a law unto itself and is a country with a very chequered history, of which more later.

- Yemen became a presidential republic with elected Heads of State and Government but officials must be Muslims and Sharia law prevails.
- Saudi Arabia stayed as a monarchy but with the King bound by Sharia law. Saudi Arabia is home to the more-extreme form of Islam called Wahhabism, host to the holy Islamic cities of Mecca and Medina, and the birthplace of Osama bin Laden.

An eclectic mix of socialism, nepotism, Islamic law and dictatorships!

But, let me concentrate first on what happened to Palestine and the Palestinians, and later on happenings in Afghanistan. Here briefly, and without judgment, is what happened in these countries.

Note: in what follows, there are references to specific events leading up to the current situation between Israel, the Palestinians, and the Muslim world at large. The Appendix at the end of the chapter contains a chronology of the main events between the early 1900s and current time (2011). You might find it helpful to read the Appendix first to get a snapshot overview and then return to the discussion below.

Palestine – Israel Conflict

The geographic region called Palestine has been described as 'the land stretching along the Mediterranean coast from what is today called Turkey to what is today called Egypt' – an area that includes parts of modern-day Syria, Lebanon, Jordan (West Bank), Israel, Gaza Strip and Egypt (Sinai Peninsula). Palestine has also been described as the 'area of land bounded by the Euphrates and Tigris rivers in the north and the Nile in the south' – that is, an area similar to the one above, but including the north-west part of Iraq. The name of the area has been tracked back to 450 BCE but the boundaries have never been precisely defined which is why parts of Palestine are now within other Middle East countries.

Islam And Armageddon 183

The Palestinian people, like those of many of the other Arab tribes that originated in the area, were originally nomadic. Home was where their herds were. Culturally and linguistically, Palestinian people are Arabs, but the origin of a national identity – being a Palestinian – is disputed by historians. Most agree that the term wasn't applied to an ethnic group until just before the First World War. Genetically, Palestinians are very closely related to Jews (somewhat ironically as it turns out given the conflict between them) and 'descendants of a core

population that has lived in the area since prehistoric times'.[163] In terms of religion, Palestinians are largely Sunni Muslims, but some are Christians.

Because of their nomadic behaviour, Palestinians never laid claim to an area of land that they might have called Palestine. Instead, their territory was ruled by the Turkish Ottoman Empire until its defeat

---

[163] http://en.wikipedia.org/wiki/Palestinian_people

during the First World War. After the area was captured by the British in 1918, a formal statement of policy by the British Government, the Balfour Declaration, recognised the existence of the Palestinian ethnic group but earmarked the geographic territory as a national home for the world's widely-displaced Jewish population. Arthur Balfour, the British Foreign Secretary at the time, was responding to pressure from Baron Rothschild, a leader of the British Jewish community and prominent player in the Zionist movement.

> *His Majesty's government view with favour the establishment in Palestine of a national home for the Jewish people, and will use their best endeavours to facilitate the achievement of this object, it being clearly understood that nothing shall be done which may prejudice the civil and religious rights of existing non-Jewish communities in Palestine, or the rights and political status enjoyed by Jews in any other country.*
> Balfour Declaration, 2nd November, 1917.

That's when the problems started! Jews started returning to the British Mandate of Palestine (it wasn't called Israel until 1948) and, by 1920, the conflict between Jews and Arabs had escalated sufficiently for the first acts of violence, the so-called Arab Riots, to take place. Conflict has raged ever since. The history of hatred, killing and political maneuverings is a lengthy one.

Realizing they had created a situation that was uncontrollable by ordinary democratic processes, the British soon reneged on the non-Jewish commitments of the Balfour Declaration and withdrew from the situation, suggesting a binational solution. The proposal was rejected by both the Palestinians and the Jews. In the meantime, the expanding Jewish population, coming in droves from the Jewish diaspora, formed the *Haganah* (literally: the Defense) national security agency, later to become the Israel Defense Force. Thus the nucleus of modern Israel was created.

At the end of the Second World War, the world's population began to understand the magnitude of the German persecution and massacre of European Jews – the Holocaust – an event that resulted in the death of over six million Jews. The Jewish people in the Palestinian lands organised a massive intake of diasporic Jews. Because world sympathy was with the Jews, blind eyes were turned to the effects of the influx on the indigenous Palestinian population. The result was that David Ben-Gurion, a prominent Zionist, was able

Islam And Armageddon

to declare independence from British rule in 1948, so creating the modern state of Israel.[164] The rest, as they say, is history.

In 1947, the United Nations tried to impose a ruling that separated the land occupied by the Israelis, as they were now called, and the Palestinians, but its mandate was ignored by the Israelis. They argued that the Palestinians had never been the rightful owners of the land. The ruling was also rejected by the Palestine Liberation Organisation (PLO), the official political voice of the Palestinian people, on the grounds that it did not give them all their land back. Since 1948, Israel has gradually increased its territorial grounds through various wars, land annexation and a superior military force.

1947 UN Israel/Palestine Partition Plan

---

[164] The Jewish war against the British 'rulers' came to a head two years earlier in 1946 when a militant right-wing group of Jewish paramilitaries, called the *Irgun*, bombed the King David Hotel in Jerusalem. This hotel was the headquarters of the British Mandate Authority of Palestine and in the resulting explosion, 91 people of various nationalities were killed and a further 46 injured. At the time, my father, a medical orderly with the British Royal Air Force, was stationed in Jerusalem and he was among the first people to enter the building after the explosion to assist those who were still alive. That's all I know about his role in the aftermath to the explosion. He would never talk about it other than to warn that this would not be the end of the conflict between Jews and Arabs. He was right.

The current situation is that those who regard themselves as Palestinians reside in one of two areas called the *Disputed Territories* by the Israelis and *Occupied Palestinian Territories* by just about everybody else, including the United Nations. The areas are the West Bank, including the east part of Jerusalem, and the Gaza Strip. Ownership of these strips of land is disputed and complex and not elaborated here. Suffice it to say that Israelis regard the land to be theirs, either by Biblical right or by annexation following recent wars, whereas Palestinians see securing these territories as the last chance to establish an autonomous Palestinian nation.

At the time of writing, the situation remains unresolved. The *impasse* is the result of the following probably-incomplete list of interlinked suspicions, disagreements and grievances:

- No agreement on geographic borders and associated rights to create Israeli settlements or re-house diasporic Palestinians. In the meantime, Israel continues to build yet more settlements in what Israelis call the *Disputed Territories*, much to the chagrin of neighbouring Arab states.
- No agreement on autonomous Palestinian control of the Gaza Strip or West Bank.
- No agreement on the future of Jerusalem. The annexation of East Jerusalem by Israel in 1980 is still not recognised by the United Nations. Muslims, Christians and Jews all regard Jerusalem to be an important religious site and reserve the right of access for pilgrimage, exploration and maintenance of religious objects and buildings.
- A deep-seated suspicion of motivations and hidden agendas in any proposals from either side.
- Continuing violence between the two parties that spills over into other nations, such as the activities of al-Qaeda and other anti-Jewish Islamic organisations.
- A feeling that the United States is heavily biased towards Israel because of the powerful Jewish representation and associated lobby in the American Government (Presidential Administration, Cabinet, Senate, Congress, Governors, Ambassadors, Mayors, leading economists), and large corporate conglomerations.
- Non-recognition of Palestinian ethnicity claims by some right-wing Israeli politicians.
- Dissatisfaction among Palestinians about the 1950 Israeli *Law of Return*, which covers displaced Jews but not displaced Palestinians, especially those who fled during the 1947-48 Arab-

Israeli War. Various United Nations mandates exist that assert the rights for diasporic Palestinians to return to their original towns or villages but with the exceptions of West Bank or Gaza Strip Palestinians, Israel has rejected these mandates on grounds of concern about security stating that the new host countries, Syria and Lebanon, should grant citizenship to displaced Palestinians. Jordan has already done so. Israel points to the behaviour of militant organisations such as Hamas in the Gaza Strip as evidence that its security concerns are very real.

- No agreement between alternative factions within the Palestinian Authority as evidenced by the recent conflicts between Hamas and Fatah.
- Israel's belief that the Palestinian Authority is corrupt and that it provides tacit and maybe also tangible support for Islamic *jihad* organisations devoted to the removal of the state of Israel. (A situation similar to the UK's perception of the relationship between Sinn Fein, the political wing of the IRA, and the militant IRA itself during the days of *The Troubles* in Northern Ireland.) As a result, Israel does not regard the Palestinian Authority capable of governing a fully-autonomous Palestinian state and so justifies its continuing control of the *Disputed Territories*.

And so the conflict has raged. Third parties, especially the United States, have made many attempts to create a settlement between the two groups of people, but all have failed. Israelis feel the land is theirs by a birthright that stretches back to Biblical times – the Promised Land. Palestinians say the establishment of an Israeli nation impinges on their traditional roaming land.

Even today, more than 60 years after the establishment of the State of Israel, the two sides continue to assert their separate rights. If anything, the enmity between them seems to be increasing. No matter who is right, the Islamic *ummah* sees Israel as an invading force in what they regard to be an Islamic country and this foments a deep-felt anger against Israel and any nation that supports Israel – especially the United States, where support for the Jewish nation is very high.

The UK is not exempt from this anger. The nation has, in the past, supplied the Israeli government with state-of-the-art military weapons, thereby contributing towards Israel's military supremacy in the region. In addition, the UK often supports America in its military campaigns – the invasion of Iraq, the war in Afghanistan, and, more recently, the attacks on Libya. Consequently, the UK is often grouped with the USA as an 'enemy of Islam'.

Influence of the war in Afghanistan

Turning to Afghanistan, here too we see a multi-faceted political history. Traditionally, Afghanistan has been ruled by the heads of its tribes, the so-called war lords. In 1979, the country was invaded by Russia acting in support of one of Afghanistan's more-socialist factions, the *Parcham*. The United States countered by supplying another faction, the *Mujahideen*, a Muslim organisation, with armaments to use against the Russians. And so another proxy war between the communist and non-communist superpowers commenced.[165] Eventually, in 1989, the Russians gave up and withdrew, leaving a power vacuum. This was filled by the extreme Muslim organisation, the Taliban, in 1996.

The Taliban was backed both by Pakistan and by the Muslim *055 Brigade*, a section of a larger *jihadist* al-Qaeda organisation founded and headed by the Saudi Arabian Osama bin Laden – of whom more later. Once in power in Kabul, the Taliban enforced the very strict interpretation of Sharia law described earlier in this chapter and commenced a series of atrocities that resulted in the rape, torture and loss of life of thousands of Afghan nationals. Osama bin Laden opened up militant training camps in Afghanistan, ostensibly to create a fighting force to support the Taliban, but also to train militant Muslims in the art of terrorism, teaching them to become *jihadists* – those who fight and kill for the supremacy of Islam. Most of the 9/11 hijackers are known to have attended al-Qaeda training camps in Afghanistan prior to mounting the 2001 attacks on New York and Washington DC.

The response to 9/11 was swift. The United States and the UK started a bombing campaign in Afghanistan with the intention of destroying the training camps and dismantling the al-Qaeda movement. Later, the aerial campaign was supplemented by an invading ground force made up primarily of American and British troops.

At the time of writing, ten years later, the war is still being waged. To my mind, the objectives are no longer clear. It also took ten years for Osama bin Laden to be located, captured and executed by

---

[165] The Korean War (1950-1953) and the Vietnam War (1955-1975) are earlier examples of proxy wars fought between the USA and a communist superpower. The Korean War was between North Korea supported by the Chinese and South Korea supported by the British and Americans. The Vietnam War was between North Vietnam supported by the Chinese and South Vietnam supported by the Americans.

Islam And Armageddon

American military personnel[166] but, in the meantime, the war in Afghanistan has created a new source of discontent in Islamic states, not because Muslims necessarily support the Taliban, but because the war represents yet another invasion of an Islamic country by infidels.

My conclusion

Osama bin Laden was a member of the Wahhabi Islamic sect. Wahhabi Muslims reject all but the very first and most basic interpretations of the Qur'an and Hadith – those created before the Sunni-Shi'a split. While possibly valid in the seventh century, these interpretations are nowadays seen to be very harsh, puritanical and authoritarian. In fact, Wahhabi rules look very similar to the Taliban rules listed earlier in this chapter, especially with respect to women's rights. For example, women in Saudi Arabia are not allowed to drive cars, must be accompanied by male guardians when outside the home, are subject to sex segregation in public places, cannot hold high office, and must wear the *niqab* (face veil) at least or, preferably, the *burqa*.

Because of its adherence to such rules, Saudi Arabia is often castigated for its attitudes towards women and its hard-line opposition to other more-tolerant branches of Islam and all non-Islamic religions. Wahhabi Muslims advocate a positive attitude towards *jihad*, the holy war against all infidels, and have provided funding for organisations such as al-Qaeda.

But, Saudi Arabia has massive reserves of oil[167] and so shares an uneasy partnership with the oil-consuming nations of North America and West Europe and, to a lesser extent, Asia-Pacific countries. It was this somewhat 'unholy' relationship that allowed American forces to set up bases in Saudi Arabia in 1991. And it was the presence of these bases that angered Osama bin Laden and motivated him to create an organisation with the declared objective of driving out foreign troops, initially from Saudi Arabia (home of the Islamic holy cities of Mecca and Medina) but eventually from all Muslim countries. He called the organisation al-Qaeda from the Arabic word meaning *base*.

---

[166] Osama bin Laden was finally located and killed by US Special Forces (Navy Seals) in Abbottabad in Pakistan on 1st May, 2011. This happened to be the day I wrote the first draft of this section!

[167] 19% of the world's oil resources and number one in size if we can believe http://en.wikipedia.org/wiki/List_of_countries_by_proven_oil_reserves

Osama bin Laden was expelled from Saudi Arabia in 1991 and the United States finally withdrew its forces in 2003 but, by then, the damage was done. By highlighting what he considered Islam's subservience to America, Osama bin Laden had succeeded in inflaming many dissident Muslims. The Saudi-Arabian-based American troops had become a potent symbol of the US government's intrusion into an Islamic country.

So, between the Israeli accessions of what most Muslims see as the rightful land of the Palestinians and the hotbed of *jihadism* in Saudi Arabia that, among other things, fostered the extreme Muslims who have carried out atrocities all over the world, one can argue that the root cause of concern about Islam is rooted in politics, not religion.

If the British, backed by the United Nations, had insisted on a proper partitioning of the lands now occupied in part by Israelis and in part by Palestinians under Israeli governance, the current *impasse* between the two ethnic groups might never have been created and the Muslim world might have been more favourably disposed towards their fellow Arabs, the Jews. And vice versa.

And if Saudi Arabia had said 'No' to the American request to set up military bases on its soil, al-Qaeda might not have had the opportunity to grow in size and power in Afghanistan and the 9/11 attacks might never have happened. 9/11 was a seminal point in history. The attacks hardened attitudes towards Islam world-wide and fomented follow-up attacks in London (7/7), Bali and Madrid, as well as against various American Embassies and military targets.

Under these might-not-have-happened scenarios, Islam might have developed to become more tolerant of non-Islamic cultures and hard-line Islamic theocracies might have been replaced with secular versions of state governance combined with a strong but separate religious structure.

Of course, this is pure *what if?* speculation – just wishful thinking. It also is never as simple as this. Natural resources, particularly oil, play a major part in Western attitudes to Islamic countries. The growth of Islamic organisations such as the Muslim Brotherhood in Muslim countries not fully controlled by Sharia law is also playing a part in how these countries are developing. Organisations like the Muslim Brothers have the declared intention of reasserting Islamic Sharia law in countries that currently operate more on West European principles. The potential rise of such organisations provides a significant cause of concern, especially as the Middle East and North African Muslim countries change the nature of their political landscapes.

Islam And Armageddon

So, back to the big question: will Islam be the cause of Armageddon? Are we being drawn unswervingly and inevitably into a conflict of ideologies based on the intransigence of Islam versus the liberalisation of secularism?

There is no simple yes/no answer. The fundamental beliefs of Muslims have certainly contributed to what we nowadays call terrorism but, on its own, I do not think Islam would have inspired atrocities such as 9/11, 7/7, and the Madrid and Bali bombings. Had the United States and certain West European countries, my own included, thought more carefully about the long-term effects of their often short-term policies, I believe the situation would have been vastly different.

I contend that the non-Muslim communities need to be more tolerant of the Muslim religion but, at the same time, help its scholars and leaders bring their religion and associated governments and social structures up-to-date. Islam is not going to go away, so the best possible outcome would be if it were updated in the light of modern-day secular democratic practices. It would, of course, be much harder for Westerners to support such a task than it has been to send in the military, but it seems the only way to make the world a better place. But, to use one of my mother-in-law's favourite expressions, 'it's not meant to be'.

I hope that, at some point in the future, she will be proved wrong, but right now I see little sign that any major non-Islamic government is working towards this end. What looks more likely is an endless conflict between Israel and the Muslim world, with faults on both sides. I see a debilitating and ineffective war continuing in Afghanistan with no clearly-defined objectives, military or otherwise, nor a concise exit strategy. I see a continuation of Islamic theocracies, some of which inch their way towards the construction of frightening weapons of mass destruction (such as Iran and its development of nuclear weapons; similarly North Korea[168]). I see heightened security against potential future terrorist acts with constant surveillance of people and their movements. And I see an ever-growing distrust and even hatred for anything that can be labelled 'Muslim'.

It should not be like this. No matter what the colour of our skin, the ethnic origin of our ancestors, the shape of our religious beliefs, or even the absence of such beliefs, we should, by now, have learnt to 'live and let live'. I don't think I will see it in what remains of my

---

[168] Not an Islamic country, admittedly, but one that's ruled by an autocracy with similar methods of populace control and suppression, censorship, personality cult and worship, and suppression of freedom of speech as found in a theocracy.

lifetime, but I fervently hope (I almost said pray!) that my granddaughters will.

A final comment: the July 22nd, 2011 Oslo Massacre

As mentioned in an earlier footnote, a massacre occurred in Oslo and on the nearby island of Utoeya on July 22nd, 2011, just as I was editing this chapter. A Norwegian, Anders Breivik, acting out of extreme anti-Islamic motives, decided the only way to convince Europeans that they were being subjugated by Islam was to commit an atrocity on a scale that could not be ignored. As a result, 77 people, many of whom were young adults, lost their lives, either when the diversionary bomb in the city centre exploded or during Breivik's subsequent indiscriminate shootings on the island.

Just before he went on his killing spree, Breivik posted a 1,516-page 778,000 word[169] manifesto on the Web called *2083: A European Declaration of Independence*. In this document, he tells how he'd been planning the massacre for nine years, creating intricate cover stories for his purchase of firearms and bomb-making chemicals.

Breivik ends his manifesto with the words, 'I believe that this will be my last entry. It is now Friday July 22nd, 12:51.' The bomb in central Oslo went off at 15:26, just two-and-a-half hours later.

In a series of booklets inside his manifesto, Breivik launches into a long anti-Islamic diatribe that includes rants against Marxism, multiculturalism, government, immigration, academia, the media, the European Union, feminism, and capitalism, sometimes using them to justify his anti-Islamic views and sometimes as evidence of the impact of Islam on European cultures and nations. At 1,516 pages, it would take many hours to try and understand what consumed Breivik, but one thing is certain: if he hadn't surfaced in Oslo, someone similar would have surfaced somewhere else in Europe. Islamophobia, an extreme or irrational fear of anything to do with Islam, is on the rise.

On average, I receive at least one anti-something e-mail a week. Mostly, they are anti-Islamic, but there's also a fair proportion of e-mails that are anti-EU or anti-immigration. There's obviously a strong undercurrent of general dissatisfaction that's building pressure so it was inevitable that someone somewhere in Europe would commit a crime similar to that carried out by Breivik.

I do not condone Breivik's actions. They were coldly planned and chillingly executed, and one mourns for the loss of life. The fear now

---

[169] Almost ten times the number of words in my book!

Islam And Armageddon

is that other extremists will emerge (there are already rumours) and we'll enter into a period of civil unrest unprecedented since the Second World War with Islam as the 'common enemy'.

I've no idea what will happen in the near future, but I see the Oslo Massacre as important an event in shaping future European policies as 9/11 was in shaping world-wide attitudes towards Islam and terrorism. These are early days, but it would appear from Breivik's manifesto that the Islamisation of Europe and the timid response of Europe's governments were major factors in determining his course of action. It is notable too that he did not target Muslims. He targeted young white Norwegian people training to become the country's future politicians.

Muslim reaction to the event was muted, leading one to wonder how they might have reacted if Breivik had slain 77 of their young brethren.

No doubt a great deal will be written about Breivik and his actions. People in high places will utter meaningless and trite statements, then do nothing. (They did.) There will be a mass out-pouring of collective grief similar to that which followed Princess Diana's death. (There was.) Analysts will pour over Breivik's manifesto. He will be considered insane simply because that's the only defence his lawyers can offer. (They have done so.) This will beg the question – what is meant by the word insanity? (If he is proved insane, why was his insanity not detected over the nine years he spent planning the atrocity?) Those with extreme or even moderate views will support parts of what Breivik stood for and be condemned for it. Muslims across Europe will wonder about the possible reaction of other anti-Islamic factions in their European country of choice, and then continue their lives as if nothing has happened. And so life will go on until the next atrocity that results in a senseless loss of life.

Breivik may be the tip of an Islamophobic iceberg or he may be a loner whose deeds will not be repeated. Only time will tell.

As Sam Harris said in a posting on his blog[170] two days after the event:

> *One can only hope that the horror and outrage provoked by Breivik's behavior will temper the growing enthusiasm for right-wing, racist nationalism in Europe. However, one now fears the swing of another pendulum: We are bound to hear a lot of deluded talk about the*

---

[170] http://www.samharris.org/blog/item/christian-terrorism-and-islamophobia/

dangers of 'Islamophobia' and about the need to address the threat of 'terrorism' in purely generic terms.

The emergence of 'Christian' terrorism in Europe does absolutely nothing to diminish or simplify the problem of Islam—its repression of women, its hostility toward free speech, and its all-too-facile and frequent resort to threats and violence. Islam remains the most retrograde and ill-behaved religion on earth. And the final irony of Breivik's despicable life is that he has made that truth even more difficult to speak about.

(^_^)

Appendix: Israel and Palestine
A short timeline of major events between 1900 and 2011

Early 1900s. While Palestine was recognised as a geographic region, the people who lived and roamed on the land were known either as Arabs, Muslims or by their local tribal names – not as Palestinians. Palestinians were only recognised as a separate ethnic group when local newspapers started using the term at the beginning of the twentieth century. Some say this was in response to the perceived territorial threat of Zionism, following its birth in 1897. Others disagree!

1917. The Balfour Declaration was made. This formal statement of British Government policy recognised the existence of Palestinians as an ethnic group, but argued that the geographic territory loosely defined as Palestine should be used to create a national home for the world's widely-displaced Jewish population. In drafting the Declaration, Arthur Balfour, the British Foreign Secretary at the time, was responding to pressure from Baron Rothschild, a leader of the British Jewish community and prominent player in the Zionist movement. The statement said:

> *His Majesty's government view with favour the establishment in Palestine of a national home for the Jewish people, and will use their best endeavours to facilitate the achievement of this object, it being clearly understood that nothing shall be done which may prejudice the civil and religious rights of existing non-Jewish communities in Palestine, or the rights and political status enjoyed by Jews in any other country.*
>
> Balfour Declaration, 2nd November, 1917.

1920. The Balfour Declaration sowed seeds of distrust between Arabs, Jews and the British authorities, which led to the Arab Riots in Jerusalem.

1922. The British Mandate of Palestine started. It was a consequence of the First World War and the capture of the territory by the British armed forces in 1918. Palestine, and Transjordan (now Jordan), were placed under the administrative control of the British following a mandate from the League of Nations, nowadays called the United Nations.

1947. Britain relinquished its mandate over Palestine. The United Nations voted in favour of a geographic partition (UN Resolution 181) that included separate areas for a Jewish state and an Arab (Palestinian) state, with Jerusalem remaining as an enclave under international control. The preamble of Resolution 181 included these words:

> *Whereas the Principal Allied Powers have also agreed that the Mandatory should be responsible for putting into effect the declaration originally made on November 2nd, 1917, by the Government of His Britannic Majesty, and adopted by the said Powers, in favour of the establishment in Palestine of a national home for the Jewish people, it being clearly understood that nothing should be done which might prejudice the civil and religious rights of existing non-Jewish communities in Palestine, or the rights and political status enjoyed by Jews in any other country.*

Note the similarity of wording with the Balfour Declaration.

Both Zionist leaders and the British government accepted the plan; Palestinian leaders and their peers in other Arab League countries did not. Britain decided not to enforce the plan but to end its mandate, thus creating a power vacuum. David Ben-Gurion, a major Zionist leader, declared Israel to be a separate state the day after the British Mandate ended. Fighting broke out almost immediately and has never fully stopped.

1947-48. The Arab-Israeli war resulted in Jordan occupying the West Bank and East Jerusalem, and Egypt occupying the Gaza Strip. An exodus of displaced Palestinians moved to neighbouring countries including Syria, Lebanon and Jordan, and regions such as Gaza Strip and the West Bank.

1950. Israel enacted the Law of Return guaranteeing Israeli citizenship to any Jew world-wide, including their spouses and their families, and allowing them the right to both migrate to and settle in Israel.

1964. The Palestine Liberation Organisation (PLO) was formed at an Arab League Summit in Cairo. The PLO is a political and paramilitary organisation recognised by over one hundred countries as the sole legitimate political voice of the Palestinian people. It was given observer status at the United Nations in 1974.

Islam And Armageddon

1967. The Six-Day War between Israel and just about all its neighbouring Arab states resulted in resounding victories for Israel, including the recapture of the West Bank from Jordan, the Gaza Strip and Sinai Peninsula from Egypt, and the Golan Heights from Syria.

1980. Israel annexed East Jerusalem and declared Jerusalem, both east and west, to be the capital of Israel.

1994. The Palestinian (National) Authority (PA), formed at a meeting in Oslo, was given responsibility for local government in the Palestinian territories. The West Bank was handed back to the Palestinian Authority, but remained under Israeli civil and military administration. The PLO became the international voice of the Palestinians.

2005. The Gaza Strip was handed back to the Palestinian Authority, but remained under Israeli civil administration.

Note that even though the three territories – West Bank, Gaza Strip and Golan Heights – are referred to as the *Occupied Palestinian Territories* (Israel being the occupier) by the United Nations and many governments, Israel refers to them as the *Disputed Territories*. Israel maintains tight control over imports and exports; access by sea, land or air; and the supply of basic services such as water and electricity.

2006. Hamas, a group within the PA, gained local representation of the Gaza Strip. Fatah, another group within the PA, gained local representation of the West Bank. Considered by Israel to be a terrorist organisation, Hamas views the Israeli-Palestinian conflict as a *jihad*, thereby justifying the continuous shelling of Israeli settlements and the use of suicide bombers. Fatah is not currently considered to be a terrorist organisation, but has been in the past. Neither organisation recognises Israel as a state. Both want to eliminate the Jewish state and return the land to ethnic Palestinians.

2006 – 11. Attempts to form a unity government between Hamas and Fatah failed and violence broke out resulting in many deaths. At the time of writing, the two organisations are again trying to resolve their differences.

2011. The search for a political solution that would give the Palestinian people autonomous control of a homeland called

Palestine, see Israel recognised by every Muslim nation, and halt militant actions against Israel world-wide continues. So far, none of these objectives has been met.

Discussions between Israel and peace-mediating bodies such as the United Nations or United States often talk about a return to the pre-war 1967 borders as a basis for a peaceful settlement. In reality, the peace-makers mean the tentative borders specified by the United Nations in 1947, prior to the 1947-48 Arab-Israeli war. If agreed, this would return the Gaza Strip and West Bank, including East Jerusalem, to Palestine and the Golan Heights to Syria. (The Sinai Peninsula has already been returned to Egypt.) Israel has repeatedly stated that its security would be put at risk if these changes were made.[171] As a result, the *impasse* continues.

(^_^)

---

[171] The latest occasion was in May 2011 when Israel's Prime Minister, Benjamin Netanyahu met the United States President, Barack Obama, in Washington DC. Obama stated that a peaceful settlement including an autonomous Palestine state must be based on the pre-war 1967 border definition. In his reply, Netanyahu said: 'While Israel is prepared to make generous compromises for peace, it cannot go back to the 1967 lines, because these lines are indefensible; because they don't take into account certain changes that have taken place on the ground, demographic changes that have taken place over the last 44 years.'

Chapter 9
The Need For A God

Eskimo: 'If I did not know about God and sin, would I go to hell?
Priest: 'No, not if you did not know.'
Eskimo: 'Then why did you tell me?'
Annie Dillard, American author

'I don't believe in God but I'm very interested in her.'
Arthur C. Clarke, English author

'I would rather live my life as if there is a God and die to find out there isn't, than live my life as if there isn't and die to find out there is.'
Albert Camus, French author and philosopher

Is there a need for a god?

Okay, I admit it! Some people need a god and the perceived comfort of an associated religion. After wandering around the archives of ancient and modern religions, digging deep into the mechanics of human reproduction and the role and transmission of genes, trying to unravel the fundamental causes of the continuing turmoil in the Middle East and its spillover into just about every corner of the world, crawling all over the contents of the Bible and the Qur'an, and trying to make sense of things like immaculate conception and miracles, I am convinced – people need gods.

But not all people.

Thinking back to conversations I had during my professional career, a couple about religion come to mind. The first was with an Iraqi colleague. During a meeting, he complained he was feeling a little light-headed. When I asked why (I knew it wasn't a hangover caused by an excess of alcohol – he was a teetotaller), he replied that he was half-way through the month of Ramadan – the period when Muslims abstain from food and drink during the hours of daylight. He was light-headed because he hadn't eaten all day. And it wasn't because he was devout – he wasn't. It was because his wife was. Had he not abstained, he said that there would have been problems at home.

The second conversation was with an American friend. During regular visits to a city just outside Dallas in Texas, I often stayed with my friend and his family at weekends rather than stay cooped up in a beige-and-light-green nondescript hotel room. Occasionally, the family – husband, wife, two small girls – attended a local church service on a Sunday morning. Whenever I was invited to tag along, I graciously declined. But I wondered why my friend went to church. He never talked about his beliefs. I suspected that, deep down, he wasn't religious in the sense that he felt it necessary to go to church. Finally, I quizzed him. He confessed that although he had a belief in God, he preferred to keep his thoughts private. He went to church more for the sake of his family and out of a sense of duty to his local community. In Texas, such things matter – it's one of the most religious states in North America.[172]

In each case, religious conformance was motivated more by a need to keep the peace than by a belief in a god. There's nothing wrong with this. There are occasions when we find it easier to conform than kick over the traces. I 'switch off my mobile phone for the duration of the flight', for example, even though there is no scientific evidence that it will interfere with the aircraft's control systems. But I wonder how many people profess to be religious just to keep the peace and to be seen as upright and righteous members of a community?

I also question why people are drawn to religions. Is there an inner need for some protective father (or mother) figure to whom we can turn in times of stress? Do we take comfort in wearing clothes that make us instantly recognisable as a member of some religious community? When religious people close their eyes, clasp their hands and enter into a world of their own called prayer, or kneel and bow down facing Mecca, what really is going on inside their heads? Are they conversing mentally with an imaginary being and, if so, what image do they have and what result do they expect? In the post-9/11 novel *Terrorist* by John Updike, the suicide-bomber-to-be Ahmad describes prayer as 'the sensation of pouring the silent voice in his head into a silence waiting at his side, an invisible extension of himself into a dimension purer than the three dimensions of this world.' Even if there was no such thing as an organised religion, would some of us feel the pressure, the urge, the need or even the desire to create a personal one to give us comfort, identity and inner peace at times of stress?

---

[172] Many years ago, when George W Bush was seeking the US Presidency, I attended a fund-raising dinner in Dallas, in the company of the same friend. We were seated at a table with six Texan blue-bloods. At one point, one of the ladies at the table asked me what religion I belonged to. My reply, 'I'm an atheist', shocked the table and, for the rest of the evening, nobody directed another question my way. Afterwards, my friend said 'You should have lied and said that you were Church of England.' My reply was to say 'It's a good job they didn't ask my opinion of the British Royal family!'

In other words, is a belief in a supernatural being and obedience to the associated (sometimes very rococo) finery of an encapsulating religion something that is buried deep inside us? Would belief and subservience surface if we weren't indoctrinated by the convictions and associated religions of parents and other childhood influencers? Is a belief in a supernatural being, and its affiliated religion, innate?

These are the types of philosophical questions that I want to explore in this final chapter.[173]

How religions develop

Reflecting on the descriptions of ancient and modern religions in chapters 5 and 6, it is apparent that the gods of primitive native shamanic religions were based either on the things people needed to survive – sun, rain, earth, fertility – or on those that threatened their existence – thunder and lightning, earthquakes, volcanic eruptions. The follow-on religions were somewhat different. They assumed the existence of an inner being – soul, *atman*, *karma*, spirit, *jiva*, *chi*, *kami* - and that something happened to one's inner being after one's death.[174] Births were welcomed but deaths were ritualized with solemn ceremonies.

But are these rituals a cover-up for something more mundane?

As examples, consider the modern funeral practices of Tibetan Buddhists (sky burials) and Hindus (funeral pyres along the banks of the river Ganges). Sky burials have been discretely observed and are recounted in *To a Mountain in Tibet* – Colin Thurbron's 2011 travelogue of his journey to Mount Kailash. They are also depicted in Lu Chuan's 2004 film, *Kekexili – Mountain Patrol*, complete with voracious vultures. Funeral pyres and associated rituals are aptly portrayed in Khushwant Singh's 1990 novel, *Delhi*.

Such ceremonies are based on a belief that although the bodily shell has expired and has no further use, the soul lives on. An appropriate religious ceremony will speed it on its way to its final destination, wherever that may be.

---

[173] As I was completing this chapter, a new book was published: *Why We Believe in God(s): a Concise Guide to the Science of Faith* written by J Anderson 'Andy' Thomson and Clare Aukofer, Pitchstone Publishing, 2011. The contents of this book relate closely to some of my subjective observations but rather than go back and edit my comments, I decided to summarise the book in a postscript to this chapter. In what follows, you will find several pointers to the postscript.

[174] As far as I'm aware, this applies not only to native religions, but to all religions.

Cynics would argue otherwise. Consider the Tibetan sky burials. At high altitudes, the ground in Tibet is very hard. It's virtually impossible to dig graves with handheld tools. Compounding the problem, there are very few trees. Cremation would be a waste – what firewood is available is needed for heating and cooking. As a result, it's better to lay the body on a charnel rock on the hill side, bereft of clothing and perhaps dissected into manageable pieces to encourage carnivores – especially vultures – to eat the flesh thereby providing sustenance for animals who, incidentally, may be hosting the *karma* of an ancestor. When picked clean, bones are ground down and mixed with barley flour, tea and yak butter or milk to make a paste that is fed to smaller birds and mammals. Nothing's wasted – the body is disposed of and the local animals are kept nourished.

Similarly, with the funeral pyres along the *ghats* (steps) that line the river Ganges in India. Bodies are cremated, usually within 24 hours of death, and the ashes disposed of in the waters of the river. In this way, one important part of the Hindu/Buddhist/Sikh birth-life-death-rebirth *samsara* cycle is completed and the *karma* of the dead person moves on to find another bodily host.

But again, cynics would argue that it's hot in India, dead bodies decompose rapidly in the heat (creating health hazards) and full-body refrigeration is expensive and not available to all. As a result, it's best for the living if bodies are disposed of as quickly as possible. Cremation is as good a way as any – and it can be encouraged by suggesting that if ashes are disposed of in the waters of the river the *samsara* cycle will be completed.

While exploring whether religious ceremonies mask non-religious reasons for carrying out actions, here's another example.

I once went to a Hindu temple called Dakshinkali, which is just south of Kathmandu in Nepal. The temple is devoted to the Hindu goddess *Kali*, a sinister 'she who destroys' blue-bodied goddess who is often depicted holding a severed head in one hand and a sword in the other, with a necklace made of skulls around her neck, multiple arms (sometimes four, sometimes ten), her tongue hanging out (some say in shame, others say to represent energy and action), and one foot on the possibly-dead body of *Shiva*, with whom she has a stormy personal relationship. She sounds to me like a goddess to be avoided, but there are plenty of Hindus who regard her as a benign and benevolent deity!

At Dakshinkali, Hindus offer male animal sacrifices to *Kali*. The animals – usually cockerels or uncastrated goats (bucks) – are paraded down to the killing pit where their throats are slit by professional butchers. I have witnessed the sacrifice – you need a strong stomach, especially when it's the turn of the goat. But why are the animals sacrificed in this way?

Whether of animals or, in the past, of humans, religious leaders advocate sacrifices for several reasons:

- To please the gods by giving them something of value: food, money, live animals, some artefact. This is called a *costly signal of commitment* by psychologists.
- To indicate obedience and allegiance to a deity.
- As evidence of renunciation (the giving up of all worldly pleasures).

The cynic's view is that, at Dakshinkali, the local guild of butchers is simply cashing in on people's need to have animals killed for meat. When their throats have been slit, dead animals are either taken home for consumption or to nearby picnic places to be cooked and eaten amid much fun and jollity.

You could also argue that the whole operation is a way of culling cockerels and bucks to prevent them becoming too numerous. A cockerel can service many hens. Experts in poultry farming say that a ratio of one cockerel to somewhere between ten and twenty hens is sufficient for fertility purposes. If there are a disproportionate number of cockerels in a chicken run, the hens suffer from too much sexual attention.[175] Sacrifices are a way of maintaining an appropriate cockerel-to-hen ratio.

So, the practices conducted at Dakshinkali fulfil both the culling and butchering needs and would probably continue in one form or another even if the Hindu goddess *Kali* was not involved. But, because she is, many people can make money from the operation – the stall holders on the pathway down to the killing pit, the butchers, the taxi drivers who transport whole families to Dakshin, the food vendors, and so on. It's a business - one that also provides outings for families and, some say, a pleasant way for people to pass their day.

---

[175] As I found out in the days when my wife and I kept ducks and drakes. In our naïvety, we thought a ratio of one drake to one duck would be okay. The ducks nearly died of sexual exhaustion! In an attempt to give them a rest, we portioned the duck pen with a wire fence; ducks on one side, drakes on the other. The ducks were fine and quickly recovered. The drakes were clearly frustrated and wore a path alongside the fence in their efforts to rejoin the ducks. Finally, we asked a neighbour to cull the drakes. Like the people of Dakshin, neither my wife nor I was able to carry out the death blows!

How religions mature

From simple gods of nature and afterlife rituals, religions, like humans, evolve and mature. Darwin's Theories of Evolution and Survival of the Fittest seem to apply just as much to religions as to animals and plants.

Religions evolve from simple native religions with just a few basic deities into massive pantheons with deities for just about everything – gods of lettuce, haemorrhoids, martial arts and women's liberation alongside the more usual gods of natural forces, fertility, and abstract concepts such as war, peace and magic. Ultimately, the pantheon becomes so large that an implosion – a deity cull - has to take place. The result is a simplified religion that admits to just one super-god, a being who is responsible for everything.

The progression of the Roman religion from a pantheon of 205 deities down to just one – God – and the way the religion was repackaged to create the Roman Catholic Church is an example. It would seem that monotheistic religions are not only easier to administer and control as they grow; they are also easier to sell to populaces in need of religious sentiments and beliefs.

The power of storytelling

> *'Give me the child until he is seven, and I will give you the man.'*
> Attributed to Francis Xavier, a sixteenth century Jesuit missionary.

Every religion has stories. Look at the huge sprawling sagas of the ancient religions, for example. Or the more-modern stories of Indian and Abrahamic religions. Scientology has stories of people in space craft. And Joseph Smith, the founder of Mormonism, created a whole new set of stories about indigenous Americans when he wrote the *Book of Mormons* in just sixty days in the 1820s. So what are we to make of the role of storytelling in religion?

Much as celebrities today employ ghost writers so they don't have to draft biographies themselves, the founders of modern religions relied on scribes and story-tellers to record their personal philosophies, beliefs, and reflections. As a result, we can safely say that just about every story relating to an ancient or modern religion has been changed or embellished in some way compared to the original verbatim version.

The Need For A God

In some ways, this is a good thing. When told properly and with emotion, there is no doubt that stories can affect how you think and even what you believe. When my granddaughters stayed with us, I used to read them bedtime stories. I quickly became disenchanted with children's story books however and I started to compose and relate my own narratives.[176] I had casts of characters – Ermintrude and her bottom-of-the-garden animal friends, followed by Edward and his farmyard animal friends, followed by the evil Picketty Witch and her dog called Spot, and, eventually, by any combination of an animal (suggested by one granddaughter) and either a fruit or a vegetable (suggested by another) around which I would weave a 20-minute story. As the girls grew older, I made the stories interactive – 'What do you think happened next?' I soon found I had the power to make them laugh and even, on one memorable occasion, cry.[177]

At one point, one of my granddaughters asked me 'Where do the stories come from, Granddad?' My reply was instant – 'Out of my head!' – and accepted with no further question or comment. But, I was never asked 'How can a giraffe speak?' Or 'How can an orange or a carrot run and jump?' The human attributes I gave to the animals, vegetables or fruit were accepted without question.

It occurred to me that the same would have happened had I been talking instead about some supernatural being called God. Children are very impressionable, very trusting and totally open to suggestions of supernaturalism. The trouble is that this means that religious beliefs indoctrinated early in life are extremely hard to displace later on – even if the knowledge children have subsequently gained of the world calls them into question. We see it in other aspects of childhood – the imaginary friend who has human characteristics, the belief in Father Christmas and the Tooth Fairy, and even the non-existent cups

---

[176] In many cases, the authors of these books had obviously never read the stories aloud. They didn't flow. Also, in some cases, the vocabulary was inappropriate for the age. And, the stories were not exciting!

[177] This was unexpected! I had told of a young female puffin who'd damaged her wing and become separated from her parents. She was rescued by a family of penguins and lived happily with them, having multiple adventures, while she waited for her wing to heal. Eventually, she was ready to say goodbye and return to her parents. As she bade farewell to the penguins, one of my granddaughters burst into tears and said that she didn't want the puffin to return to her parents as she'd been so happy with the penguins! The tears were totally unexpected and left me momentarily speechless, not knowing how to progress the story. Eventually, I managed to persuade my granddaughter that the puffin would be better off with her parents but I solemnly promised that she'd return at least once a year to visit the penguins who'd rescued and nurtured her. This was accepted and, to my relief, the tears dried up.

of tea or pieces of cake handed out during make-belief tea parties. I have gorged on such fare!

Evangelism and other excesses of religion

Evangelists exploit the power of storytelling. If I was in the United States on business and stuck in a hotel room over a weekend, I used to watch the Sunday-morning God channels on television. I found them hilarious. Either a white-haired elderly man looking like everyone's image of a much-loved grandfather or a similarly white-haired elderly lady looking like an adorable grandmother would come on stage and start to spout all sorts of nonsense – some based on passages from the Bible, some on other sources of religious exhortation. Somewhere during the proceedings, the evangelists would claim a hotline to God and that the only way viewers could achieve salvation would be to purchase sets of tapes, videos, or books for some 'meagre' price - $9.99 (why not $10.00 and be done with it?) plus postage - to receive a starter kit. Meanwhile, saintly purple-surpliced choirs would burst into seraphic or happy-clappy song every now and then and programmes would be interrupted every ten minutes or so with advertisements for items such as automobiles, double-whopper cheese burgers and religious materials 'essential' for one's spiritual development.

I thought it was a hoot but I could only take so much. The programmes did have an impact on me however – just not the one the evangelists might have hoped for.

Ultimately, it was those programmes that inspired the title of this book: *The Religion Business: Cashing in on God*. In my mind, it was very clear that TV evangelists were just salespeople selling products. The only difference was that the product was the god of their choice, not a double-whopper cheese burger, a carbonated soft drink, or a luxury car.

Evangelism has been with us ever since the first founders of religion discovered their powers of storytelling. Abraham was an evangelist. Jesus Christ was an evangelist. Muhammad was an evangelist. But none had the advantage of modern mass-media communication technology.

This is where modern-day evangelists are different. Television, the Internet, iPods, Twitter, Facebook and mass-produced printed materials have increased their power and influence enormously. The development of such techniques has heralded a new order of evangelism.

One of the first to exploit the new opportunities was Granville Oral Roberts – the evangelist and faith-healer who realized the money-spinning power of TV evangelism. He founded the Oral Roberts Evangelistic Association in 1947, claimed he had millions of followers and established Oral Roberts Ministries as a highly-profitable family business. Today, the business is managed by his son.

I've never listened to Oral Roberts, but I do recall the American evangelist Billy Graham's visit to the UK in 1984. By then, my conversion to atheism was complete. As a result, I was amazed how many people he attracted to his open-air meetings. They were held in football stadiums – the only venues big enough to accommodate the thousands who flocked to hear him speak. 'Here's a man with storytelling powers', I mused but I wasn't tempted to attend any of his meetings. Retrospectively, perhaps I should have gone along just to judge the power of his oratory skills and see if he could persuade me back into the Christian faith.

To catch something of the flavour of evangelistic revival and faith-healing meetings, watch the 1992 Paramount movie, *Leap of Faith*. Directed by Richard Pearce, the film stars Steve Martin as fraudulent revivalist and faith healer Jonas Nightengale, and Debra Winger as his I'm-in-the-game-to-make-money sidekick. The film brilliantly captures the tricks of the trade and Martin gives what for me is one of the finest performances of his acting career.

Spoiler alert. If you haven't seen the film, you may want to skip the next paragraph.

During the film, Jonas comes across a young lad, Boyd, who has been crippled by a hit-and-run truck driver. Boyd (played by Lukas Haas) genuinely believes Jonas can cure him. Jonas says 'I believe in the power of belief. I've heard mutes sing and seen cripples walk' but we, the audience, are not sure if he is being genuine or whether it's all part of the act. Much to everyone's amazement – the evangelist included – Boyd is cured at one of Jonas's revival meeting.

It's an interesting film – one that captures the nature of revival meetings and the people who lead them, and one that I recommend if only so you can see what goes on behind the scenes at such meetings.

The ending is pure Hollywood, but don't stop watching when the credits start to run. Read them and you'll find the usual disclaimer: *The persons and events in this motion picture are fictitious. Any similarity to actual persons or events is unintentional.* Are fictitious? Does this include God and Jesus Christ, both of whom are mentioned many times in the film? Or are they excluded from the 'persons' category? Just a thought!

Okay ... returning to Roberts; his success inspired an army of TV evangelists. You can find them on channels all over the world. Some are connected to modern religions such as the Seven Day Adventists, Jehovah's Witnesses (why do they refuse life-saving blood transfusions?), Mormons (did they feel guilty in their early days of polygamy and paedophilia?),[178] Christian Scientists (who forego modern medicines), Pentecostals (who take the words of the Bible as literal), and many more. Among them are some loners who give a particular spin to their preaching. In marketing, you'd say they were people selling products with a *unique selling point*. Take George Hensley, for example. He founded the Church of God with Signs Following centred on the ability to handle snakes, especially poisonous ones. The church is based on the following passage from the New Testament:

> *And these signs shall follow them that believe; In my name shall they cast out devils; they shall speak with new tongues; they shall take up serpents; and if they drink any deadly thing, it shall not hurt them; they shall lay hands on the sick, and they shall recover.*
>
> Mark 16:17-18

Hensley was reported to have been bitten by snakes more than 400 times. He recovered from every bite without medical assistance – except the last one. It killed him!

But, as we've said, evangelism is not just an American phenomenon. India is well-known for its God-men – people who make vast profits from their 'ability' to create miracles, cure the sick and provide spiritual sustenance while relieving you of all your money. One – Sai Baba – came to my attention while I was writing the book. (Baba died in May 2011.)

Described as 'India's revered spiritual guru', Baba made items appear from nowhere – holy ash (*vibhuti*, a substance made from burnt cow dung and said to have healing properties!), watches, other jewellery. He presented these items to visiting dignitaries, thereby earning their gratitude and life-long support.

Baba was born of a virgin, or so he said. His mother's reaction to this statement is not known. At the age of thirteen, he was stung by a

---

[178] I used to visit a company just north of San Diego in southern California. On the drive up Interstate 5, near a place called La Jolla (pronounced La Hoya, as I found out to my embarrassment!), I would pass a very large ornate Mormon temple. My reactions were varied: what a huge waste of money, where did the money come from, what was the point of such a monument to man's extravagance?

scorpion, an event that's usually fatal. He recovered, miraculously acquiring the ability to speak Sanskrit, or so the story continues.

Baba maintained he was an *avatar* of *Shiva*. He claimed every god – Yahweh, God, *Allah, Shiva, Vishnu* – was a different manifestation of the one Supreme Creator. This was a clever move on his part. It meant you could be a Sai Baba devotee without renouncing your existing religion.

But Baba was accused of illusion and of using sleight-of-hand to perform his so-called miracles. He was also accused of sexually abusing young boys: fondling their genitals, having oral sex and, allegedly, engaging in sodomy. Many saw him as a fraud but attempts to expose him were consistently quashed by the Indian authorities – notably by those in power who had previously received private audiences or gifts. Whatever the truth, the Sai Baba organisation became worth a lot of money. At the time of Baba's death in 2011, the organisation was worth $6 billion – a huge amount of money bearing in mind it was earned using standard magic tricks by someone with a spectacular afro hair style, a dismal record of healing, but an inspirational presentation style.

So, what is the truth? Are evangelists and God-men just cashing in on people's requirements for something to believe in? Is a belief in a supernatural being an innate belief, or are we easily conned by those who trade on superstition, are accomplished orators, and have more than a passing acquaintance with magic tricks. I will return to the question of innateness later on. First, though, a more fundamental question ...

Does God exist?

I am drawn to try to answer this question, but Richard Dawkins has done a far better job in his 2006 book, *The God Delusion*. He approached the question from the opposite end – can we prove that God does not exist? He does a credible job but he doesn't prove – undeniably prove with cast-iron evidence – the non-existence of God. As Dawkins says, the probability of his existence might be infinitesimally small, but it is not zero.

But Dawkins postulates that research biological chemists are on the verge of solving the mystery of the origin of life. Their success, when it happens, will be the final nail in the belief of a Supreme Creator and Dawkins is convinced that it'll happen. I am of the same mind, albeit not with Dawkins's depth of biological knowledge, but close enough in my scientific training to accept what he says.

That's not to say I don't have my own views on God's existence or non-existence. I do and I set them out in the following sections.

Cause-effect analyses

Some philosophers have used cause-effect arguments to demonstrate the existence of God.

Cause-effect sequences can be either linear or cyclical. Linear sequences work something like this:

> An event, cause A, triggers an effect, B
> B now becomes a cause in its own right, triggering an effect C
> C becomes a cause, triggering an effect D
> And so on...

The cause-effect sequence never ends.

Here's an example that may be extrapolated to prove the existence of God.

> God (A) created the earth and all its content in six days (B)
> The earth's contents (B) reproduced to produce yet more contents (C)
> The multiplied inhabitants (C) grew hungry (D)
> Hunger (D) created a need to learn how to grow food and harvest the result (E)
> The new farming techniques (E) created horse-drawn ploughs to ease the tilling of the land (F)
> And so on...

There is no direct proof that there was a god who triggered this sequence but, given that the rest of the cause-effect sequence is true, one could conclude the first step is as well – that is, that God either exists or existed in the distant past.

A cyclical cause-effect sequence closes the loop. Here's an oft-used example:

> 'I cannot get a job in astrophysics.'
> 'Why not?'
> 'Because I've no experience of astrophysics.'
> 'Why not?'
> 'Because I cannot get a job in astrophysics!'

The Need For A God

Another example, close to my heart, occurred when I temporarily relocated to California to work for an American company for a period of eighteen months in the mid-1990s. The company paid for me to live in a hotel for two months while I looked for an apartment. I duly found an apartment but the renter wanted me to set up a monthly US-dollar payment order. I did not have a US-dollar bank account so I went to a local branch of Wells Fargo (I liked the stagecoach-and-horses logo!) and had a meeting with one of the managers – they are called traders in the Wells Fargo bank! The conversation went something like this:

'Can I set up a bank account?'
'Yes, where are you living?'
'In a local hotel.'
'We need a permanent address to set up the account. A hotel address isn't sufficient.'
'But I need a bank account to set up a permanent address.'
'Sorry, I cannot help!'

A classic *Catch-22* scenario![179]
Eventually, I worked out how to break the cycle. My company wrote a letter confirming I was an employee, stating my salary and agreeing to pay the money into a Wells Fargo bank account if one was established in my name. On that basis, the bank set up the account using the company's address as my temporary address and, hey presto, I was able to rent the apartment!
More philosophically:

God (A) created the earth and all its contents including humans (B).
The humans (B) accepted that God was their creator (C/A).
Ergo God exists.

This is a neat explanation of the origin of, say, the belief in God's existence. But the philosophical question remains – how was the first cause created? Who created the creator? How do you break the cycle to prove the point – just as I did in the case of the Wells Fargo no-deal cycle? *Ra*, the Egyptian sun god, was said to be self-creating, as was the Hindu god *Brahma*. As far as I know, the Abrahamic God

---

[179] Catch-22: an unsolvable logical dilemma, or logical paradox, from Joseph Heller's 1961 novel of the same name. The well-known song *There's a hole in my bucket dear Liza, dear Liza* is yet another example of a cyclical Catch-22 cause-effect cycle.

(Yahweh, God or *Allah* – make your choice) makes no claim to self-creation. He just was, is and forever will be – that is, he is eternal.

So what is the truth? Philosophers have argued – and will continue to argue – about cyclical sequences of causes and effects. I will leave them to their deliberations. For me, the argument doesn't work. Self-proving and self-serving statements mean nothing without evidential proof.

God and mathematics

> *'We can never prove a theory right; we merely fail to prove it wrong.'*
> Attributed to the Austro-British philosopher Karl Popper.

Could mathematics help? It is the foundation of science and engineering, so could we apply it to prove God's existence?

People have come up with several mathematical postulates that purport to prove God's existence – some weird and wonderful and most definitely the work of conspiracy theorists. Here's an example – a simple mathematical 'proof' attributed to a character in Aldous Huxley's novel, *Point Counter Point*.

> Let X equal any number, assumed positive for simplicity
> Then X divided by zero is equal to infinity: $X/0 = \infty$
> Transposing the equation, we get $X = 0 \times \infty$. In words, X is the product of nothing (zero) multiplied by infinity
> Therefore, if we interpret X to be a variable representing the universe and all its contents, it was created by an infinite being, God, out of nothing.

Neat, huh? But is it what it claims to be – a mathematical proof of the existence of God? I don't think so. Mathematics is based on axioms – statements that cannot be proved but which are accepted to be true. In the attempted proof of God's existence above, the fact that any number X divided by zero is equal to infinity is an axiom. Thus, the argument is self-defeating. If you accept the axiom then, yes, the equation could be interpreted as a proof (at a stretch!). But what happens if you do not accept the validity of the axiom?

Are calculations that attempt to define the probability of God's existence any better? I am inclined to reject them outright. God either exists, or he doesn't. There's no in-between percentage – the probability is either 100% or 0%. That is why I don't understand agnosticism.[180] God just cannot 'possibly exist'. *Yes*, it might rain tomorrow and *yes*, I might go shopping tomorrow – that's where probabilities do apply. But God? Why create massive religious facades if you are not sure he exists?

I suggest that in mathematical terms, God's existence has to be Boolean – TRUE or FALSE. There's no room for probabilities. There's no room for a lack of precision of any sort.

When he formulated his *Investigation of The Laws of Thought on Which are Founded the Mathematical Theories of Logic and Probabilities* in 1854, George Boole had no idea that his calculus of reasoning would, one day, fuel a revolution in engineering: digital electronics. Modern electronic gadgets are controlled by microprocessors whose computing capabilities are based on the Boolean algebra resulting from Boole's treatise. And those who are steeped in this algebra, as I am, are as prone to ask direct questions as they are to reject fuzzy replies.

Here's an example. Consider the following statement:

> *Eat five portions of fruit and vegetables a day.*
> Nutritional advice from the UK Government to its citizens, originating from the recommendations of the World Health Organisation in 1991.

The 'and' is confusing. Merriam-Webster's definition of the word contains the following: *used as a function word to indicate connection or* <u>*addition*</u> (my underlining) *especially of items within the same class or type* ...

Based on this definition, does the advice mean that one should eat five portions of fruit <u>and</u> five portions of vegetables a day, that is ten portions of these food types a day? Or does the advice mean that one should eat five portions of fruit <u>or</u> five portions of vegetables a day? If the latter, is a mix of fruit and vegetables okay as long as the total number of portions comes to five?

We know the answer: five, not ten, portions a day and a mix is acceptable, but the grammar is ambiguous. A more precise way of exhorting us to eat a healthy mix would say:

> *Eat five portions of either fruit or vegetables, or a mix of fruit and vegetables, a day.*

---

[180] Strictly speaking, agnosticism is admitting to neither the existence nor non-existence of God – 'I don't know if he exists'. For me, this translates into a might-exist belief – 'I don't know if he exists. He might or he might not!'

But that's a mouthful (no pun intended!) and so we stick to the simpler directive and assume that people will work out its true meaning.[181] Or maybe they assumed it did mean ten portions a day, thereby contributing to their expanding waistlines?

What is the relevance of this to God? Simply that if God's existence is a binary variable, TRUE or FALSE, he must succumb to the logic of binary algebra. Agnosticism cannot exist in the Boolean world. So now I am waiting for a Boolean proof of God's existence!

What is a soul?

All major modern religions include the concept of a soul: *karma* in Jainism and Buddhism, *soul* in the Abrahamic religions, *atman* in Hinduism, and so on.

But what really is a soul? It's a question that has kept philosophers awake for hours but, for me, it's simple. My body is my physical manifestation but my thoughts, my analysis, my hidden judgments, my opinions, my awareness of the environment and my reactions to it constitute something which I like to refer to as my 'self-awareness' – my soul.

I suspect people who go off to the desert for forty days to contemplate the nature of the human soul are really just trying to put structure on their self-awareness. You do not need to invent a mythical supernatural being to do this. 'I think, therefore I am' is fine. My body is my *yin*; my self-awareness my *yang* – it's that simple. But, the brain that houses my soul – my self-awareness – is vital to my well-being.

A person can survive the loss of an arm or leg, but not the loss of their head. The head houses the brain; the command centre for both the physical body and its self-awareness and truly a remarkable piece of physiological engineering. If we include the tongue's ability to feel and taste, the head houses all five basic senses – touch, sight, smell, hearing and taste. As countless French nobles, and Anne Boleyn, would tell you if they could, they were lost without their heads!

The mind is a pliable organ, open to suggestion. If at five years old you tell me that it's an entity created and controlled by a supernatural

---

[181] We can express this requirement, call it X, in Boolean algebra. Let A = fruit and B = vegetables. Then the extended version of the statement becomes X = A + B + AB. This equation reduces to X = A + B. In words: Eat five portions of fruit or vegetables a day. In Boolean terms, the 'or' in this version implies the inclusive OR, not the exclusive OR. Grammatically, however, the ability to mix the portions isn't obvious. Such is the whimsical charm of the English language!

being, I'll believe you. Later, when I've developed my intelligence and attained the ability to reason, I might reject your explanation, just as I might eventually reject claims that Father Christmas and the Tooth Fairy exist (even though they were enjoyable at the time).

So, what are souls, spirits, or *karma*? Do they really live on in some way after we die? Do they pass to another life form or do they rest in peace if we've achieved *nirvana*? Or do they 'ascend to heaven' to be greeted by St. Paul at the Pearly Gates?

I don't know but perhaps the more important question is why should I care? I observe that when people die, that's it. Their bodies decay, rot away, decompose, and do so irreversibly. Dead is dead. Even if the deceased possessed something that did move on, neither I nor anybody else has any scientifically-proven knowledge of it or its destiny. I refuse to believe that my actions as a living person will influence this 'something' after my death. Where's the proof? There's none. Why should I spend my life – 60, 70, 80 years of what should be an enjoyable experience – preparing myself for something completely unknown and unproven? You'd have to be crazy or deluded to do this.

Is there a God gene?

Let me return to the question of innateness: is a belief in God innate?

First what is meant by innate? Based on Merriam-Webster's definition, it means:

1. *existing in, belonging to, or determined by factors present in an individual from birth:*
2. *belonging to the essential nature of something:*
3. *originating in or derived from the mind or the constitution of the intellect rather than from experience.*

That is, innate implies qualities or characteristics that are part of one's inner essential nature and not acquired after birth.

Instinct is different. Here's part 1 of a definition. (The second part follows later.) Based again on Merriam-Webster's definition, an Instinct is:

Instinct – part 1:
An inherent inclination of a living organism towards a particular behaviour: something that is performed without prior experience (although may be improved with experience)

An example of animal instinct is the young bird's ability to fly out of the nest even though it has no previous experience of flying. It also knows it needs to fly with its mouth open to catch food. Its parents did not teach it to do that either.

The two nouns, innateness and instinct, are often used interchangeably. I prefer to think about innateness as a property and instinct as its manifestation.

First, is there a grammar gene?

Because our entire physical make-up is defined by the genes in our chromosomes at the point of conception, people have asked 'Is there a God gene?' Among the thousands of genes in our DNA, is there one, or perhaps a group that creates a belief in a supernatural being?

People have also asked 'Is there a grammar gene?' Language acquisition is more tangible than God acquisition, but both are complex processes – much more complex than learning, say, to add or subtract. But with language acquisition we can see, or rather hear, the evidence that it happened.

On the assumption that an understanding of language acquisition could shed light on God acquisition, I would like to digress and take a look at our current understanding of how we learn to speak a language. My main reference is the linguist Steven Pinker's book, *The Language Instinct*, published in 1994 by Penguin Books. Guy Deutscher's 2005 book, *The Unfolding of Language*, published by Arrow Books, is also worth a read.

Drawing on such sources, here is a summary of current thinking on language acquisition and the existence, or otherwise, of a grammar gene.

First, let's define the word *grammar* to be the classes and functions of words plus a set of rules for combining the words. Pinker claims our ability to acquire a language is innate. Contrary to popular opinion, we do not learn basic grammar from our parents. Parents teach us vocabulary and *prescriptive* grammar rules for a particular language, but the ability to create sentences expressing ideas greater than those implied by any individual word in the sentence is based on an innate universal grammar called a *generative* grammar.

A generative grammar is a set of rules that determines the form and meaning of words and sentences in a language as spoken within a particular community. For example, in the English language, we usually order words in a sentence as subject noun – verb – object noun

– as in *the cat sat on the mat*. We could adopt an alternative ordering of subject noun – object noun – verb, *the cat the mat sat*. We don't, but Germans and Russians do.

A prescriptive grammar is a set of arbitrary rules for how one 'ought' to speak the language. In English, we do not say *the cat was sitted on the mat*. While this would be generatively correct, prescriptively, it would be wrong.

In his book, Pinker postulates that the rules for a generative grammar are coded in our genes – in grammar genes - and as a result babies are born with them wired into their brains. Parents simply nurture development, adding the prescriptive rules and associated vocabulary a child needs to speak its native language. (Writing comes later.) A child born of French-speaking parents will learn to speak the French language whereas a child born of Russian-speaking parents will learn the Russian language. Because of the prescriptive differences between their languages, neither child will be able to communicate easily with the other.

By the age of three to four, children will be reasonably fluent in their mother tongue – able to create whole sentences that have meaning, even if the child has never heard or expressed the idea before. Children will also have an innate understanding of word types (nouns, verbs, adjectives, adverbs, and so on), syntax order (subject noun before verb before object noun) and tenses (past, present, future).

Once achieved, the ability to speak the language is there for life – like swimming and riding a bicycle. Assuming you continue to live in the same country or in one that speaks the same language, this is great. But if you want to move from, say, England to France later in life, it can be a problem. While our generative grammar remains intact, it will have been tainted by our first prescriptive overlay – sometimes seriously so. To learn a second language, you have to 'delete' the prescriptive rules and vocabulary of your first language and replace them with the different attributes of the second language.

Very few of us can do this in a way that leaves no trace of an accent, or telltale constructs or expressions. The time to learn a second language is at the same time as you learn the first – when you are very young. Two of my granddaughters are doing this as I write this book. They live on the border of France and the French-speaking part of Switzerland and although English is spoken at home (and by us when we visit), they speak French at crèche and school. Even though they are only five and three years old, they appear to be coping well, and it is truly fascinating to see their simultaneous progression in the two languages.

Linguists such as Pinker and Deutscher assert that all the languages in the world can be broken down into a basic generative grammar with specific prescriptive overlays that condition the generative grammar into a definitive language.

So back to the question: is there a grammar gene? Is there a gene that somehow hard-wires the generative rules of grammar into our brains? If so, this will account for why tribes discovered in the rain forests of the Brazilian/Peruvian Amazon or hidden plateaus of New Guinea have developed languages. Even though their languages appear primitive, linguists have discovered they are every bit as sophisticated in their syntactic structures as modern developed languages.

Look at the vocabulary of the English language. It has come a long way since Samuel Johnson compiled his dictionary in 1755. It contained 42,773 entries. Today's Oxford Dictionary contains 171,476 current-use entries and a further 47,156 entries that are no longer used. (I use the term *entries* rather than *words* as it is difficult to define the word *word* precisely. If a word has, say, two different meanings, such as *doctor (noun)* – one who heals – and *doctor (verb)* – to alter deceptively – is this one word or two? It isn't as easy to count words as you think!)

Vocabulary, the set of building blocks from which a language is constructed, evolves. New words enrich our ability to write prose, poetry, great dialogues in plays, express emotions in more figurative terms, remove (or create!) ambiguities, and so on.

Some words die. 'Didst thou go to the pictures?' is now 'Did you go to the cinema?'

Some words fight to survive. The Academie Française advises speakers of the French language to use *logiciel* instead of *software*, *courriel* instead of *e-mail*.

And languages evolve. The Creole language spoken in parts of Louisiana has evolved from an earlier pidgin version of the French language, originating from migrants from the French-speaking part of Canada. Creole is now so different from French that it is classed as a separate language. Before going to the next footnote, can you guess the meaning of 'Mo laimm twa'? Even if you have a knowledge of the French language, I suspect your answer will be 'no'. If so, see the footnote.[182]

---

[182] 'I love you.' The original French is ' Je t'aime.' Even Jane Birkin would be challenged to breathe sex and eroticism into 'Mo laimm twa'! The words sound ominous and sonorous, more suited to a Tibetan Buddhist chant.

Languages die out either because the number of people using them shrinks or because speakers turn to another language (as happened when many native American Indians adopted the English language of those who invaded their country).

I travelled often to the Netherlands on business. While I was there, I observed that just about every Dutch person not only understood my English but also replied in English. A similar situation prevailed in Sweden, another country I visited regularly. But not so in France. The French remain reluctant to either understand or speak English, and who can blame them? Their language is French, and they are keen to protect it. I hope they succeed. But the Dutch and the Swedes? They may not be so lucky. Because there are fewer of them, they have more incentive to adopt other languages. The Dutch and Swedish languages could progressively die out.

Were this to happen, it would just be an example of Darwinian evolution. It seems to apply as much to vocabulary and languages as it does to humans and other species. And given evolution is a matter of selecting genes based on which is fittest for the carrier's environment, it seems natural to ask: is there a grammar gene?

Darwin himself asked this question. In his 1871 book, *The Descent of Man*, he asked whether language is the result of 'an instinctive tendency to acquire an art?' And he postulated about the evolution of instincts as well as organisms.

Before proceeding, let's refine our understanding of the word *instinct*. I'll borrow freely not just from Pinker's book, but from the many websites I found that discuss instinctive behaviour.

Instinct, Part 2:
An *instinct* is a *subconscious process involving the cerebral cortex in the brain, and based on a primitive reaction that we may or may not be able to control.*

Although we're born with all our natural instincts intact, not all of them manifest themselves at birth. Some develop as we mature.

Here are some examples of instant and latent instincts:[183]

- New-born babies seeking a mother's breast for nourishment.
- The tendency in young girls to pre-puberty coquettishness. These actions are a precursor to their post-puberty instinct to attract a

---

[183] The summary of Thomson and Aukofer's book at the end of this chapter contains a longer list of innate and cognitive behaviours that, through adaptations, can be linked to a belief in God.

mate for reproduction. At seven years old, it might provoke a comment like 'She's cute'. At fifteen, the same behaviour might attract 'You're not going out dressed like that!'
- The wide range of maternal instincts present in just about every female shortly after birth. (Between the ages of five and ten, two of my granddaughters were forever playing Mummy and Baby.)
- Male reproductive instincts, such as aggressive sexual advances, and protective instincts, such as fighting with intruders. Mostly, these are suppressed or heavily modified by conventional and acceptable social mores and behaviours.
- The survival instinct, probably one of the strongest instincts we possess.

Instincts often improve with experience – babies suck better after a few practice runs – or when reasoning is applied – if we jump off a high building without any flying apparatus, we will probably die when we meet the ground.

We may also confuse instincts with reflexes. A reflex is a physiological event – a neural mechanism that responds to a physical stimulus. It is confined to the nerve centre. We reflexively, not instinctively, withdraw our hands from hot surfaces and react to sudden loud noises or flashes of light.

But back to language and the possible existence of a grammar gene ...

If, as Pinker and other linguists postulate, the basic structure of a language is innate, can we identify the gene that carries it and, by so doing, come up with a way to identify the supposed God gene?

'Grammar gene found!'
'First language gene discovered.'
'Better grammar through genetics.'
'The power of language may all be in the genes'
'Poor grammar? It are in the genes!'
A sample of headlines from UK newspapers circa 2000.

A gene that might be responsible for our understanding of grammar – a grammar gene – was identified in the mid-1990s. Called *Forkhead Box P2* (FOXP2), it was isolated to a common mutant gene in a close-knit British family of Pakistan origin, known as the KE family. Fifteen out of thirty-seven KE family members suffer from a particular speech deficiency. Because they have trouble controlling fine movements of their lower jaws, they are unable to articulate certain basic units of sound (*phonemes*) and the words that use them. They also have difficulty creating lists of words that begin with a particular letter and creating sentences with embedded relative clauses. (Example: the dog, *which only has three legs*, likes chewy biscuits.) It is these additional difficulties that suggest the root cause of their problem lies deeper than their physical disability.[184]

But, while the headlines screamed 'grammar gene found', linguists were – and still are – sceptical. They point out that there could be confusion between cause and effect. Is the inability to speak properly the result of damaged genes affecting the construction of the part of the brain that houses and controls the understanding of grammar? Or is the physical damage to the sufferers' speech organs restricting their ability to express ideas correctly even though their innate linguistic abilities remain intact?

Pinker is of the latter opinion. He is a strong advocate for the existence of the grammar gene (see Chapter 10, *Language Organs and Grammar Genes* in his book), but he is not convinced it has been found. It is easier to isolate genes that modify phenotypes (physical attributes) than to isolate ones that modify the ability to think at high levels of abstraction, pursue philosophical topics and, ultimately, postulate the existence of God.

Basically, the business of linking genes to behaviour is still in its infancy compared to that of linking them to a phenotype. In the case of FOXP2, it is now known that it can have many different phenotypic effects depending on which other genes it teams up with. Whatever FOXP2 is, it would appear not to be a grammar gene. Remember, genes contain instructions on how to build a particular protein, and protein builds us. If a protein is not built, or is built incorrectly, or is built somewhere else, the gene can have an indirect influence on behaviour. But attempts to attribute changes in behaviour to individual genes have proved fraught with difficulty. When, having seen a child behave in the same way as one of its parents, we say 'She has inherited her father's genes', the truth is that we are nowhere near understanding whether genes play any role in copy-cat behaviour.

That's clear, then ...

But there is one more thing we need to sort out before returning to the question of the existence of a God gene – the role and meaning of intelligence when commenting on instinct.

---

[184] http://en.wikipedia.org/wiki/KE_family See also Pinker, *The Language Instinct*, p. 323 et seq.

The words 'intelligence', 'reasoning' and 'cognition' are often used to mean the same thing. Linguists, biologists and psychologists argue over the precise meaning of these words so, in the spirit of defiance and ignorance, let me say how I am using the words. I will let the lexicographers sort out the final definitions.

- *Intelligence* is the ability to learn, understand or deal with new situations in a novel way; the ability to apply knowledge to a concept, situation or environment.
- *Reasoning* is a process, methodical or otherwise, for arriving at a conclusion working from a set of facts, deductions and observations.
- *Cognition* is the act or process of knowing something including both awareness and judgment.

The meanings overlap, but the words are not synonymous. The first is an ability, the second a process, and the third an action.

Many instincts are improved and even vastly modified by experience. Experience can influence intelligence, and intelligence is influenced by reasoning. So when modified by reasoning, instincts might evolve to the point that they no longer seem to be such. For example, I do not walk the streets of my home town consciously suppressing the instinct to engage in courtship with females that catch my reproductive eye. This natural instinct has been conditioned by reasoning, intelligence, social conventions and age(!) to the point where it is no longer dominant. Attractive females may catch my eye, but that's all.[185]

Back to the God gene

Let's return to the question of the need for a God and whether there is a God gene dictating the need.

In what follows, I will assume just one god, called God, but the arguments can be extended to cover a pantheon of gods.

First, I will explain the reason for phrasing the question in terms of God rather than in terms of a religion. There are many websites and books that investigate the answer to the question 'Is there a need for religion?' – indeed, this was the initial title of this chapter. But on reflection, I changed it.

---

[185] As my wife said to me many years ago when we first ventured onto the topless beaches of the South of France, 'You can look but don't touch.' I obeyed!

I see religion as an outgrowth of a belief in God, not the other way round. First, we establish a belief in a supernatural being, God. Then we build a superstructure around the belief – sacred buildings, sacred books, ritualized observances, worship techniques, and so on. On this basis, I think belief in God is the cause and religion is the effect. If there was no belief in a God, there would be no need for religion.[186] Hence the form of my question – is there a need for God and, if so, is it an instinctive need based on some form of a God gene?

As I've already pointed out, children are impressionable. At an early age, they believe almost anything you tell them if you look sincere, haven't been caught lying in the past, and are in a position of authority. They believe in Father Christmas and the Tooth Fairy because the evidence for their existence is over-whelming – gifts at Christmas and money under the pillow replacing last night's loosened tooth.

Typically, these characters are adult-induced, not innate, but children do create their own beliefs in things unevidenced, invisible, or intangible – the Bogeyman, or monsters in the wardrobe for example.[187] But as children grow older, their various beliefs are modified by reality. In various ways – through older siblings or school friends, by spying through the upstairs railings, from parents who reveal all, or by opening the wardrobe door – they work out that these mythical entities do not exist. They were inventions – products of their own creative minds and those of others. So, with regret for some and relief for others, they pass through one of the stages of childhood and put their childish notions away.

What about a belief in God? If small children are told that there is a God somewhere in a place called Heaven, do they come to the same 'it's not true' conclusion as they grow older? Sadly, not always. God and the often very decorative and mystical adornments of the religions that surround him can persist into adulthood. Although adults know that there are not fairies at the bottom of the garden, some cannot bring themselves to make the same doesn't-exist statement about God. At worst, they become trapped by the conventions of their religion. At best, they express doubts and duck out of ritual behaviours and meetings, but never quite shake off the feeling that someone, somewhere, is observing and noting with pleasure (or otherwise!) their thoughts and actions.

---

[186] Although Theravada Buddhists might disagree with this statement. But it depends on whether your definition of religion mandates a belief in a supernatural being, or not.
[187] Thomson and Aukofer ascribe these types of beliefs to empathy plus what's called Hyperactive Agency Detection Device. See the appended postscript for more details.

Let's return to the small child for a minute. Paul Bloom, a Professor of Psychology and Cognitive Science at Yale University, has suggested that children have a natural tendency to separate body from mind (called *dualism*); what we might term 'body and soul'. Any leanings toward religion – beliefs in unknown deities, fear of the unknown, demons and monsters – are by-products of this separation.[188]

The concept of dualism pervades just about every religion I've studied – the *karma* in Jainism and Buddhism, the *soul* in the Abrahamic religions, the *atman* in Hinduism, and so on. It is easy to see that the concept I described as self-awareness can take on an existence of its own. Once the idea has been put in someone's mind, it's very hard to displace or replace it. This would be especially true if separation of soul from body and the associated belief in God were instinctive, the result of a God gene.

We know, simply by observation, that small children take comfort from imaginary friends and have an elementary trust in friendly authoritative adults. Is this instinctive? I suspect yes. Is the instinct caused by an identifiable gene? I don't know – but what I do know or, better still, what I observe is that as small children pass through puberty to adulthood, the need for imaginary friends is often replaced by the need for idols of one form or another. Celebrities, for example – sports stars, pop stars, film stars, manufactured celebrities, reality TV stars, and the British Royalty. This adulation has spawned a huge industry – look at the rise of celebrity magazines such as *OK* and *Hello*. Why do people read these magazines? Is it envy, jealousy, aspiration, curiosity, or adulation? Or all of the above?

I consider adulation to be a form of worship, an *extravagant respect or admiration for or devotion to an object of esteem* (Merriam-Webster). These celebrities have become substitute gods in a world that has veered from spiritual to material. I don't denigrate the people who read such magazines – I just don't understand why they do it. I am curious to know whether those who are deeply religious also read such magazines, or whether their religious beliefs fulfil their need for someone or something to worship?

Do memes help?

Recall Dawkins's concept of a meme – a replicating unit of cultural inheritance; beliefs, ideas, behaviours, styles, tunes or catch-phrases that propagate through social groups. Something that moves from one

---

[188] Also discussed further in the appended postscript.

human brain to another similar in concept to genes that move from one human body to another. Memes might explain the evolution of both personal and organised religions similar to how genes explain the evolution of mankind. Let's explore them and see ...

First, let's distinguish between personal and organised religions.

A personal religion is some inner set of beliefs that an individual may or may not share with others. People develop them for all sorts of reasons: for comfort at times of stress, in exultation of an event like the birth of a baby, as a means of closure (such as burial rites), or as a substitute for family. It could just be something they contemplate after meditation.

An organised religion is one that has standard and documented beliefs, rituals, rules and regulations, taught by a priesthood authorised by church elders to pass on their knowledge and understanding. The doctrines foster group identity, thereby encouraging group cooperation and strength in numbers.

Just as genes can self-replicate, mutate, or become extinct, so can memes. For self-replication, look at the phenomenon of information transmitted via Twitter, or the speed at which a YouTube video can go viral, or the proliferation of a runaway e-mail. For meme mutation, look at how rumours spread and become distorted. As Mark Twain said, 'The report of my death is an exaggeration.'

Similarly, just as genes usually work in groups (gene complexes) to produce a specific physical manifestation (the phenotype), memes work in groups called meme complexes, or *memeplexes*.

Religions could be defined as a memeplex. As an example, recall the Apostles' Creed of the Roman Catholic Church:

1. I believe in God, the Father Almighty, creator of heaven and earth.
2. I believe in Jesus Christ, his only Son, our Lord.
3. He was conceived by the power of the Holy Spirit and born of the Virgin Mary.
4. He suffered under Pontius Pilate, was crucified, died, and was buried.
5. He descended to the dead. On the third day he rose again.
6. He ascended into heaven and is seated at the right hand of the Father.
7. He will come again to judge the living and the dead.
8. I believe in the Holy Spirit,
9. (I believe in)The holy Catholic Church, the communion of saints,
10. (I believe in) The forgiveness of sins,

11. (I believe in) The resurrection of the body,
12. And (I believe in) life everlasting.

Each of these twelve statements can be considered to be a religious meme: units of religious beliefs. Statements 1 to 8 and 10 to 12 define Christian religions other than Roman Catholicism. It's statement 9 that qualifies the memeplex to create the Catholic religion. Alternatively, if you modify statements 1 (replace God with *Allah*), 2 (replace Jesus with Muhammad and delete the Son of God connotation), 7 (replace Jesus with *al-Mahdi*), and 9 (replace Catholic Church with Islam) and take away statements 5 (no resurrection), 6 (no ascension) and 11 (no resurrection again), you have the basis for a working definition of Islam.

Now consider what happens when memes mutate. In terms of religion, we call the effects of such mutations *schisms* – splits in the church. Islam split into the two main classes – Sunni and Shi'a. Christianity split into Roman Catholic (the parent) and Protestant (the mutated offspring). And so on.

We could continue in this vein analysing the evolution of religions in memetic[189] terms, drawing on analogies between genes and genetics and memes and memetics, but memetics has its critics. Some point out that there's no memetic equivalent to the biological substance and function of DNA; others point to the possibility that very high mutation rates in memes would result in cultural chaos rather than cultural evolution.

Such inadequacies are evident in the discussion about memeplexes defining religions. Where is the meme that mutated and caused the Catholic/Protestant split? Meme 9? If so, what was the cause and nature of the mutation and the effect on meme 9? How would we quantify the mutation if there is no code script? We may need to add more memes, or sub-memes, to the memeplex to try to explain the nature of the meme mutation and the resulting schism.

Similarly, what does it really mean to say 'I believe in *God, the Father Almighty, Creator of Heaven and Earth*'? What lies behind the word *God*? What are God's properties? What lies behind *Father Almighty*? Conceptually, what do the words mean? Father of what? Is *Father Almighty* a synonym for *God*? If so, why repeat it? What lies behind *Creator*? Can I believe that God created the earth but then evolution

---

[189] Memetics: defined to be the study of the concept and transmission of memes; the heredity and variation of cultural units.

took over? And what is *Heaven*? What did God create that's referred to as *Heaven*?

As always, the devil lies in the details (no pun intended!). The structure of memes is less defined than that of genes. Because there is no coding script comparable to the gene's base-pair coding sequences in DNA, the application of memetics to the definition and evolution of religions is so fraught with pitfalls and ambiguities that, in my view at least, it doesn't merit further pursuit. However, before we leave the subject, let's take one more look at the question of the existence of a God gene – something in our genetic makeup, coded into one or more of the genes housed in our chromosomes.

The question of a grammar gene remains unresolved but, as several authors have pointed out, even if such a gene existed, its prime phenotype may not be the ability to speak one or more languages. Genes create proteins that create us, and the 'us' includes our brains and speech organs. However, the combination of the two to understand and make use of a language is, to my mind, a consequence of genes' creation of the physical organs, not the primary effect of a specific gene.

What I do believe is that there is a language instinct, as postulated by Pinker. But how the instinct, or any instinct come to that, relates to our genes is not clear to me nor, it seems, to others who are more knowledgeable about such things. I don't think there's a one-to-one correspondence between higher-order functions, such as language acquisition, and the genes that control the manufacture of the body parts involved – the brain, mouth, throat, tongue, lips and so on. I think that we still have some way to go before we understand exactly how the coding in our genes causes us to be born with an innate understanding of a generative grammar. I accept that a generative grammar is innate – just not that it's related directly to some segment of DNA.

I've reached the same conclusion about a God gene. It doesn't exist. Would a child invent Father Christmas if sacks of toys never appeared on December 25th and his name was never mentioned? Children invent mythical characters but it is doubtful if he would be included. What would cause children to invent him? There is no innate belief in Father Christmas. Similarly, if a small child believes in God, the idea must have been planted by an adult or some other external agent such as a story book. Once planted, however, this particular belief could well stay with the child into adulthood for various reasons:

- The adult feels comfortable with the concept and sees no need to question it.
- The belief in God outweighs any rational objective reasoning.
- The adult feels comforted by the idea of God, especially in times of stress – sickness, loss of a family member or close friend – or in times of danger.
- The adult is engulfed by one or more of the trappings of the belief, that is, by any of Ninian Smart's seven dimensions: doctrinal, mythological, ethical, ritual, experiential, social and material.

Note that none of these reasons would apply to an adult's continuing belief in Father Christmas. If this conviction continued into maturity, it's for some other possibly strange reason.

An interesting question that sometimes arises is this: What would happen if we took a number of new-born babies, less than six months old say, and placed them on an uninhabited island with all the basic needs to survive – food and drink, shelter, warmth, medicines and whatever else is required to nourish and sustain them as they grew to adulthood, but without adult carers? Would they develop a belief in one or more supernatural beings? Would some form of a religion emerge to encompass the belief?

This is a hypothetical question, of course. Any speculation as to the answer would be just that – speculation. It could not happen in practice. Even if such an experiment was set up, there would have to be adult carers to foster the first few years' growth and their presence would inevitably influence the intellectual development of the group. But one novelist, William Golding, postulated the outcome – albeit with a more-mature group of children. In his 1954 novel, *The Lord of the Flies*, Golding tells the story of what happens to a group of young English schoolboys (the oldest is thirteen) stranded on an island following a plane crash. They start out trying to behave as a civilised community but their behaviour degenerates into primal savagery with religious overtones. The multi-layered story can be read at three levels:

- As an entertaining *Boy's Own* story of invention and adventure.
- As an allegory of how the removal of the constraints of law and order causes regression to a primitive and lawless society.
- As an allegory of the development of a primitive native religion and the ensuing battle between Good and Evil.

The Need For A God

With reference to the last allegory, we see how:

- a conch shell originally used to confer authority to speak at a group meeting becomes more of a religious symbol denoting power.
- the younger boys, called *littluns*, invent a monster called 'The Beast' and how their fear of the monster eventually causes one of the older boys, Simon, a *bigun*, to be mistaken for the Beast and inadvertently killed during a primal dance.
- the group fractures into two separate groups, one Good (headed by Ralph), the other Evil (headed by Jack).
- Jack starts using body and face paint and elevates himself to the status of a demigod inspiring awe and fear in the *littluns*.
- torture develops, first of a pig, then of some of the *littluns* and eventually of one of the *biguns*, Piggy, resulting in his death.
- both groups descend into proto-religious behaviour with offerings to the Beast including the head of the dead pig mounted on a stick. As the head decomposes, it becomes covered in flies, the *Lord of the Flies* of the title.

I first read this book sometime in the 1960s. The picture it painted of a group of civilised English schoolboys regressing into savagery has never left me. The book appears in many *100 Best ...* lists and contributed to William Golding's award of the Nobel Prize for Literature in 1983. I recommend it.

Thomson and Aukofer postulate that a belief in God and an enjoyment in a religion can be ascribed to adaptations of various innate and cognitive behaviours developed originally as primal survival instincts. They suggest that the creation of supernatural beings and related religions is man-made. 'God did not make man. Man made God.' Our primitive instincts lend themselves to beliefs in supernatural beings and, once established, we cling to our beliefs because they are comforting and easier to believe than not to believe. Their arguments are highly plausible and the evidence they offer supports my own views on why we have a tendency to believe in God, especially when we are young and not yet in a position to reason about his existence.

Read more about their suggestions in the postscript to this chapter.

The future of religion

What might we conclude from this journey through the many facets of God and religion? Does God exist? Or is he the invention of a fertile mind looking for a way to make money? Is religion just an organised business? Should we be looking for a God gene or is this a hiding to nothing? Will Islam be the cause of Armageddon? Is Theravada Buddhism the answer? If so, what's the question?

These questions, and many others, have been the subject of this book. When I started writing it, my intention was to capture my thoughts in an essay for the benefit of my granddaughters, to be read when and if needed. Over time, the essay evolved into something much, much greater. The subject is enormous and I've learnt a great many things by studying it. The intricacies of gene transmission through the mechanics of human reproduction turned out to be a fascinating subject – one quite unlike anything I had studied before. I knew the practice of course – how else would I have grandchildren? – but the theory is far more complex and, dare I say it, far more wonderful than anything I could have envisaged. If there were a God, this would have been one of his most awe-inspiring creations. As it happens, though, I am firmly on the side of the evolutionists. It is evolution that created the masterpiece that is mankind – not a supernatural being.

That is pretty much the end of the matter as I see it, but to conclude this chapter – and indeed the whole book – here are a few final thoughts.

One of the lessons of Golding's *Lord of the Flies* – one that arises repeatedly as you read around the subject of religion in general – is that organised religions are simply ways for small groups of people to control the lives of much larger populations and in so doing accumulate power and wealth. Cicero, the great Roman orator of Julius Caesar's Senate, was said to have acknowledged 'the necessity of religion as a form of social order despite its obvious irrational elements'. This theme has occurred time and again throughout the book: in the ancient religions, in the modern religions, in the crackpot cults of David Koresh, Jim Jones, L Ron Hubbard and others;[190] in the establishment and application of Islamic Sharia law; and, these days, in the quack religions of evangelists and cult leaders of every type and

---

[190] Including one who came to light as I was finishing this chapter: Warren Jeffs. Jeffs was the self-proclaimed prophet and president of the Fundamentalist Church of Jesus Christ of Latter-Day Saints, an offshoot of the Mormon Church. He is now (August 2011) a convicted polygamist and child abuser serving a life sentence in a Texas prison.

persuasion. If you strip the mysticism that surrounds a belief in a supernatural being away from the organised religion of which it is 'head', what emerges is a business, a very lucrative and, at times, ruthless business.

Consider the following paragraph, lifted verbatim from Chapter 1.

There is a product. In fact there are several products, very similar in nature but coming from an organisation whose history includes violence and life-threatening addictions. There are also several myths perpetuated about the product, including its origin, its make-up, holders of secret knowledge, and what it can do for you. In fact, there is considerable mystery as to the exact nature of the product but there is a very capable, some might say ruthless, marketing team coupled with an efficient distribution channel such that the product is readily recognisable and available in every corner of the world. But, despite this, people consume this product with an implicit belief that it solves an immediate problem and does so in a way that does not harm the consumer. There are also competitive products, including abstinence from any of the products, and sometimes the market chooses to adopt one of the competitive products in preference to the real thing but, in most cases, the differences between the various products are slight or even indiscernible. But, despite which product you consume, the variety of products is ubiquitous, always available, comforting and very lucrative for the merchants and peddlers involved.

Now consider the next two embellished versions of the paragraph.

Version One:

There is a product. *It's called Coca-Cola.* In fact there are several products, very similar in nature – *Diet Coke, Coke Zero, Dasani, Minute Maid, Sprite, and many more* - but coming from an organisation whose history includes violence *(the accusations and ensuing court cases of the Coca-Cola Company's alleged complicity in the murder of eight trade-union employees by paramilitaries at a Colombian bottling plant[191])*, and life-threatening addictions *(the original 1865 medicinal product contained both cocaine and alcohol).* There are also several myths perpetuated about the product, including its origin *(in 1865 by pharmacist John Pemberton in a drugstore in Columbus, Georgia, originally as a coca wine called Pemberton's French Wine Coca, and possibly inspired by a European coca wine called Vin Mariani),* its make-up *(including a mysterious ingredient*

---

[191] The allegations were not proved in a court of law but visit the following website, and many others, to read more.
http://en.wikipedia.org/wiki/Criticism_of_Coca-Cola#Bottling_plant_murders

called Merchandise 7X[192]), holders of secret knowledge *(only two executives have access to the exact formula of Coca-Cola with each executive knowing only half the formula[193]),* and what it can do for you *(refreshes, exhilarates, revives, sustains, adds life – extracts from Coca-Cola advertising slogans since 1886).* In fact, there is considerable mystery as to the exact nature of the product *(Merchandise 7X again, plus the 'does it still contain cocaine?' question[194])* but there is a very capable, some might say ruthless, marketing team *(who, when it comes down to it, just want to sell a flavoured carbonated sugar solution thereby contributing to the obesity of many young, and not so young, people[195])* coupled with an efficient distribution channel *(with manufacture, bottling, and distribution outlets in over 200 countries in the world[196])* such that the product is readily recognisable and available in every corner of the world. But, despite this, people consume this product with an implicit belief that it solves an immediate problem *(the bodily need for liquid)* and does so in a way that does not harm the consumer. There are also competitive products *(from Pepsico and Cadbury Schweppes, the main competitors to the Coca-Cola Company),* including abstinence from any of the products *(an abstainer from any carbonated soft drink),* and sometimes the market chooses to adopt one of the competitive products in preference to the real thing *(another Coca-Cola advertising slogan)* but, in most cases, the differences between the various products are slight or even indiscernible *(they are all based on a flavoured carbonated sugar, or sugar-substitute, solution).* But, despite which product you consume, the variety of products is ubiquitous, always available, comforting and very lucrative for the merchants and peddlers involved *(generating $31 billion revenue with $6.8 billion net income for the Coca-Cola Company in 2009[197]).*

---

[192] Merchandise 7X is now known to be a mix of the following oils, spices and flavourings: orange, cinnamon, lemon, coriander, nutmeg and neroli plant oil (produced from the blossom of a bitter-orange tree).

[193] A well-known urban myth but, apparently, the truth is slightly different. The Coca-Cola Company does have a rule restricting access to only two executives but each executive knows the entire formula and others, in addition to the prescribed duo, also know the formulation process.

[194] The answer is 'no'.

[195] A harsh judgment, I know, but it's only very recently that the Coca-Cola Company has reduced the amount of sugar in its products, the lower-calorie or zero-calorie offerings, and also turned to non-carbonated healthier drinks such as fruit juices and water.

[196] The United Nations currently recognises 195 countries. It would appear that the Coca-Cola Company knows about countries not yet known to the UN. Or is it creative marketing?

[197] According to http://www.wikinvest.com/stock/Coca-Cola_Company_(KO)

The Need For A God

Version Two:

There is a product. *It's called God.* In fact there are several products, very similar in nature – Yahweh, Father Almighty, Allah - but coming from an organisation whose history includes violence *(see Hosea 13:16, Isaiah 13:16, 2 Kings 10:7-8, Leviticus 20:13, Romans 1:24-32, Deuteronomy 21:18-21, 1 Samuel 18:27, Isaiah 13:16, Numbers 31:17-18, Exodus 21:7-11 and many more instances in the Bible)* and life-threatening addictions *(fasting, scourging, extreme self deprivation, voluntary and involuntary suicide).* There are also several myths perpetuated about the product, including its origin *(a self-creating creator who created everything else in six days, the product of an immaculate conception),* its make-up *(the Son, the Father, the Holy Ghost, all rolled into one),* holders of secret knowledge *(Papal infallibility, Kabbalah, God-men, evangelists, Operating Thetan courses),* and what it can do for you *(absolve your sins, prepare you for the afterlife).* In fact, there is considerable mystery as to the exact nature of the product *(does God exist, who created him, is there an afterlife?)* but there is a very capable, some might say ruthless, marketing team *(priests, cardinals, imams, bishops, and other high-church officials)* coupled with an efficient distribution channel *(churches, mosques, synagogues, temples, TV , Web)* such that the product is readily recognisable and available in every corner of the world. But, despite this, people consume this product with an implicit belief that it solves an immediate problem *(a manufactured need for spiritual sustenance)* and does so in a way that does not harm the consumer. There are also competitive products *(Christianity, Judaism, Islam, Hinduism, and more),* including abstinence from any of the products *(atheism),* and sometimes the market chooses to adopt one of the competitive products in preference to the real thing but, in most cases, the differences between the various products are slight or even indiscernible *(they are all based on a belief in a mythical supernatural being, or set of beings).* But, despite which product you consume, the variety of products is ubiquitous, always available, comforting and very lucrative for the merchants and peddlers involved *(it is impossible to discover the financial worth of organised religions since they are mostly classed as charitable benevolent and tax-exempt organisations. They pay no capital-gains nor property nor corporate tax, do not have to produce income statements or disclose any other financial data, receive many grants and other subsidies from governments, own vast amounts of land and property, and are major investors in large corporations. Entering 'How much is XXX religion worth?' into a search engine produces virtually no results of substance. There is plenty of speculation and plenty of minutia – the diocese of so-and-so owns x thousand shares in some company and y acres of land ... - but rarely does one find a single authenticated statement of revenue and net income. But, one thing is for sure. Organisations like the Roman Catholic Church are immensely rich, far richer than any major corporation such as the Coca-Cola Company, and with a complicated organisation designed to disguise their true wealth.[198])*

As I said before, religions are just the same as businesses. And some of them are extremely lucrative. Sai Baba was said to be worth $6 billion at his death in 2011; Hubbard accrued $200 million in 1982. For this reason alone, it is hard to imagine religions will die out – there's too much money invested in them and they are far too profitable.

But, despite the absence of an organised competitive atheist movement, God/religion is on the decline in certain parts of the world, particularly in Western Europe. We see the evidence in the following:

- Falling church attendances.
- The commercialization of religious festivals such as the Christian Christmas and Easter.
- The cross-fertilization of religious and secular concepts caused by increasing migration of people of one religion moving to a country with a different dominant religion. For example, people from Islamic countries migrating to non-Islamic countries (it rarely happens the other way round!).
- Rising living standards in first world countries reducing the need for spiritual comfort in times of hardship.
- Longer lives postponing the need, if it exists, to prepare for the afterlife.
- A reduction in the power of a church to entice you back into the religion as an active member.

From that point of view, it's worth asking what religions have to offer these days.

The early religions developed when survival was a struggle – the basic needs of food, warmth and shelter were hard to come by.

---

[198] It's impossible to assess the wealth of the Roman Catholic Church. Estimates on various websites vary from millions of dollars to billions of dollars but all are guesses. In any case, what's meant by wealth? How are assets such as buildings, land, and works of art valued? Can they be purchased? If not, their book value is effectively zero. The organisation of the Church is also complex. It's not a single entity. It would take a mammoth effort to unravel the true wealth of the Church but the impression is that the Church is not poor, not after centuries of existence and power.

The Need For A God

Religion used to be the *opium of the masses* (Karl Marx) but, nowadays, few thinking people feel the need for the protection and assistance of supernatural powers. They have all the food, warmth and shelter they need. They also have man-made celebrities to engage their need for someone/something to follow. Why bother about supernatural gods when there's an alternative so readily to hand? And anyway, evolution is on the verge of explaining our origins. Strip all those things away and religions are just a way of relieving people of their money.

As I walk by churches, I see all sorts of 'promotions', as retailers would call them – *Jesus Lives, Let God Guide You, Come And Be Saved, Believe in Jesus, There Is Only One God, The Holy Spirit Moves*, and so on. What do these slogans mean? Are they designed for believers or non-believers? Would they entice me into the church? I would be more intrigued if the sign said *Buy One God, Get One Free!*

At least some of the notices are humorous. Enter 'Church Sign Boards' into a search engine and you'll find examples like these:

- Church car parking. Trespassers will be baptised!
- We are the soul agents in this area
- All we want for Christmas is your presence
- Staying in bed shouting 'Oh God!' does not constitute going to church
- The meek shall inherit the earth, if that's OK by you
- There are some questions that cannot be answered by Google
- Forgive your enemies. It messes with their heads

And on car bumper bars you will find examples like 'Honk if you love Jesus; text while driving if you want to meet him!'.

Another thing that puzzles me is why there is such a bewildering choice of religions. If there's only one God, why is there more than one religion? Having read this book, you'll know my view – it's because they are competitive businesses vying for your patronage. But how would someone who is thinking of joining a religion (it does happen!) work out which one to join?

Beyond that, there's the question of whether there has ever been a time in the history of *homo sapiens* when a social group existed that did not have a need to invent or follow a religion.

Communism is a false *yes*. From 1917 until the collapse of the Soviet Union, religions were practiced behind closed doors. Now, they are back in full swing. The Russian Orthodox Church, a branch of

Christianity similar to Roman Catholicism, is very much alive and well.

Okay, so what about North Korea – the hardest hard-line communist state in the world? The current *Dear Leader*, Kim Jong-Il,[199] is promoted as a god in the sense that he is to be revered and even worshipped by his country's people. The result may appear to be a personality cult *par excellence*, but the reality is different. Buddhism, Confucianism and Christianity are tolerated in North Korea but those who practice religions overtly run the risk of persecution, especially if they are Christians. (For a first-rate account of life in today's secretive state of North Korea, read Barbara Demick's illuminating 2010 book, *Nothing To Envy*.)

Religions exist – that's a fact of life. And they are big business, so the chance they will all die out any time soon is extremely remote.

The best we can hope for is to tame their excesses and educate our offspring about the alternatives to belief in mythical supernatural beings. If we do that, there is hope that we, the human race, will emerge from the mystical world of superstition we have created so far and into a new world of enlightenment about nature, evolution and the wonder that is us.

I'm almost tempted to end with 'God willing!'

(^_^)

---

[199] Now replaced by his son, Kim Jong-un, following Kim Jong-Il's death in December 2011.

Postscript: The Science of Faith

Summary of Thomson and Aukofer's book

'Like religious ideas and beliefs, religious rituals are by-products of mental mechanisms originally designed for other purposes.'
Thomson and Aukofer, p. 82

One of the problems with writing a technical book is that new or previously-unseen publications turn up during the fingers-to-keyboard writing stage. It becomes a temptation to read through the new material, assess the content and go back and edit what has already been written. The danger, of course, is that the process never stops and the book is never finished.

Consequently, I took a decision to 'freeze' the writing stage in July 2011 and ask a former colleague to review the manuscript prior to final publication. And then another book caught my attention: J Anderson ('Andy') Thomson and Clare Aukofer's *Why We Believe in God(s): a Concise Guide to the Science of Faith*, published by Pitchstone Publishing, 2011.

It was the word *science* that convinced me to make an exception. The lead author, Andy Thomson, is a forensic psychiatrist who has made a special study of the psychology of suicide bombers. He has now turned his attention to why we might be pre-ordained to create gods and associated religions. I could not resist the temptation to read the book and, as expected, it turned out to be both interesting and pertinent to some of what I had already written in this last chapter. But, rather than go back and edit my earlier comments, I decided to leave my comments and conclusions as they were and summarise Thomson and Aukofer's book in a separate postscript. Here's the summary, with links back to some of my earlier observations.

First, recall the definition of an innate behaviour. It is something we're born with and which either manifests itself at birth (a baby instinctively sucking at a mother's breast) or which develops as we mature (the mating instinct that develops post-puberty).

We also acquire behaviours by the mechanism of cognition: the act or process of knowing something including both awareness and judgment. That is, something that we deduce, understand, become aware of, apply judgment to based on our intelligence and observation of the world around us. For example, I will not launch myself off a high cliff because I perceive that those animals that can fly and land safely have wings and I don't have wings.

Innate and cognitive behaviours are often linked. In my jumping-off-cliffs example, the survival instinct, a basic innate behaviour, kicks in when I work out the possible consequences of jumping without wings.

Thomson and Aukofer assert that we have adapted these various types of behaviours to create ideas, beliefs and rituals associated with supernatural beings, god(s), and religion.

Here's a summary of the major forms of both innate and cognitive behaviours and their adaptations to religion. The first six entries are broadly categorised as innate; the rest are usually considered to be cognitive.

Behaviour 1. Forming *attachments* and the need for a caretaker. Attachments are part of teamwork (buddy), reproduction (sexual mate), kinship (mother, father, siblings, offspring and extended family members), comfort (friend, family pets), and protection/survival (child-parent bond). We also form attachments to inanimate objects such as a fluffy toy, rabbit's foot, lucky charm, or small child's blanket.

Forming attachments is probably the most important innate behaviour that transfers easily to a belief in a supernatural being.

Adaptation. Attachments are extendible by *transference* to a supernatural parent/friend/protector. In fact, religions encourage blood-family-to-supernatural-family transference by using close family titles such as Father Almighty (God), Father (priest), Son of God (Jesus Christ), Sister (nun), Mother Superior (chief nun), Brother (monk), Holy Father (Pope), Mother of God (Mary), God the Father (God), Holy Mother Church (the Roman Catholic Church).

The use of titles that imply close family relationships draws on our tendency to favour kin over others. The kinship people feel makes it easier for them to accept group religions and harder to leave them.

Behaviour 2. *Tribal instinct.* A willingness to work as a member of a team for the common good (cooperation and cohesion).

Adaptation. Extendible to conformance to common doctrines specified by a particular religion.

Behaviour 3. *Primary foraging theory.* A craving and over-indulgence in things that we like: foods high in sugar, salt or fat; sex; mind-altering drugs. Such things cause the release of neurochemicals. For example,

The Need For A God

dopamine gives us a good feeling and triggers a 'give me more' response. See later for more about neurochemicals.

Adaptation. It is suspected that many religious activities and experiences cause the release of the same pleasure-inducing chemicals in the body. More detail below.

Behaviour 4. *Dualism*, the mind-body split already mentioned earlier in this chapter. *Dualism* is connected to our sense of perception. We automatically separate the perception of physical attributes (things we can touch, see, smell, taste and hear) from non-physical attributes (abstract concepts such as death, emotions, predatory intent). This separation is the default setting of the brain and lends itself to the consideration that our self-awareness is something quite different to our physical self. This being so, it's only a small step to convert 'self-awareness' into a religious entity called a 'soul' and thus adapt the innate behaviour into the domain of a religious belief.

Adaptation. Dualism enables complex social interactions and relationships with unseen human beings and, by extension, unseen imaginary supernatural beings.

Dualism might explain why we are confused when we see magicians or illusionists at work. The mind wants to accept that Liu Qian passed his hand through a glass tabletop. The body knows it is not possible.

Behaviour 5. *Hyperactive Agency Detection Device (HADD)*. Automatically assigning a possibly predatory human or animal cause to something that happened rather than a non-threatening inanimate cause. An out-of-sight door slam is attributed to an intruder rather than the wind; a twig snapping in the forest is attributed to a grizzly bear rather than a timid fawn.

Adaptation. Extendible to natural phenomena and supernatural beings. The sound of thunder implies that 'God is angry' or 'God's moving the furniture around'; rain that 'God is crying'. HADD encourages a belief in paranormal beings such as ghosts and spirits. The 'who's there?' question is extendible to a two-way dialogue with an imaginary presence – prayer.

Behaviour 6. Innate sense of personal *morality* and associated community *ethics* of behaviour: an instinctive feeling for what's right and what's wrong. (Harris, *The End of Faith*, and Dawkins, *The God Delusion*, both devote a whole chapter to this topic.)

Adaptation. Leads to an acceptance of religious doctrines such as the Ten Commandments as long as they are not markedly different to our own innate morals and ethics.

Behaviour 7. *Empathy*: Ability to think like others; putting ourselves in their shoes in order to predict a response; feeling the same pain. You bump your head, I go 'ouch'. You yawn, I yawn. Reactions like these are attributed to *mirror neurons*: neurons in the brain that fire in an observer in sympathy to those that fire in the person observed.

Adaptation. Empathy can lead to the creation of imaginary friends and, by extension, to imaginary deities. The use of crucifixion symbols and images evoke an empathetic pain reaction.
Empathy also encourages conformance so as not to upset others: 'I go to church to please my community.'

Behaviour 8. *Decoupled cognition*. The ability to decouple ourselves from our environment while still engaging the mind: day-dreaming, replaying past conversations, planning future conversations, meditation, becoming involved while watching a film or reading a novel.

Adaptation. Decoupled cognition gives us the ability to create and become immersed in religious thoughts and sentiments such as prayer, meditation, and religious rituals. It allows us to think about others even though they are not physically present. This ability extends to a belief in communication 'beyond the grave': séances, conversing with ancestors.

Behaviour 9. *Minimally counterintuitive behaviour*, also called *intuitive reasoning* – basically, 'filling in the blanks' or 'bridging the gaps'. The ability to turn incomplete pictures into complete ones. In the illustration (Thomson and Aukofer, p. 66), you infer the existence of a white square from the four black shapes even though there is no square defined by lines.

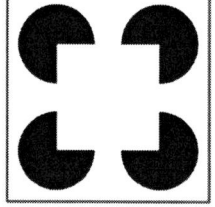

Adaptation. Gaps in our belief system are filled or bridged if we attribute human properties to deities: human shape (God), human behaviour (Jesus died, just like you and I will), use of human artefacts (*Kali* brandishes a sword, known to be a dangerous weapon).

It also works the other way round. The Confucian Chinese Emperors, Egyptian Pharaohs, Roman Emperors and Inca Kings were all revered as living gods. The Pope is infallible.

Small gaps don't test our credulity as much as big ones.

Behaviour 10. *Over-reading determination*: assigning events to things that cannot be true – 'It rained because I forgot my umbrella!', 'It always rains when I go on holiday', 'It's not meant to be!' (my mother-in-law's expression). Who decreed it wasn't meant to be?

Adaptation. Blame can be assigned to a supernatural being, and is extendible to offers of placatory gifts including, as we have seen, human sacrifice.

Behaviour 11. *Teleology*: the need to understand the design or purpose of something as evidenced by a small child's relentless asking of the who, what, where, why and how questions – why is the sky blue, the grass green, sugar bad for you, cabbage good for you, ...?

Adaptation. If you do not know the answer, or it has been a long day, or the question is embarrassing ('Where do babies come from?'), it is sometimes easier to invoke a supernatural being or create a make-belief answer – 'God painted the sky blue', 'The stork brings them'.

We have an innate need to understand the meaning of life and religion can help fulfil that need

Behaviour 12. *Deference to authority*. We have a tendency to obey a person who is in a perceived or elected position of authority: a policeman, a person in uniform, a teacher, even when we know the command to be wrong.[200]

---

[200] Thomson and Aukofer cite the famous Milgram experiments in the 1960s in which participants were asked by an authority figure to inflict ever-increasing electric shocks on unseen subjects. Although no shocks were actually applied, the participants didn't know this and some increased the voltage far higher than expected. The experiment has oft been repeated always with the same result. The conclusion is that most people will defer to a command by an authority figure even though the command is in breach of their personal morals. Visit http://en.wikipedia.org/wiki/Milgram_experiment to read more.

Adaptation. Extendible to deference to a god and to the commands of his earthly spokesperson: the Pope, Indian God men, priests, and so on.

Behaviour 13. *Reciprocity.* 'You scratch my back; I'll scratch yours.' The informal exchange of goods or labour. Reciprocity builds an 'I owe you, you owe me' bank.

Adaptation. Extendible to prayer and associated rituals or promises. 'If you make me better, I promise to be good', or 'Here's a goat as a sacrifice. Now can you make it rain?'

Behaviour 14. *Deceit* and *self-deception.* The ability to deceive both ourselves and others regarding a belief: the alcoholic believes she has her drinking under control; the husband convinces himself that his wife is not having an affair with another man. The basis of hidden agendas.

Adaptation. Extendible to a belief that a supernatural being exists even when reasoning suggests otherwise.

> *'Genuine morality is doing what is right regardless of what we may be told; religious morality is doing what we are told.'*
> Thomson and Aukofer, p. 78.

So, there we have it. Thomson and Aukofer's argument is that this set of interlinked behaviours could account for the origins and development of religious beliefs and thus represent a science for the cause of religion. They support their theory with commentary about the release of chemicals in parts of the body or brain caused by certain events or actions, typically with pleasurable results. Here's a summary of the chemicals and their effects.

Note: a *neurotransmitter* is a chemical that helps to relay signals from one part of the brain to another, whereas a *hormone* is a chemical that is released by a cell or a gland in the body and that sends out messages to other parts of the body.

Serotonin (Neurotransmitter): Causes a feeling of well-being, good self esteem and influences the brain cells associated with social behaviours, sexual desire, memory, ability to learn, body-temperature regulation, sleep and appetite. (The anti-depressant *Prozac* is designed to boost serotonin levels.) Even though it isn't a hormone, serotonin is often called the *Happy Hormone*.

Dopamine (neurotransmitter): Comes from pleasure in food, sex and mind-altering drugs. Urges a do-it-again response to repeat the pleasure. Dopamine causes increased heart rate and blood pressure, and influences brain cells associated with movement, motivation, punishment-reward-pleasure, sleep, attention focus, mood, memory and learning. Seen to be a reward chemical.

Adrenaline and Noradrenaline (neurotransmitter hormone): Increases heart rate, provides temporary bursts of strength by triggering the release of glucose to muscles (perhaps to escape a predator), focuses attention, and underlies the *Fight or Flight* response.

Oxytocin (hormone): Released during childbirth and breastfeeding and strengthens attachment. Oxytocin is also released during sexual intercourse and especially during orgasm. Generates feeling of love, generosity, trust and empathy and sometimes referred to as the *Love Hormone*.

Endorphin (neurotransmitter): A natural non-addictive opiate (narcotic), similar in effect to morphine found in the opium poppy and capable of temporarily suppressing pain and enhancing social bonding. Produced by exercise, excitement, pain, eating spicy food containing capsaicin (the active component of chilli peppers), and sexual orgasm. Has an analgesic effect (pain suppression) and produces feelings of well-being and even euphoric exhilaration (the *Endorphin Rush*) especially if released as part of a group activity such as a ritual associated with communal worship. Basically, a survival chemical.

Thomson and Aukofer suggest that religious activities can stimulate the production of some if not all these chemicals and thus induce the same feelings of well-being. Activities to which they attribute this effect include: trance induction, repetitive swaying, deep meditation, awkward postures held for a long time (as in yoga), fasting, rhythmic drumming or other forms of repetitive music, chanting, dance, singing, music,[201] rituals involving mind-altering drugs, devout prayer, and other forms of ritual worship.

In summary, the argument is basically that once religion has developed as a by-product of innate and cognitive behaviours, the rituals associated with it cause the release of pleasure-inducing chemicals in our bodies and thus serve to strengthen and increase the religious experience. It's an interesting thesis – one that plugs the gaps in some of my subjective observations.

I recommend the book and Thomson's 54-minute lecture to the American Atheists in 2009. The video is available on YouTube: http://www.youtube.com/watch?v=1iMmvu9eMrg

I leave the last words to Andy Thomson and Clare Aukofer:

> '*Religion may offer comfort in a harsh world; it may foster community; it may incite conflict. In short, it may have its uses – for good and evil. But it (religion) was created by human beings, and this will be a better world if we cease confusing it with fact.*'
>
> Thomson and Aukofer, p. 116.

(^_^)

---

[201] I can attest to this. Before I became hard-of-hearing, I was an avid listener of music, all sorts ranging from thirteenth century chants to twenty-first century techno and trance and embracing all styles of classical music plus most modern western and world music. I've many times been reduced to tears by a piece of music: *Mars* from Holst's Planets would do it, as would the *1812 Overture* by Tchaikovsky and the last movement of Sibelius's *Symphony No. 2*. Stravinsky's *Rite of Spring* would leave me breathless. *Classic CD* magazine once ran a quiz to determine what pieces of music had what it called the *tingle factor*. I recall that the results were all over the musical map but one thing was for sure – in the right environment and with the right company, music is a very powerful aphrodisiac!

Epilogue: A Letter From A Granddaughter

'What a distressing contrast there is between the radiant intelligence of the child and the feeble mentality of the average adult.'
Sigmund Freud, Austrian Psychoanalyst

'In childhood our credulity serves us well. It helps us to pack, with extraordinary rapidity, our skulls full of the wisdom of our parents and our ancestors. But if we don't grow out of it in the fullness of time, our ... nature makes us a sitting target for astrologers, mediums, gurus, evangelists, and quacks. We need to replace the automatic credulity of childhood with the constructive scepticism of adult science.'
Richard Dawkins, *Unweaving the Rainbow*, 1998, page 142–3

'If so, the absence of textbooks and teachers in most schools who are conversant and concerned enough with the difficulties of the theory of evolution to accurately present its hypothetical character, places a moral obligation upon all Muslim parents. They are obliged to monitor their children's Islamic beliefs and to explain to them (by means of themselves, or someone else who can) the divine revelation of Islam, together with the difficulties of the theory of evolution that will enable the children to make sense of it from an Islamic perspective and understand which aspects of the theory are rejected by Islamic theism (tawhid) and which are acceptable.'
Sheikh Nuh Ha Mim Keller, Islamic scholar,
http://www.masud.co.uk/ISLAM/nuh/evolve.htm

'When I was a child, I spake as a child, I understood as a child, I thought as a child: but when I became a man, I put away childish things.'
1 Corinthians 13:11

While writing this book, I had a conversation with Ella, the oldest of my four granddaughters. She'd just turned twelve when we spoke about religion and she showed me an essay that she'd written at school. The essay was in the form of a letter to one of her teachers, Mrs. Allan, who taught about religions. The subject of the essay was along the lines of 'Write a letter expressing your feelings about religion being taught at school'. I reproduce Ella's essay below with no changes other than the correction of a couple of minor spelling errors.

Dear Mrs. Allan,

Some people still believe in religion but there are not so many people in the UK who believe in religion so I think we don't have to study it.

Although studying religions may be important for the future we don't really need to study it right now. If we wanted to learn about religion when we are older, we could go to university or college. However, some people still believe in a religion because it gives people hope. So, maybe you could start an RE[202] club after school if enough people are interested.

Religion could be a bad thing for some because if some people in your family believe in a religion and some might not, it could lead to fights.

There are lots of different religions such as: Hinduism, Buddhism, Christianity, Sikhism, Judaism and Islam so all over the world, different people believe in different religions.

I think that we don't need to study religion at school because not everyone believes in religion or they don't think that it is important to learn. I think people should respect other people's beliefs.

Yours sincerely,

Ella Bennetts
(December, 2010, age 11)

There's hope!

(^_^)

---

[202] Religious Education

A Sam Harris/Richard Dawkins Dictionary

During the course of my readings of the books written by Sam Harris and Richard Dawkins, I had occasion to look up many words in the dictionary, either because they were new to me or just to check my *a priori* understanding. Here is the Sam Harris/Richard Dawkins dictionary I created. You may find it useful if you ever read their books. Note: there is some overlap with the words defined in Chapter 2.

Abridgement: Shortening, reduction.
Adduce: To offer an example, reason or proof in discussion.
Altruism: The behaviour of an animal that is not beneficial to and may even be harmful to itself but that benefits others of its species. The opposite of selfishness.
Animus: Basic attitude, usually spiteful, malicious.
Aphasia: Unable to comprehend the meaning of words, usually caused by brain damage.
Anthropocentrism: Considering human beings as the most significant entity in the universe. Interpreting the world in terms of human values and experiences.
Apostate: One who renounces or abandons a religious faith.
Canard: False fabricated report.
Casuistry: A specious argument, false look at the truth.
Chauvinism: An attitude of superiority.
Confabulation: Gossip, often embellished.
Conflate: To fuse, to join.
Construal: The noun derived from the verb *to construe*. How a person sees, understands and responds to his or her environment.
Cosmology: A study of the nature of the universe and its contents. Part of metaphysics.
Desacralize: Divest of sacred properties.
Dichotomy: Division into two contradictory or mutually-exclusive sub-groups.
Didactic: Designed or intended to teach; intending to convey instruction or information as well as pleasure and entertainment.
Disavow: Deny responsibility, refuse to acknowledge.
Disingenuous: Lacking in candour, false.
Divisive: Creating disunity or dissension.
Dogma: A point of view that cannot be proven.
Echolocation: Echo location.

Ecumenical: Promoting worldwide Christian unity.
Efficacy: Result.
Efflorescence: Blossoming, developing, unfolding.
Enteroreception: Intestine reception.
Epiphany: Appearance of a divine being.
Epistemology: A study or theory of the nature and evidence of knowledge, usually with reference to its limits and validity. Epistemology answers questions such as 'What is meant by knowledge? How is it acquired? How is it validated?' Part of metaphysics.
Eschatology: A belief in and the trappings of an afterlife.
Ethology: The scientific and objective study of animal behaviour
Eucharist: Spiritual communion with God.
Exculpatory: To clear from an alleged fault or guilt.
Exegesis: Critical explanation or interpretation.
Exigency: A state of affairs that makes urgent demands.
Felicitous: Pleasant, well-suited.
Filariasis: A disease caused by the parasitic filarial worm.
Genotype: Type of species, genetic constitution of an individual or group.
Hegemony: Domination.
Hermeneutics: Interpretation.
Heterodox: Holding unorthodox opinions.
Inchoate: Imperfectly formulated.
Ineluctable: Inevitable.
Inerrant: Free from error.
Internecine: Marked by slaughter.
Infidel: One who has no religious beliefs; one who is not a Christian/Muslim or who opposes Christianity/Islam.
Kinesthesia: Reception of a stimulus received by end organs.
Liberal: Not bound by authoritarianism, orthodoxy or traditional beliefs or forms.
Maladaptive: Badly adapted.
Meme: A replicating unit of cultural transmission such as tunes, ideas, catch-phrases, fashion. Something that moves from one human brain to another similar in concept to genes that move from one human body to another. A term invented by Richard Dawkins.
Memetics: The study of the concept and transmission of memes.
Mendicant: Having no goods or possessions, a beggar.
Metaphysics: A branch of philosophy concerned with the fundamental nature of being and based on cosmological, epistemological and ontological considerations. Metaphysics is a

notoriously difficult word to define and is usually explained within the context of a particular subject, such as religion.
Obfuscate: To make obscure.
Obscurantist: Opposition to the spread of knowledge.
Omnipotent: Unlimited authority.
Omniscient: Knows everything.
Ontology: A study of the nature of being, existence, reality. Part of metaphysics.
Paradigmatic: An outstandingly clear or typical example, archetypical.
Phenomenology: The study of a phenomenon.
Phenotype: The bodily manifestation of a gene, or gene complex, such as curly hair, blue eyes, and so on.
Phylogenic: Evolutionary history.
Phylum: A direct line of descendant within a group.
Pluralism: A state of society in which members of diverse ethnic, religious or social groups maintain an autonomous participation in and development of their traditional culture or special interest within the confines of a common civilization.
Piety: The state or quality of being dutiful to religion.
Plebiscite: Acceptance by majority vote.
Pragmatism: A practical approach to solving problems or situations.
Precept: A command, law.
Prestidigitation: Sleight of hand.
Proprioception: Reception of stimulus received within an organism.
Proselytize: Recruit into a faith.
Psychotic: Mentally deranged.
Ramify: Separate into divisions.
Rapine: Pillage and plunder, not rape.
Ratiocination: Reasoning.
Redactor: Author, editor.
Reflexivity: Turning back on itself, reflection.
Regnant: Reigning, dominant.
Reify: To regard something abstract in a material or concrete way.
Reparation: The act of making amends.
Rococo: Excessively ornate.
Roiling: Disturbed, muddied.
Scrofulous: Diseased run-down appearance, morally contaminated.
Secular: Of, or relating to the world: not specifically bound by religious beliefs.

Selfishness: The behaviour of an animal that is beneficial to itself but not beneficial and may even be harmful to others of its species. The opposite of altruism.
Sentient: Responsive to stimulus.
Squassation: A form of mediaeval torture, variant of *strappado*.
Syllogism: Deductive reasoning.
Tautology: A statement that is always true – for example, 'I am alive or I am dead'. Grammatically: an unnecessary repetition such as in 'free gift'.
Theocracy: A state governed by religious leaders.
Transubstantiation: A belief that wafer and wine becomes the flesh and blood of Jesus Christ.
Unitary: Undivided, whole.
Vastitude: Immensity.
Vicissitudes: Difficulties, hardships.
Zygote: Fertilized egg, developing individual.

(^_^)

Acknowledgements And Further Reading

Websites

I am heavily indebted to the many anonymous authors of Wikipedia articles, www.wikipedia.com. Where possible, I cross-checked facts I found on Wikipedia but I recognise that some non-Wikipedia sites are based on or derived from the corresponding Wikipedia articles.

Other notable websites are normally referenced in text or via the footnotes but one that deserves special mention is www.godchecker.com Truly a fascinating website, listing all the known deities and giving a brief appraisal of their origin, attributes and current status. The website listed 3,700 deities when last I looked!

Books

1. Bowker, John, *World Religions: The Great Faiths Explored And Explained*, Dorling Kindersley, 1997
2. Bryson, Bill, *A Short History Of Nearly Everything*, Black Swan, 2004
3. Darwin, Charles, *On the Origin of Species*, 1859, Oxford University Press, 1996 or available as a free PDF download from many websites including http://www.talkorigins.org/faqs/origin.html
4. Dawkins, Richard, *The Selfish Gene*, Oxford University Press, 1976, 2006 (30th Anniversary Edition)
5. Dawkins, Richard, *The God Delusion*, Black Swan, 2006
6. Dawkins, Richard, *The Greatest Show On Earth: The Evidence For Evolution*, Bantam Press, 2009
7. Deutscher, Guy, *The Unfolding of Language*, Arrow Books, 2005
8. Harris, Sam, *The End of Faith: Religion, Terror And The Future Of Reason*, Free Press, 2005
9. Harris, Sam, *Letter To A Christian Nation: A Challenge To Faith*, Bantam Press, 2007
10. Hitchens, Christopher, *God Is Not Great: How Religion Poisons Everything*, Twelve, 2007
11. *Holy Bible*, available as a free PDF download from many websites including http://www.gasl.org/refbib/Bible_King_James_Version.pdf Quotations in the book are taken from this version unless otherwise noted.
12. Hosseini, Khaled, *A Thousand Splendid Suns*, Bloomsbury Publishing Plc, 2007, p.248

13. Humphreys, John, *In God We Doubt: Confessions Of A Failed Atheist*, Hodder & Stoughton, 2007
14. Keown, Damian, *Buddhism: A Very Short Introduction*, Oxford University Press, 1996
15. McGraith, Alister & McGraith, Joanna Collicut, *The Dawkins Delusion: Atheist Fundamentalism And The Denial Of The Divine*, SPCK, 2007
16. Pearce, Richard (Director), *Leap Of Faith*, 1992 Paramount movie starring Steve Martin, Debra Winger
17. Pinker, Steven, *The Language Instinct*, Penguin Books, 1994
18. *Qur'an*, available as a free PDF download from many websites including: http://www.nooremadinah.net/Al-Quran/EnglishTranslation/Download/QuranEnglishTranslation.pdf. Quotations in the book are taken from this version.
19. Sen, K M, *Hinduism*, Penguin Books, 1961
20. Thera, Narada Maha, *Buddhism in a Nutshell*, Buddhist Cultural Centre, Sri Lanka, 1933
21. Thomson, J Anderson 'Andy' and Aukofer, Clare *Why We Believe in God(s): a Concise Guide to the Science of Faith*, Pitchstone Publishing, 2011
22. Waines, David, *An Introduction to Islam*, Cambridge University Press, 2004

Acknowledgments

Colin Maunder

In the mid-70s, a young BT electronics engineer, Colin Maunder, attended a short course I gave at Southampton University. We have remained colleagues and friends ever since, collaborating on many technical projects, workshops and papers and sometimes co-presenting short courses in industry. Colin went on to spearhead the ground-breaking IEEE standard on boundary scan, a revolutionary new way of testing electronic components and boards loaded with such components. He left BT in 2004 to set up a business with his wife, Viv, concentrating on all aspects of business communication. Their company, called the Writing House, can be found at www.writinghouse.co.uk

I approached Colin to see if he would volunteer to proof-read the first draft of the book. Not only did he agree, he did so with an enthusiasm and depth of grammatical knowledge that far exceeded my expectations. His conversion of my sometimes pedantic prose into

Acknowledgements And Further Reading

a more-lively version transformed the book and I am forever indebted to his contributions. Thank you Colin.

Andy Thomson and Clare Aukofer
During the closing stages of writing, a new book came to my attention. The book *Why We Believe in God(s): a Concise Guide to the Science of Faith* by Andy Thomson and Clare Aukofer looks at the adaptation of innate and cognitive human behaviours to the tendency to create supernatural beings, god(s), and their associated religions. I was unable to resist the temptation to read the book even though I was 'almost done'. As it happened, this turned out to be a good thing. The ideas expounded in the book provided a scientific base for many of my subjective observations in Chapter 9 and I decided to include a summary as a postscript to the chapter. I am indebted to Andy Thomson and Clare Aukofer for reviewing and correcting an earlier summary of their book. Any residual misunderstandings in my summary are due to my inability to grapple competently with the psychology of innate and cognitive behaviours.

Valeria Wrigglesworth
When I completed the appendix on human reproduction and gene transmission in Chapter 6, I looked for someone more knowledgeable than me to review the content. Valeria Wrigglesworth, a lecturer at Fareham College, volunteered. Valeria teaches the Genetics and Genetic Engineering unit of an Applied Science course and she did an excellent job of correcting my misunderstandings and improving the description. As with the previous acknowledgement, any residual errors in the appendix are due to my inability to understand what, to me, was a fascinating but complex subject.

(^_^)

Index

0

055 Brigade · 188

7

7/7 · 35

9

9/11 · 33, 171, 188

A

Abraham · 70
Adam and Eve · 70, 76, 96
Adamson, Marilyn · 4
Adrenaline · 243
Afghanistan
    Taliban · 159
    War against the Taliban · 188
Agnostic (Defn.) · 16
Ahura Mazda · 41
Aisha · 79
    The Jewel in the Medina · 167
Allah · 16, 157, 165
Allah's Brothel · 168
Alleles · 121, 126
Almah · 150
al-Mahdi · 81
al-Qaeda · 186, 188
    9/11 atrocity · 33, 171, 188
    origin of · 189
Ammonite fossil · 107
Amritsar · 65
Animism · 16, 68
Anti-Semitism · 31, 75, 143
Apocalypto (film) · 51
Apostate · 16, 80, 163
Apostles' Creed · 78, 225
Apostolic socialism · 31
Arab Riots · 184, 195
Arab Spring · 164, 174
Armageddon · 16, 33, 81, 157, 191
Artha (Hinduism) · 53
Ascetic (Defn.) · 16
Atheist (Defn.) · 16
Atman (Hinduism) · 53
Atonement · 76, 77
Attachments · 238
Aukofer, Clare · *See* Thomson, Andy
Autosome · 104, 121, 124
Avatars · 16, 54
Ayatollah · 43, 170
Aztec Religion · 49

B

Ba'ath party · 181
Baba, Sai · 208
Balfour Declaration · 184, 195
Balfour, Arthur · 184, 195
Baron Rothschild · 195
BCE · *See* Before Common Era
Before Common Era · 38
Begum, Hena · 175
Behaviour
    cognitive · 238
    innate · 238
Belief (Defn.) · 16
Ben-Gurion, David · 184, 196
Beslan · 34
Besra, Monica · 154
Bhakti (Hinduism) · 54
Bhikkhunis (Buddhism) · 59
Bhikkhus (Buddhism) · 59
Bible · 70, 77
    bad behaviours · 155
bin Laden, Osama · 174, 182
    execution of · 188
BIOS · 134
Blaine, David · 152
Blasphemy (Defn.) · 16

Index

Bloom, Paul · 224
Bodhisattvas (Buddhism) · 63
Boole, George
    Laws of Thought · 213
Boolean mathematics · 213
Bootstrapping · 134
Bowker, John
    World Religions · 30
Brahma (Hinduism) · 54
Brainwashing · 173
Branch Davidians · 32
Breivik, Anders · 178, 192
Brown, Derren · 152
Bryan, William Jennings · 110
Buddha · 60
    Enlightened One · 60
Buddhism · 59
    Buddha · 59, 60
    Chinese · 67
    Four Noble Truths · 60
    Is it a religion? · 22, 63
    Mahayana · 62
    Noble Eight-Fold Path · 61
    Pure Land · 67
    Tantra · 63
    Therevada · 62
Burqa (burka) · 157

C

Calvin, John · 145
Canaan · 70
Cartoons of Muhammad · 166
Catch-22 · 211
Catechism · 78
Cause-effect analyses · 210
CE · *See* Common Era
Celebrity magazines · 224
Cell · 103, 121, 124
    Diploid, 2N · 121
    Division · 121
    Haploid, N · 122
    Nucleus · 104, 122
Celtic Religion · 46
centromere · 135
Chi (Taoism) · 67

Child prodigies · 62
Chinese Buddhism · 67
Chosen People · 72, 143
Christianity · 70, 75, 141
Christmas · 145
chromatids · 135
Chromosomes · 103, 104, 121, 124
    Homologous · 122, 125
    mutation · 137
    Replication · 123
    X chromosome · 123
    Y chromosome · 123
Church of Scientology · 88
Coca-Cola · 231
Cognition · 222
Cognitive behaviour · 238
Common Era · 38
Communism
    religion without a god? · 31
Confucianism · 65
Confucius · 65
Cosmology · 16, 247
    geocentric · 143
    heliocentric · 143
Creationism · 108
    taxonomy · 113
Creed (Defn.) · 17
Crick, Francis · 103, 129, 131
Crossing over · 105, 121, 136
Cytokinesis · 121
Cytoplasm · 104, 121

D

Dakshinkali · 202
Dalai Lama · 63
Daoism · 66
Darrow, Clarence · 111
Darwin, Charles · 5, 97
    On the Origin of Species ... · 99, 100, 251
    story of · 97
    The Descent of Man · 219
Darwin, Erasmus · 97
Darwinism (Defn.) · 17
Dawkins, Richard · 12, 112, 154

Dictionary · 247
meme concept · 224
The Blind Watchmaker · 112
The God Delusion · 11, 12, 36, 209, 240, 251
The Greatest Show on Earth · 109, 251
The Selfish Gene · 15, 17, 93, 106, 108, 251
Unweaving the Rainbow · 245
Day of Judgment · 81
Deceit and self-deception · 242
Decoupled cognition · 240
Deference to authority · 241
Deism (Defn.) · 17
Deity (Defn.) · 17
Déjà vu · 62
Demick, Barbara
Nothing to Envy · 236
DeoxyriboNucleic Acid · *See* DNA
Dervishes · 82
Design-For-Test · 25
Deutscher, Guy · 218
The Unfolding of Language · 216, 251
Dharma (Hinduism) · 53
Dharmachakra (Buddhism) · 61
Dianetics · 88
Diaspora · 17, 74, 184
Diet of Worms · 144
Disputed Territories · 186, 197
Divine (Defn.) · 17
Divinity (Defn.) · 17
DNA · 103, 121, 128
fingerprinting · 129
mitochondria · 129
replication · 130
Dogma (Defn.) · 17
Double helix · 104, 129
Dualism · 224, 239
Dynamo (Frayne, Steve) · 152

E

Egg cells · 105
Egyptian Religion · 40
Embryo · 122
E-meter · 89

Emmanuel College · 113
Empathy · 240
Engrams · 88
Enlightened One · 60
Enlightenment · 60
Epistemology (Defn.) · 17
Eschatology (Defn.) · 17
Ethics · 21, 239
Evangelists · 206
  Baba, Sai · 208
  Graham, Billy · 206
  Hensley, George · 208
  Leap of Faith (film) · 206
  Roberts, Granville Oral · 206
Eve · *See* Adam and Eve
Evolution · 97, 105
  inheritance of acquired characteristics · 139
  Lamarkism · 139
  of languages · 218
  of marine iguanas · 98
  of religions · 204
  of stories · 97
  of the human eye · 112
  theory of · 101

F

Fact (Defn.) · 17
Faith (Defn.) · 17
Fallopian tubes · 136
Fatah · 197
Father Christmas · 29, 205, 215, 223, 227
Fatwa · 17, 160, 166
Feng Shui (Confucianism) · 66
Fertilization · 105, 122
Fight or Flight response · 243
First World War · 184
Five Pillars of Islam · 81
Five Vows (Jainism) · 58
Flood Geology · 114
Flying Spaghetti Monster Church · 87
Folk Shinto · 69
Four Noble Truths (Buddhism) · 60
FOXP2 · *See* Grammar gene

Index

Funeral pyres · 201

G

Galileo · 143
Gandhi, Indira · 65
Gandhi, Mahatma · 58
Gap Creationists · 115
Garden of Eden · 70
Gautama, Siddhartha *(Buddha)* · 59
Gaza Strip · 186, 196, 197
Gene complex · 106
Generative grammar · 216
Genes · 103, 104, 122
    alleles · 121, 126
    body as survival machine · 106, 130
    collaboration program · 128, 134
    crossing over · 105, 121, 136
    dominant · 126
    genetic bootstrapping · 134
    God · 215, 222
    grammar · 216, 227
    mutation · 105, 134, 138
    recessive · 126
Genesis, Book of · 70, 93
Genome · 103, 105, 122, 129, 132
Gentile · 73
Germ cells · 105, 137
God · 17
    Ahura Mazda · 41
    and mathematics · 212
    cause-effect analyses · 209
    definition of · 17
    does he exist? · 209
    gene · 215, 222
    the need for · 199
god (Defn.) · 17
Godchecker website · 28, 39
God-men · 208
    Baba, Sai · 208
Gods of nature · 84
Golan Heights · 197
Golden Rule (Confucianism) · 66
Golden Temple, Amritsar · 65
Golding, William
    Lord of the Flies · 228

Grammar
    generative · 216
    prescriptive · 217
Grammar gene · 216, 227
    FOXP2 · 220
    KE family · 220
Grave goods · 39, 85
Greek Religion · 42
Guru Gobind Singh · 64
Guru Granth Sahib (book) · 64
Guru Nanak Dev · 64

H

Hadith · 18, 80
    and martyrdom · 172
    attitude to suicide · 170
    definition of · 18
    origins of · 80
    rewards in Paradise · 168
Hajj (Islam) · 82
Hamas · 187, 197
Hanukkah (Judaism) · 75
Happy Hormone · 243
Hare Krishna · 54
Haredi Jews · 74
Harmandir Sahib · 65
Harris, Sam · 34, 154
    at war with Islam · 161
    Dictionary · 247
    quotations from the Qur'an · 162
    The End of Faith · 11, 12, 18, 52, 141,
        149, 157, 161, 162, 164, 240, 251
Hasadic Jews · 74
Hasan, Usama · 119
Hawking, Stephen · 109
    M-Theory · 109
    The Grand Design · 109
Heaven (Defn.) · 18
Heavenly Mandate (Confucianism) ·
    66
Hell (Defn.) · 18
Hensley, George · 208
Heresy (Defn.) · 18
Hermaphrodite · 151
Herzl, Theodor · 75

Hezbollah · 80, 167
Hijab · 157
Hinduism · 53
   and evolution · 117
Historical Dimensions (Ninian Smart) · 21
Hitler, Adolf
   was he a Christian? · 30
Holocaust · 31, 184
Holy Ghost · 149
Holy See · 153
Holy Spirit · *See* Holy Ghost
Homo sapiens · 101
Homologous · *See* Chromosomes
Hormone · 242
Hosseini, Khalid
   A Thousand Splendid Suns · 159
   The Kite Runner · 159
Houri · 169
Hubbard, L Ron · 88, 234
Human Biology · 121
   summary · 104
Human Genome Project · 132
Humphreys, John
   In God We Doubt · 28
Hydrogen bonds · 129
Hyperactive Agency Detection Device · 239

I

Ibrahim (Abraham) · 70
Imam · 170
Immaculate Conception · 76, 150
Imperial Household Shinto · 69
Inca Religion · 48
Incarnation · 18, 145, 151
Indulgences · 144
Infidel · 18, 80
Innate · 18
   behaviour · 238
   definition of · 215
   language · 216
Inquisition
   Medieval · 142
   Portuguese · 142, 143
   Roman · 142
   Spanish · 142
Instinct · 18
   definition, part 1 · 215
   definition, part 2 · 219
Intelligence · 222
Intelligent Design · 111
   love of gaps · 113
Intuitive reasoning · 240
Iran · 13, 20, 41, 80, 175, 181, 191
Irreducible complexity · 112, 119
Islam · 70, 78
   and adultery · 175
   and censorship · 165
   and evolution · 117, 245
   and intolerance · 176
   and martyrdom · 170
   and war · 162
   hard-line · 157
   knowledge by revelation · 83
   Middle Age development · 83
   origins of · 79
   support of violence · 163
Islamic Golden Age · 83
Israel · 182, 184
   Ben-Gurion, David · 185, 196
   Disputed Territories · 186, 197
   events timeline · 195
   Law of Return · 186, 196
   Netanyahu, Benjamin · 198
   Six-Day War · 197

J

Jacob · 71
Jainism · 56
   is it a religion? · 57
   Triple Gems · 57
Jerusalem · 186, 196, 197
   King David Hotel bombing · 185
Jesus Christ · 75
   Genealogy · 145
   Immaculate Conception · 76
   Incarnation · 151
   Resurrection · 76, 151
Jews · 31, 72

Index

and anti-Semitism · 31, 75, 143
and Palestinians · 183
and the Balfour Declaration · 184
and Zionism · 75
diaspora · 74
Haredi · 74
Hasadic · 74
Holocaust · 31, 184
Orthodox · 74
Reform · 74
Sephardic · 143
Jihad · 18, 161, 197
Jilbab · 157
Jiva (Jainism) · 56
Jnana (Hinduism) · 54
Johnson, Samuel · 218
Jones, Jim · 31
    apostolic socialism · 31
    People's Temple · 31
Jones, Sherry
    The Jewel in the Medina · 167
Judaism · 70, 72
Jyllands-Posten · See Muhammad

K

Ka'ba · 81
Kabbalah (Judaism) · 72
Kaccha (Sikhism) · 64
Kakars (Sikhism) · 64
Kali · 202
Kama (Hinduism) · 53
Kama Sutra · 53
Kami (Shintoism) · 68
Kamikaze · 68, 173
Kangha (Sikhism) · 64
Kara (Sikhism) · 64
Karma · 30, 54, 61
KE family · 220
Kesh (Sikhism) · 64
Khalistan · 65
Khalsa (Sikhism) · 64
King David · 71
Kirpan (Sikhism) · 64
Kony, Joseph · 35
Koran · *See* Qur'an

Koresh, David · 32

L

Laity (Defn.) · 19
Lamarck, Jean Baptiste · 139
Lamarckism · 139
Language
    generative grammar · 216
    prescriptive grammar · 217
Law of Return · *See* Israel
League of Nations · 181
Leap of Faith (Film) · 207
Lord's Resistance Army · 35
Love Hormone · 243
Luther, Martin · 110, 144
Luxenberg, Christoph
    Syro-Aramaic Reading of the Qur'an · 169

M

Madrassas · 174
Mahayana Buddhism · 62
Marine iguanas · 98
Martyr (Defn.) · 19
Martyrdom · 170
Mary · 76
    immaculate conception · 150
Mecca · 79, 82
Meditation (Defn.) · 19
Meiosis · 105, 122, 134, 135
Memeplex · 225
Memes · 224
    application to religion · 226
    memeplex · 225
    memetics · 226
Memetics · 226
Mendicant (Defn.) · 19
Messiah · 73, 75
Middle East · 181
Milgram experiments · 241
Mind control · 173
Minimally counterintuitive behaviour · 240

Miracles · 19, 152
Mitochondria · 122, 129
Mitosis · 122
Moksha · 53, 61, 65
Monotheism (Defn.) · 19
Morality · 239
Moses · 71
Mother Teresa · 154
   Monica Besra · 154
MRSA · 108
M-Theory · 109
Mufti · 170
Muhammad · 78
   and Aisha · 79
   and martyrdom · 172
   background · 78
   images of? · 165
   Jyllands Posten cartoons · 166
   rewards in Paradise · 168
Mujahideen · 188
Mullah · 170
Muslim Brotherhood · 164, 175, 190
Muslim(s) · 19
   and world population · 177
   becoming a Muslim · 81
   definition of · 79
   jurists · 83
   protesters · 166
Mutation of genes · 105, 134, 138

N

Native Religions · 84
   origins of · 84
Neanderthals · 39, 102, 106
Neurotransmitter · 242
New Religious Movements · 86
New Testament · 76, 145, 150
Newman, Cardinal John · 153
Newton, Isaac · 7, 24
Niqab · 157
Nirvana · 60, 215
Noah · 70
Noble Eight-Fold Path (Buddhism) · 61
Noringa, Motoori · 68
Norse Religion · 44

North Korea · 191, 236
Nucleotides · 128
Nucleus · 122, 124

O

Obama, Barack · 198
Occupied Palestinian Territories · 186, 197
Oil · 189
Old Shinto · 69
Old Testament · 75, 77, 150
   Ten Commandments · 73
   use of violence · 163
Operating Thetan · 90
Organelles · 104, 122
Origin of life · 102, 109, 130, 209
Original sin · 76
Orthodox Judaism · 74
Osama bin Laden · *See* bin Laden, Osama
Oslo Massacre · 192
Over-reading determination · 241
ovum · 137

P

Palestine · 181, 182
   events timeline · 195
   Occupied Palestinian Territories · 185, 197
   Palestine Liberation Organization (PLO) · 185, 196
   Palestinian Authority (PA) · 187, 197
Palestine Liberation Organization · 185, 196
Palestinian Authority · 187, 197
Pali Canon (Buddhism) · 60
Pantheon (Defn.) · 19
Paradise · 18, 19, 163, 168, 169, 171
Para-Historical Dimensions (Ninian Smart) · 21
Parcham · 188
Parsis · 41

Index

Parthenogenesis · 151
Passover (Judaism) · 75
People's Temple · 31
Phenotype · 106, 123, 225
    Definition of · 123
Pinker, Steven · 112, 220
    The Language Instinct · 39, 97, 112, 216, 221, 252
PLO · 185, 196
Poetic Edda (Norse) · 44
Polar bodies · 137
Polytheism (Defn.) · 19
Pope · 77
    Benedict XVI · 153
    papal infallibility · 77, 144
Prescriptive grammar · 217
Primary foraging theory · 238
Princess Diana · 193
Progressive Creationists · 115
Promised Land · 71, 75, 187
Prose Edda (Norse) · 44
Protein · 123
Protestants · 37
    and Evolution · 117
Pure Land Buddhism · 67

Q

Qian, Liu · 152
Qur'an · 19, 70, 79, 157
    and *Allah's* Brothel · 168
    and suicide bombers · 171
    attitude to suicide · 169
    interpretation of *houri* · 169
    origins of · 79
    rewards in Paradise · 168

R

Radicalize (Defn.) · 19
Raja (Hinduism) · 54
Reasoning · 222
Reciprocity · 242
Reflex · 220
Reform Judaism · 74

Reformation
    European Protestant · 77, 144
Religion · 12, 19, 21
    activities inducing good feelings · 242
    adaptations of human behaviours · 238
    ancient religions · 38
    and Creationism · 117
    and money making · 29
    as a business · 234
    as a cause of wars · 36
    conflict with science · 110
    definition (advanced) · 21
    definition (basic) · 19
    excesses of · 206
    how religions mature · 204
    modern religions · 52
    origins of · 38, 201
    special 'promotions' · 235
    the future of · 230
Renaissance · 179
Resurrection · 76, 151
Reward chemical · 243
RNA · 131
Roberts, Granville Oral · 207
Roman Catholic Church · 77, 141
    and celibacy · 151
    and contraception · 28
    and evolution · 117
    and indulgences · 144
    and miracles · 153
    and sainthood · 153
    and the Inquisitions · 142
    Apostles' Creed · 78, 225
    wealth of · 234
Roman Religion · 43
Ryan, Congressman Leo · 31

S

Sabbath (Judaism) · 75
Sacred explosions · 168
Sadhus (Hinduism) · 54
Saints · 153
    creation of · 153

in Islam · 80
Salat (Islam) · 81
Samsara (Hinduism) · 53
Sangha (Buddhism) · 60
Sawm (Islam) · 81
Schism (Defn.) · 19
Scientific approach · *See* Scientific method
Scientific method · 25, 129
 founder of · 143
Scientology · 88
Scopes Trial · 111
Second Coming · 76
Second World War · 30, 184
Sect Shinto · 69
Secularism (Defn.) · 19
Self-awareness · 214, 224
Sen, K M
 Hinduism · 55
Seven Seals · 33
Shahadah (Islam) · 81
Shakyamuni (Buddhism) · 62
Shamanic religions · 84
Shamans · 69, 84
Sharia law · 43, 80, 158
 death of Hena Begum · 175
Shavuot (Judaism) · 75
Shi'a Imams · 80
Shi'a Muslims · 80
Shintoism · 68
Shiva (Hinduism) · 54
Shrine Shinto · 69
Shruti, (Hinduism) · 53
Siddha (Jainism) · 57
Sikhism · 64
Sinai Peninsula · 197
Singh, Khushwant
 Delhi · 201
 Train to Pakistan · 56
Six-Day War · 197
Sky burials · 201
Smart, Ninian
 Seven Dimensions of Religion · 21
Smith, Joseph · 204
Smriti (Hinduism) · 53

Soul · 20, 85, 214, See also Atman, Chi, Jiva, Kami, Karma, Self-awareness, Siddha, Spirit
 and dualism · 239
 early indicator of a religion · 39
Species · 101
Sperm cells · 105
Spirit · 84
Split personality · 62
Storytelling · 204
Sufis · 82
Suicide bombers · 167
 and white grapes? · 169
 rewards in Paradise · 168
Sullivan, Jack · 153
Sunnah · 158
Sunni Muslims · 80
Superhuman (Defn.) · 20
Supernatural (Defn.) · 20
Supreme Creator (Defn.) · 20
Survival chemical · *See* Endorphin
Survival machine · 106, 130
Survival of the Fittest · 101
Syncretism · 20, 69

T

T'ai chi ch'uan (Taoism) · 67
Taliban · 159, 174, 188
 impositions on Afghanistanis · 159
Talmud (Judaism) · 72
Tanakh (Judaism) · 70
Tantra Buddhism · 63
Taoism · 66
Teleology · 241
Ten Commandments · 72, 75, 154
 listed · 72
 morality and ethics · 240
 what they don't say · 154
The Troubles · 187
Theism (Defn.) · 20
Theocracy (Defn.) · 20
Theology (Defn.) · 20
Theory of Evolution · 101
 versus the Book of Genesis · 102
Thera, Narada Maha

Index

Buddhism in a Nutshell · 29, 59
Theravada Buddhism · 62
Thetan · 89
Thomson, Andy · 201, 237
Thomson, Andy and Aukofer, Clare
  Why we believe in god(s) · 201, 237
Thurbron, Colin
  To a mountain in Tibet · 201
Tirthankars (Jainism) · 58
Tooth Fairy · 29, 205, 215, 223
Torah (Judaism) · 70
Totemism · 20, 68
Transtheism · 20, 57
Transubstantiation · 20, 28
Tree of Life · 101
Tribal instinct · 238
Trimurti (Hinduism) · 54, 62
Tripitaka (Buddhism) · 60
Triple Gems (Jainism) · 57
Tushita Heaven (Buddhism) · 63
Twin Towers · *See* 9/11

U

Ummah (Islam) · 177
  attitude to Israel · 187
United Nations · 195
Updike, John
  Terrorist · 173, 200
Ussher, James · 115

V

Vedas (Hinduism) · 53
Vishnu (Hinduism) · 54

W

Wahhabi Muslims · 80, 189
Wailing Wall · 72
Wallace, Alfred Russel · 99
War lords · 188
Watson, James · 103, 129
Wedgewood, Josiah · 97
West Bank · 186, 196, 197
Whirling Dervishes · 82
White Nights · 32
Wilkins, Maurice · 129
Witch doctors · 84
Witchcraft · 142

X

Xenu · 91

Y

Yahweh · 70
Yang · 66
YHWH · *See* Yahweh
Yin · 66
Yom Kippur (Judaism) · 75
Young Earth Creationists · 115

Z

Zakat (Islam) · 81
Zionism · 75
Zionists
  Baron Rothschild · 184
  Herzl, Theodor · 75
Zoroaster/Zoroastrianism · 41
Zygote · 105, 123, 133

(^_^)

Lightning Source UK Ltd.
Milton Keynes UK
UKOW050651220812

197911UK00001B/31/P